BRITAIN'S NO 1
Art Forger

MAX BRANDRETT
The Life of a Cheeky Faker

WRITTEN WITH ANTHONY VALENTINE

First published in Great Britain by Gadfly Press in 2022

Copyright © Max Brandrett and Anthony Valentine 2022

The right of Max Brandrett and Anthony Valentine to be identified as the authors of this work has been assert-ed by them in accordance with the Copyright, Designs and Patents Act 1988. All rights reserved

No part of this book may be reproduced, stored in a retrieval system or transmitted in any form or by any means (electronic, mechanical, photocopying, recording or otherwise) without the prior written permission of the author, except in cases of brief quotations embodied in reviews or articles. It may not be edited, amended, lent, resold, hired out, distributed or otherwise circulated without the publisher's written permission

Permission can be obtained from gadflypress@outlook.com

This book is a work of non-fiction based on research by the author

A catalogue record of this book is available from the British Library

Typeset and cover by Jane Dixon-Smith

SPELLING DIFFERENCES: UK V US

This book was written in British English, hence US readers may notice some spelling differ-ences with American English: e.g. color = colour, meter = metre and = jewelry = jewellery

UK REGIONAL ACCENTS

The dialogue was written with regional
accents spelt as pronounced: e.g.

"Ee, but 'e were such a fast alley-cat!" she smirked.
"Me friend Margaret warned me against 'im.
But would I listen? Would I 'eck!"

This book is dedicated to the memory of Dorothy Harris

With thanks to:
Martina Brandrett
Marie Mayo
Marian Camp
Anne Kelly
Susan Hove
Bobby Cummines OBE
Mark Fealy
Marcus Fuller
Tasha MacLellan
Sammy MacLellan
Simon Barden and crew
Justin Wadey
Chris Ellison
Jim Hartley
Micky and Trixie Openshaw
Simon Potel
Carol Anne Macauley
Tony Valentine

CONTENTS

Chapter 1: Calamity and Kindness	1
Chapter 2: Worms and Elephants	23
Chapter 3: Giblets and Songsters	52
Chapter 4: Injecting Donuts and Swaying Palm Trees	70
Chapter 5: Flirting and Flannel	90
Chapter 6: The Gilded Frame and Popping Champagne	114
Chapter 7: Hard Beds and Soft Beds	143
Chapter 8: Up the Prom and Down the Hill	169
Chapter 9: Foreign Affairs and Home Truths	192
Chapter 10: Champions and Choppers	211
Chapter 11: Hard Knocks and Happy Endings	231
Other Books by Gadfly Press	259
Hard Time by Shaun Attwood	269
Prison Time by Shaun Attwood	276

CHAPTER 1:
CALAMITY AND KINDNESS

When I heard the clicking heels descending the concrete steps to our poky flat in the basement, I stopped drawing for a moment, listening for the doorknocker and my mum's broad Yorkshire tongue as she lashed a visiting rent collector or tallyman. But today was different. The footsteps were different. The voices were different. My mum was speaking softly, to a woman, muffled behind the closed door of our tidy parlour. I was carefully shading in Mickey Mouse's mouth and eyes, planting a broad grin across his face when the glimmering electric bulb above my head fizzled to nothing.

"Mum!" I called out.

A burst of light suddenly struck me as my mum opened the cupboard where I was sitting in the darkness.

"He likes to do 'is drawings in 'ere," my mum explained to a stocky lady in bulging blue stockings who was peering in at me. "Come on, out tha come."

"He has a lot of hair, doesn't he?" observed the lady, as I sprang from my cubbyhole.

"His father was same," my mum huffed.

I showed my picture to the lady and she smiled, squinting against the low October sunshine which streamed through the rips in the curtain.

"It's jolly good," praised the lady. "You like tracing?" she asked.

I shook my head and told her, "I never traced it. It's a sketch."

"Really?" she uttered, somewhat surprised, then asked my mum, "How old is he?"

"Six."

The lady glanced at my grubby feet and inquired, "Does he have any shoes?"

My mum explained, "His brother's got 'em at present. He's t'up school today."

"That's perfectly alright," the lady assured her, smiling sympathetically. "We have plenty." They went outside and I heard the lady say, in a hushed tone, "It's for the best, Mrs Harris."

After the lady had gone, my mum dug deep to find a tanner to put in the meter, and I returned to the privacy of my enchanted cupboard to continue with my sketch.

When my brother Tony returned home, my mum called out from the scullery, "Max! In 'ere. I need to speak to ya." We slurped mushy Weetabix biscuits in water as she told us, "Tomorrow you're goin' away on a wonderful trip. Just you two. Not your brother Kenny, nor your sister. Just you two. You understand?"

"How long we goin' for, mum?" asked Tony.

"Not long. And you'd better behave yourselves," she warned. "And just to make things easier, Joe you'll use ya proper first name," she told Tony. "And *you*," she said, turning to me, "will call yourself Harold."

"Harold!" I shrieked.

"Harold Harris," she confirmed.

"But why?" I grizzled. "Me name's Max Brandrett, ain't it?"

"Your brothers are 'arris, your sister's an 'arris, and you'll be an 'arris. Harry Harris," she decreed. "Whoever 'eard of Max Harris? It don't sound right!" Then, hugging us both tightly, she sniffled, "Joe and Harry, me two boys, me two precious boys."

The next morning, Joey and I ran up the steps and sat on the wall outside the house to wait for whatever it was we were supposed to be waiting for. The ornate iron railings were missing, commandeered maybe ten years earlier (in the early 1940s) to make Spitfires or tanks, and it meant that us boys could drop down to our flat like intrepid parachutists rather than use the steps. Above our flat were three further storeys housing half a dozen families or more. The neighbours were friendly and they loved my mum. My mum wasn't the tallest, but she was pretty, and despite her second-hand clothes and scant makeup, she always looked well-groomed and fashionable. But it was her kindness and generosity which made her special. Spotting a neighbour, she would cry out in her loudest Guisboroughese, "Ee, don't stand there leek wet week! Come in for cuppa and fag!" She would have given away her last penny.

Our road, Buckingham Road, Brighton, was a wide street of large Victorian terraced houses, mostly split into humble flats occupied by railway workers and hotel skivvies like my mum. Some entire houses were the homes of rich families, and the reason my mum had moved south was to enter domestic service for the Powells, and particularly to care for an elderly gentleman. My mum held down four jobs, presumably because she couldn't hold down a husband. I didn't know my father. She had mentioned to me once that he was tall and handsome, theatrical and flamboyant, with a magnificent mane of wavy hair. I'd also heard her tell others that he was a "womanising rat" and a "no-good spiv" who made a living by duping punters into paying for his spurious racing tips.

A shiny green Morris Minor Traveller came into view up the street, chugging slowly in our direction. A man in the passenger seat was peering and pointing at the house numbers, gesticulating to the lady who was driving. Eventually they came to rest alongside us. My heart pounded.

"Hello," said the man in a loud, clear voice as he stepped out of the car. "Are you the Barnardo's boys?"

We shrugged at him. He looked like a park keeper in his rough, navy-blue jacket. I didn't like him. The lady, however, was tall and elegant in a grey, velvet-trimmed coat and matching hat, and she wore spectacles like a schoolteacher.

"Hello boys," she greeted. "Where is your mother?"

We led them down the steps and through to the scullery at the back. My mum was outside in the yard, wringing a pinny through the mangle. She stopped abruptly and prinked her hair.

"I'm Mrs Gibson," said the lady, smiling and shaking my mum's hand. "This is Mister Odin."

"Here," said Mister Odin, "we brought these for the boys," and he handed Tony and I a pile of neatly pressed clothes.

Joey and I were sent to the bedroom to dress, while the adults went into the parlour. We excitedly ripped off our ragged shorts and pullovers, flinging them into a messy pile on the floor, and adorned ourselves in their smart grey replacements. I pulled up my new, itchy wool socks, and Tony helped me lace up my generous black shoes. I think my mum was quite shocked when she came from the parlour and saw us.

"Do they have anything else to bring with them?" asked Mrs Gibson, and my mum sheepishly shook her head.

I grabbed my pencil and my pair of stubby, wax crayons, one green and one yellow, and my thin wad of thick, coarse paper, and I was ready to go.

"Joseph looks a little bow-legged," observed Mister Odin.

"Rickets?" inquired Mrs Gibson.

My mum nodded and sighed deeply, "I've tried to... But I just couldn't... It's all been so..." and I could see that she was overwhelmed and fighting to hold back her tears.

"It's alright," comforted Mrs Gibson. "We'll soon have him right."

Outside, on the kerb, my mum hugged us and kissed us on the cheeks. Then, wiping her eye, she turned to Mrs Gibson and asked pleadingly, "Will I be able to..? I mean, will I ever see..?

"They'll be well taken care of, Mrs Harris," Mrs Gibson assured her.

"Harold!" Mister Odin called out, holding open the rear door of the Traveller. "Harold!" he snapped again.

It was a moment before I realised that Harold was *me*. Joey and I climbed into the car and sat bolt upright on the back seat, as instructed. It was a lovely motor, with tan leather seats and a gleaming chromium steering wheel. The next-door neighbours, Mr and Mrs Russell, had come out to see us off, she with her fuddy-duddy nineteen-forties' hairstyle and he in his dapper waiter's waistcoat and bow tie of the Southern Railway. As we drove away, I glanced back through the rear window and saw my mum fall into Mrs Russell's arms.

"Would you like a lollipop?" asked Mrs Gibson.

Somewhere en route to wherever it was we were going, Mrs Gibson stopped to drop Mister Odin off. She pulled over by a park gate, and I nudged my brother in the ribs and whispered to him, giggling, "I told ya 'e was a park keeper."

When we set off again, I saw Mrs Gibson's kindly eyes smiling back at me in the mirror. "Boys," she said gleefully, "I am taking you to a wonderful place."

As I observed the changing landscapes, I drew cows and sheep, buildings and cranes, cars and horses. I felt almost overawed with subject matter.

"This is it," Mrs Gibson announced, some hours later, as we slowed down and turned in through a set of broad metal gates. "Can you read the sign?" We looked bemused. "It says, 'Doctor Barnardo's Village'. This is where you're going to live."

We gawped out of the windows with bulging eyes, our heads spinning frantically from side-to-side. A vast garden opened up before us: Lawns with circular beds of flowers and shrubs; fountains and gazebos; a village green; a sports field; a swimming pool; dozens of pointy-roofed cottages; a church; and a hospital; all encircled by a jungle of giant trees. It was magical.

"This way, Harold," instructed a lady called Mrs Carter as I tried to follow Joey, who was being led off in the opposite direction. "You are staying in Joy Cottage because you're a bed-wetter. If you can be a good boy for seven nights, then we may let you join your brother."

There were lots of boys in my dormitory. Obviously, I was the new boy. I knew no-one and I knew nothing. Mrs Carter showed me to my bed and introduced me to Dougie, who had the bed next to mine.

After bread and jam, and the Lord's Prayer read by Mister Carter, we settled in our beds and Dougie explained the drill: "At 'alf-past-eleven, George comes."

"Who's George?" I asked.

"'Sewer George', the sewer man," said Dougie. "He takes us to the bog if we're desperate for a slash. You'll see."

The light went out and I snuggled under my blanket, cheering myself up that it wouldn't be long before I was going home again.

What seemed like a moment later, a man's voice echoed in the darkness: "*You* want to go? Do *you* want to go?" When the voice was above my head, I peered out and saw in the torchlight that Dougie was putting on his slippers. He beckoned me and I followed. We filed downstairs to the latrine and relieved ourselves. I went back to bed with a relieved mind and an empty bladder, but still I squeezed my legs together as tightly as I could.

A woman's voice startled me and the lights flashed on. I was so shaken that it took me a moment to realise that I had slept through the night and it was morning. The boys all leapt from their beds and I did likewise. We lined up, two lines of fifteen boys, and stood in silence as a fat nurse executed a bed inspection. She passed along the rows of beds, flicking back the blankets and wiping her chubby palm across our sheets. "Good boy, nice and dry... Yes, good boy... Good boy... You dirty boy! Get this sheet off at once and wash it!" It was still pitch black outside as the naughty boys were banished to the middle of the green to publicly scrub their bedsheets clean in a trough of icy-cold water. The humiliation was seen as a cure for wicked and wilful bed-wetters.

And so I got used to the routine. I counted down the nights on my fingers. I had succeeded in not wetting the bed for six nights on the trot. Next was night seven, hopefully my last night away from my dear, dear brother Tony/Joey, as long as I could hold it in. I went to bed. I was missing my brother immensely. I kept thinking about him. I was excited. I was anxious. I was tired. I was warm. I was warm. Then I heard Sewer George's voice in the darkness: "*You* want to go? Do *you* want to go?" I realised then that it was too late for *me* - I had already gone! My heart pounded. I lay still, totally still, not moving and not breathing, but waiting. "*You* want to go?" and I heard Dougie stir and put on his slippers, and the padding of eager feet disappearing away down the steps. Under the cover of darkness, I slipped out of bed, yanked off my sodden bedsheet, grabbed Dougie's dry one, swiftly swapped them over, and was, as far as anyone was concerned, still fast asleep when they returned. I heard Dougie get back into bed, then wriggle and moan uncomfortably.

In the morning there was a hell of a furore. "You dirty boy, Dougie! Dirty!" Nurse yelled. And then to me, "Oh, good boy, Harold. That's seven dry nights. What a good boy you are."

That evening I was sent to Angas Cottage, where I slept soundly under the watchful eye of my beloved brother.

The weeks rolled by and we ate three square meals per day, including meat, attended daily lessons at school, and the pain which Joey suffered because of his rickets began to ease off, thanks to regular doses of revolting castor oil and cod liver oil prescribed by the fat nurse. Joey was always looking out for me and standing up to any bullies that I couldn't sort out myself. We loved the fact that we had a proper football pitch at our feet, and we were each given our own football kit, Arsenal for me and Chelsea for him. We wanted for nothing, except a cuddle from our mum. I think I missed her more than Joey did, although I suspect he put on a brave face so as not to upset me. We did receive letters from her, telling us that she missed us and loved us, and urging us to behave ourselves. It was a great comfort and I felt sure that any day soon Mrs Gibson would arrive and take us back to Brighton.

Although I did cry most days, as many of the children did, the Village was a happy place. And I was luckier than most because I could escape into my drawings. I had been supplied with pencils and crayons and paper, and I would while away any spare moments escaping into my own little private world. It was exciting because Christmas was coming, and I did pictures of the landscape and cottages all covered in icicles and snow, and cheeky grey squirrels and robin redbreasts. We all helped decorate a huge Christmas tree with tinsel and baubles, and sprigs of holly and pinecones plucked from the trees. The boys all took it in turns to help the girls stirring the Christmas pudding in a giant bowl. Father Christmas came and handed us each a bulging pillowcase. I was flabbergasted when I put my head inside and discovered a kingdom of toys. There were soldiers and horses, a car, a lorry, a lion, a jack-in-the box and an aeroplane, all chipped hand-me-downs, but I was as happy as a lark. Later, after we were stuffed with roast and pudding, and had given thanks to the Lord, we were each called up onto the stage in the main hall and presented with another, special toy. Mine was a wooden duck on a cart, with a rope to pull it along. It only had three wheels, but I thought it was smashing.

We had been at Barnardo's in Barkingside for a year or so when Mrs Gibson came back for us. She smiled warmly and ushered Joey and I into the back of the Morris. This time we actually had *things*, such as clothes, to take with us.

"Are we going to see my mum?" I asked Mrs Gibson, as we drove away from the waving children and carpets of fresh bluebells under the trees.

"You're going to stay with the Andersons," she replied. "You remember the Andersons, don't you?" I remained silent, disappointed and sad that I wouldn't be seeing my mum. "They are the kind American family who visit the Village sometimes, and bring toys for the children. You liked them when you met them. And they especially like *you*."

The concrete prefab houses quickly gave way to green fields and twittering hedgerows. We passed a farmer with a giant shire horse, and some boys playing on top of a pillbox, and an airfield with bombers.

At the end of a leafy lane, I recognised the car immediately. It was maroon, almost purple, and big. Behind it stood a large white house with black wooden beams and four tall chimneys. Mister and Mrs Anderson and their two sons came out to greet us. They had their own television set, with a magnifying glass which enlarged the people's heads to the size of our own. We had wonderful times, all of us playing hide-and-seek in the orchard and outbuildings. We polished the car and did chores in the garden. But most of all, we adored the drives out into the countryside for picnics, and to the seaside to play baseball on the beach and swim in the sea. Mister Anderson owned a washing machine factory; he was rich!

"Sit down, boys, Mrs Anderson and I would like to talk to you," said Mister Anderson. "The thing is, boys, we have grown fond of you over these past months, and we were wondering whether you would like to live with us all the time?"

"Yes please," Joey and I both said together.

"Great! But here's the thing," he continued hesitantly, "we're moving back to America. So we'd have to adopt you, and we'd all live in America. How does that grab ya?"

"The only thing is," Mrs Anderson cut in, "we'd have to ask your mom for her permission first, before we could do anything. She'd have to agree, or..."

The news wasn't good. Mum didn't agree. Mrs Anderson hugged me, and as she said goodbye, I wept bitterly and mourned what might have been.

"I've got you some lollipops," smiled Mrs Gibson, as we drove away.

Watts Naval Training School was a Barnardo's home which was pretty much as close to being on a ship, whilst remaining on dry land. It had extensive grounds and a main, vast old building, three storeys high, which looked more like a cathedral than a ship, but was run exactly like a ship. I was put in a dormitory with Joey, up on the second floor, on Lincoln Landing. The 'ship's company' comprised of three hundred boys or more, and we worked to a rigid naval timetable. At 6.30 A.M. the bugle would wake us up and we would jump out of bed, wash face, brush teeth, brush hair (clipped short by the barber), dress in uniform shirt and shorts, ronnick (polish) the wooden decks, attend prayers and eat our breakfast in the mess hall. Then, at 9 A.M., we were marched out onto the parade ground at the front of the building and drilled up and down, in perfect unison. In the centre of the square was a towering mast, commandeered from a bygone warship called H.M.S. Woodlark. Standing to attention, we would be inspected by the captain, and God help us if we didn't pass muster! Any untidiness or imprecision and we were hoicked out for punishment.

I was a 'grog boy' (tea boy), which kept me on the right side of the masters, but unfortunately it meant that I had to wait outside the cookhouse door for delivery of a giant teapot, and couldn't eat until I had poured out dozens and dozens of cups of tea. Sometimes, when I did get to sit down at one of the long tables, the prefect would tease me and think it funny to deprive me of food. It was as a result of this that I got dysentery. Hungry and scrumping for pears in the orchard one day, one of the fruits must have been dirty and I ended up being as sick as a dog in the infirmary. A week after I was discharged, I still couldn't face any food, despite the fact that it was my seventh birthday. One of the masters, a kindly soul called Colonel Dean, and his lovely wife who was always respectfully addressed as Ma'am Dean, invited me for a celebration tea at their cottage. She served me paste sandwiches and cake, but when she had left the room, I threw them out of the window.

The next day she summoned me to see her. "Guess what the gardener's dog found, just *there*, outside the window?" she asked me.

"Dunno, Ma'am," I shrugged.

"I think you do," she insisted. "But I'm worried about you. You're very thin. You must eat," and she leaned forwards to give me a corned beef sandwich.

"Ma'am Dean," I moaned, staring up at her wide-eyed, "you never kissed me on my birthday."

She chuckled and smiled, "And if I give you a kiss, Harold, do you promise me that you'll start eating again?"

I nodded enthusiastically, grinning from ear-to-ear, and her warm lips brushed my cheek, and I was instantly cured of dysentery.

"I have something else for you," she said, and handed me a

large and expensive colouring-in book. "I know how much you love to draw, and I've seen how beautiful your pictures are."

"Thank you," I politely acknowledged.

Sometime later in the garden, she looked over my shoulder and asked, "May I look?" I could see that she was puzzled as she flipped through the pages of printed, black line-drawings. "But you haven't coloured any of them in!"

"I'm sorry, Ma'am Dean," I said, looking at the ground, shamefaced, "but I don't like colouring. I like drawing."

Then, flicking through the formerly blank pages on the reverse side, she gasped, "Did you do these?"

I nodded nervously as she examined my work: a dramatically shaded autumn landscape; a sketch of the school chapel; a respectful and glamorous cartoon of *her*; plus various pictures of cars, boats, trains and hedgehogs.

"Well Harold, you really are quite the John Constable!" she praised.

She obviously passed on her glowing approval to the masters, as I was called to one side by a teacher called Mister Runcie and presented with a box of watercolours, oil paints and art paper. And, in order to avoid the boys who liked to deride and antagonize me, I was also granted special permission to paint my pictures in the peace and privacy of the school's museum. It certainly suited me, and it proved to be a wonderful advertisement for the school when visiting dignitaries paused to watch me paint.

Joey and I were told that we had been accepted for placement in a foster home in Suffolk. It was considered that I might benefit from the surroundings, and my brother would be taken in with me. Mrs Gibson arrived and we climbed onto the back seat of the Traveller, on our way to another adventure.

"I haven't actually met the Reverend," said Mrs Gibson, "but I feel sure that he's a very nice man."

"What's a reverend?" I asked.

"A rector," she replied. "You know what a rector is, don't you?"

"It's like a vicar," said Joey.

"Oh," I sighed. "Will he be taking us to America?"

Mrs Gibson passed us each a lollipop.

"Now, follow me. Up here, boys," directed the Reverend Soden, stooping as he went upstairs and onto the landing, his pipe smoke trailing behind him like a steam train. "This is *my* office… And in here… This is where Lord Nelson's mother was born."

"Are there any ghosts?" asked Joey.

"Of course there's no ghosts in the rectory," huffed Mrs Fish, the housekeeper. "Well I've never seen one."

"And along here…" continued the Reverend, "is *your* bedroom." Joey and I peered inside at the two little beds which were almost lost in such a large room. "The Cavaliers hid from the Roundheads in the rectory during the English Civil War."

"Are these pictures all yours?" I asked, as we trotted along behind him through the maze of passageways and rooms, upstairs and downstairs.

"Most of the portraits belong to the church," he answered. "Personally, I prefer landscapes."

Barsham Rectory was beautiful. We climbed the trees in the surrounding woodland and swam and fished for tiddlers in the River Waveney. The nearby school was a cheerful place and, when I wasn't chasing the girls, I painted. I did a watercolour of the Anglo-Saxon church and an oil painting of Lord Nelson, which I copied from a book. It was a busy house, with visitors coming and going, and we had wonderful meals, but when I felt lonely or sad, I would sit next to the fishpond and think about my mum.

The Reverend Soden was a kind and gentle man. "I'm very sorry, boys," he apologised one day, coughing weakly into his handkerchief, "but I'm afraid that it's no longer possible for you to stay here."

Mrs Gibson arrived and told us that Mrs Fish, the Reverend's housekeeper, and her husband, were prepared to take us in. Much to our glee, we were delivered to a village sweet shop, which was run by Mister Fish. He was a nice, if naïve, man and the temptation of living above a limitless supply of Horlicks tablets and

Mars bars proved too much for us. In a matter of weeks it was noted that the stock of sweets was much depleted. Mrs Gibson returned to collect us, and this time there were no lollipops to console us on the long and silent trek back to the naval training school.

The school had its own railway station, and when boys were old enough to leave, they would take the short walk up Bintree Lane to board a train to freedom. A special, made-up song would ring out as they left, expressing a widespread desire to escape. On occasions, pupils would run away as far as the station, only to perish under a train. It wasn't talked about.

My brother and I kept our noses clean and managed to ingratiate ourselves to the masters sufficiently that we were included in a school camping trip to the north coast of the county. Seventy boys travelled the short distance by railway and hiked the final mile to an empty field above the beach. Upon arrival, we built our tents and dug latrines, before plunging into the cold grey waves for swimming races. As well as football and cricket, the masters had also planned a devilish cross-country race. Although Norfolk was supposedly a flat county, the circuit would include running up a hill to the peak of an impossibly tall cliff, referred to by locals as 'Beeston Bump', then back down again, then away across some miles of scrubland, then back up to the pinnacle to the finishing line. It was a daunting challenge, but the winner would receive the mouth-watering prize of half-a-crown. It was, I decided, an opportunity too good to miss. As I padded breathlessly through the heavy mounds of sand, I spotted my chance to cut out a huge chunk of the exhausting route by hiding in some bushes. I crouched down and waited there, and presently, when the three leading boys came chugging by, I darted out behind them and ran like the clappers. My ears were suddenly ringing with the cheers and yells of the enthusiastic masters, "Go on, Harris! Go on, boy!"

As I sprinted past my weary competitors and flung myself through the winner's tape, they gasped begrudgingly, "Well done, Harris," although there was more than a hint of suspicion in their tone.

"Never had you down as a runner, Harris. Well done," said Colonel Dean, as he shook my hand and awarded me my silver half-crown.

My victory didn't go unnoticed and, apart from the cash, it earned me a kiss the following day from a girl on the beach. She had blonde curly hair, but not only on her head! I couldn't help but notice that she had a sprig of fluff sprouting from the side of her swimming costume. It fascinated me, so much so, that I made a sketch of her, complete with her frizzy adornment.

I was later confronted by an outraged teacher who pointed at the offending matter with disgust and demanded, "And what..? What is *this*, boy?"

"It's public hair, sir," I answered, quite innocently, and was summarily corrected for my insolence.

It was always slightly nerve-racking to be summoned down into the basement of the school where the offices were located.

Joey and I were called in and told, "Your mother is coming to see you."

We hadn't seen her for some years, and I was both excited and apprehensive.

"She ain't coming," sneered a couple of the boys on the playing field, and I scrapped with them until they were bruised and bloodied and ran away.

It was a crisp, bright morning, and I eagerly washed, dressed, prayed and ate, aching with pent-up excitement. I waited for the whistle to blow, then fell into rank and marched smartly out onto the parade square. I uplifted my chin and raised my feet higher than usual, and marched along with a spring in my step. Although the drill dictated that we maintain 'eyes front', I felt my gaze wavering, spontaneously seeking out my mum's wavy, coiffured locks. It was Joey who spotted her and subtly gestured for me to raise my attention upwards. On the next pass, I glanced up and saw her standing aloft on the top floor balcony, with shorter hair and a strange man on her arm.

"Tummy rumbling?" the captain asked, as I stood to attention for his inspection.

"I've got the collywobbles, sir," I told him, which caused a titter amongst the boys.

"Pull your socks up, boy," he commanded. Then to his aide, "Hole in sock. On report."

Before the obligatory punishment of standing out on deck for half-an-hour, I was granted permission to see my mum for ten minutes.

She hugged Joey and I together, squashing us and planting soppy red kisses across our mouths and cheeks, then shrieked, "By 'eck, boys! Look 'ow ya grown! They must be feedin' ya reet!" Smiling doe-eyed at her companion, she announced to us, "Boys, this is Sid." He was a stocky man with large, hairy hands which barely protruded from the sleeves of his black, oversized jacket. "Sid's livin' with me now," said my mum. "He's from Newcastle. You'll love 'im. He used to work down pit."

"Aye, I love this woman to death," purred the Geordie coal miner. And suddenly he burst into song, serenading my mum with a rendition of, 'On the Street Where you Live', filling the cold air with how tall and heartened he felt, just to have my mum nearby. My mum stared sweetly into his eyes, and they kissed on the lips.

"Mum, are we going home?" I asked.

"Not today, darlin'," she sighed.

She gazed at me longingly, and stroked my face, her smile bathing me in a moment of warmth. Her eyes sparkled with sadness. She didn't cry. None of us cried. And then she was gone.

My favourite spot at school, when I wanted to be completely alone, was down on the riverbank, beyond the open-air swimming pool. I would sit there and weep, reflecting upon the quietly passing water, and sing an Irish ballad about people who found themselves a long way from home: *"If you ever go across the sea to Ireland, Then maybe at the closing of your day, You will sit and watch the moonrise over Claddagh, And see the sun go down on Galway Bay, Just to hear again the ripple of the trout stream, The women in the meadows making hay..."*

I didn't know what it was called, or where I'd picked it up from, or truly what it was about, but it made me feel better.

Mrs Gibson came and took us to a place called Bell Farm, somewhere near Ipswich.

"Best behaviour, boys," Mrs Gibson warned us. "This could be your last chance at being fostered."

When we arrived, the shabby wooden door squeaked open, and a little man with a handlebar moustache appeared.

"Who is it?" boomed a woman's voice from indoors. "Is it the orphans?"

"Yes, ma dear, it's the orphans," the man called back. Then to Mrs Gibson, with a pronounced Suffolk burr, "I'm Arthur. Come in, come in. Come in, lads."

A hairy-faced woman in a billowing frock came bouncing into the overcrowded parlour and flung her flabby arms around us, and slobbered all over us.

"This be Mabel, my missis," grinned Arthur.

The woman spurted, excitedly, "We're so excited! Aren't we, Arthur?"

"Yes, ma dear," Arthur instantly replied, "most excited."

Mrs Gibson left us boys with a telling raise of her eyebrow.

"Oh, look at ya! You're so adorable!" drooled Ma'am Mabel. "Gi's a kiss."

Mister Arthur giggled nervously as his wife accosted us with her tongue.

"Have you 'ad yer dinner?" she asked. "I've got dinner. Now you sit down 'ere and…"

"May I go to the toilet, please?" I requested.

"Toilet, toilet, yes, yes, this way," she bade me. "Now what's yer name again?"

"Harold," I said.

"Harold. What a lovely name," she complimented, as I followed her through the tight, smoky kitchen.

Opening the back door, she pointed outside to an ancient brick privy, and handed me some pages of old newspaper. There was no lavatory or cistern, just a metal bucket.

"There, sit down at the kitchen table, young Harold," she prompted, when I had returned from my pee. "Arthur! You lay out the plates. Hurry up, or it be cold! Arthur!"

"Right, my love," he uttered, and quickly set out some crackled, off-white dinner plates.

Ma'am Mabel carefully lowered a large, steaming, sizzling pot onto a landing-pad in the centre of the table. We looked on excitedly as she lifted the lid and great puffs of delicious steam erupted from the vessel. She dipped her blackened ladle into the depths of the bowl, then sploshed out some disgusting grey, greasy gloop onto our plates.

"Don't be shy!" she slurped, spitting projectiles of chomped-up chicken-skin into our faces.

We held onto our stomachs and stared at our plates, trying to ignore the horror as she slobbered her way through flesh and bones, devouring legs and wings and the parson's nose. When she had finished, she let out a series of short belches, slumped back on her creaking chair, and instructed us to clear up the dishes and wash them. Arthur assisted us and gave us directions on how to pump up water from the well. Mabel departed and we later found her in the parlour, drifting away on the tiny sofa, humming along to Bing Crosby on the wireless.

"Do light the lamp, Arthur," she grumbled.

There was an unfamiliar hiss of gas and then a glowing white illumination from the brass lamp on the wall. Almost every inch of the walls and shelves were filled with pictures and trinkets, mainly miniature jugs and floral plates. There must have been hundreds of them.

"Sit here, sit here," she urged us, patting the dusty cushions on either side of her. We sat down and she spread her weighty arms across our shoulders. "Bing Crosby was called Harold," she divulged, kissing me wetly on the cheek. "Harold Lillis. Did you know that?" I didn't. "There! You're famous!" she beamed, kissing me again and again.

In the morning, we were woken up at 6 A.M. We washed

ourselves down in the yard, and given vile bread-and-dripping. The local school was two miles away, as the crows flew, but further on foot. It was obvious from the moment we walked through the gates that we weren't welcome.

"Stick with me," said Joey, as a dozen sets of hostile eyeballs followed us across the playground.

At playtime, a ruffian snarled at me, "Oi, foundlin'! Can yer fight?"

Joey wasn't there. I was on my own. The boy was bigger than me. Kids circled round to watch. I punched him in the face. He grabbed my throat and tried to pull my head down. I overbalanced him and we rolled around on the tarmac, wrestling and kicking. Suddenly I found myself suspended by the collar, my feet dangling above the ground.

"You want to fight, lads?" boomed the gorilla-like man with curly sideboards who held myself and my combatant aloft, one in each hand.

Apart from semaphore signals and swimming, Watts Naval School taught you to be tough. Kitted out in giant boxing gloves, I socked the bully in the face and guts, and didn't stop, even when he was quivering and sobbing in a heap on the ground.

The thatched roof at Bell Farm was in disrepair and prone to leaks during heavy downpours. Joey and I would cuddle our stone hot-water bottles and huddle under an old patchwork bedspread in an attempt to dodge the drips. I was normally sent to bed at 7 P.M. There, I would listen to Johnnie Ray and Doris Day on a crystal set which I'd made myself, while Joey would have to stay downstairs in the parlour and listen to the likes of 'Mrs Dale's Diary' and the 'Archers'.

Although we hated having no running water or toilet or electricity, the Christmas we spent at the farm was a happy one. We helped to decorate a glorious Christmas tree in the parlour, Arthur built a blazing log fire in the hearth, Mabel cooked a tasty goose, we sang lively carols, and I was given a smart pen-and-pencil set. It was bitterly cold outside, but we enjoyed jumping around in the snow, flinging snowballs, and making snowmen and snowwomen. My paintings of winter landscapes, horses and military generals were much loved by Mabel and Arthur, as well as by the teachers at the school.

I was dozing dreamily, half asleep under the bedcover one evening, as David Whitfield crooned, *"I'll make you mine, Forever mine, On this our wedding day, The bells will ring, The choir will sing -"*

"Thud!" The room shook. I jumped up with a start and looked frantically all around in the darkness. I nervously got out of bed and crept down the stairs to the parlour, my heart racing. The door was open. Joey looked over at me, shocked. Mabel was lying flat on her back on the floor. Arthur was kneeling next to her. He was gently slapping her cheeks. She groaned.

"Quick! Get help!" Arthur yelled. "Quick!"

I ran up the lane, barefoot and breathless and slammed the neighbour's doorknocker. We ran back. Arthur was crying. Mabel was still. More neighbours came. Arthur looked pale and drank brandy. They covered Mabel's body with a sheet. The doctor arrived. A gang of men lifted Mabel up and laid her on the kitchen table. Joey and I were sent to bed.

When Mrs Gibson came in the morning, she was truly sympathetic, and gave us lollipops. She didn't take us back to Watts. "Where we're going is a marvellous school," she told us. "It's a technical school where you can learn to be a motor mechanic or an electrician."

Its official title was the William Baker Technical School, but it was known simply as 'Goldings', a name retained from its former glory as one of the grandest country houses in the whole of Hertfordshire.

"So boys, what sort of thing would interest you?" inquired Mister Wheatley, the mild-mannered headmaster, leaning back in his chair and twiddling his thumbs.

Joey shrugged his shoulders, and I replied, "Painting, sir."

"Ah!" Mister Wheatley exclaimed, jolting his head back and

smiling. "Excellent Harold! We teach boys painting and decorating here, and I feel certain that we will make an excellent tradesman of you."

Joey and I decided to learn printing, in preference to decorating, boot-making, tin-bashing or gardening. I hated it, although I was encouraged to paint in my spare time, pictures rather than walls, when Mister Wheatley realised that I had a talent for art. There was a printing press in the old stable block, and there I tried to understand the tedious and laborious intricacies of typesetting, which even our teacher of typography admitted was a, "puzzling business." Life at Goldings was less strict than the military-style regime which we had been used to and, therefore, was open to a dash of disrespect and recklessness. Although the teachers were generally committed to furnishing us two-hundred-and-fifty boys with a brighter future, some seemed to look upon school life as a war between them and us. We named our enemies 'The gestapo' and their most ardent member was a bullyboy called Baldwin.

Outside the upstairs landings there were fire escapes, and these were seen as, and sometimes used as, stairways to freedom. And so, on a warm summer's night, I instigated a daring escape plan. Seven of us, including my brother Joey, carried supplies commandeered from the cookhouse, and went over the top, descending undetected onto the garden below. Creeping silently across the lawn, we observed the enemy fraternizing in the downstairs mess. We proceeded with caution, using the cover of the bushes until we were far enough away to make a run for it. And we didn't stop running until we were away and into the woods. Beyond the trees lay our goal, the magnificent River Beane where we planned to set up a basecamp on the riverbank. When we reached the water's edge, we larked around in the moonlight, laughing and joking, but falling silent with fear every time a twig snapped, or the undergrowth rustled, or a dog barked in the distance.

We woke up with a shiver in the morning, and the river was blanketed with a cloud of floating mist. Water rats scampered about, ducking and diving in the swirling currents amongst the weeds and rushes. We ate some of our plain biscuits, and some bread and jam, then charged around playing football and cricket. The sun rose and we lazed about on the grass, making the most of not having to do chores or studies, and not being told what to do. As the day warmed up, we all stripped off and jumped in the river, and swam and splashed around like a bunch of crazy kids. In the afternoon, we snapped off some branches to make a shelter, before plunging into the cool, clear water once again.

The next morning, after a comfortable night's rest on beds of leafy twigs and grass, we had our breakfast and played in the sunshine, rejoicing in the fact that we were free. We made spears out of sticks and tried to stab fish, but failed. There were enough biscuits and bread to keep us going, although minor pangs of hunger were quite normal to us anyway. The river water was fresh, and we sploshed about, frolicking and laughing like a pack of boisterous hyenas. Suddenly there was a whinny and the clip-clopping of hooves. We stood up and stared. A farmer was sitting on a hay-cart, a distance away, staring back at us. A girl in a long frock was sitting next to him, also staring. We were naked. The man smacked his horse and they disappeared.

"D'ya think he'll tell anyone?" the other boys nervously asked me.

"Nah, he won't be bothered," I reassured them.

We were all still bathing and roughhousing when the expeditionary force burst out of the woods.

"Harris!" yelled the gestapo leader, Herr Baldwin.

Baldwin's devil-eyed lieutenant, Herr Pratt, stood smirking at his side. And his smirk remained when, later, he thrashed my bare arse in front of the entire school. My cohorts were less severely dealt with, based upon the presumption that I was the ringleader.

It was Joey's time to leave school. At sixteen years old he was considered to be a young man, old enough to make his own way in the world. As he walked away towards the railway station, I stood with a tear in my eye and sang him the old song from Watt's Naval School, *"Leaving down Bintree Lane..."* Life dragged on.

They persisted in trying to teach me about the print trade, despite my total lack of enthusiasm. I managed to stand it for another year, filling my time as much as possible with painting.

Finally, I received my call into Mister Wheatley's office. I was given ten pounds and a train pass, along with his wise words: "Be lucky. Be happy. And stay out of trouble, Harris."

"Yes sir, I'll be keeping well out of trouble, sir," I grinned.

And so, with some odd bits of clothing and my paints in a haversack, I stepped out into the big wide world to begin my life.

CHAPTER 2:
WORMS AND ELEPHANTS

It was half an hour's walk to Hertford railway station. The ticket collector punched my one-way ticket to Brighton and directed me onto the platform to await the next London-bound service. I tried yanking open the drawer on a vending machine, but ended up having to spend sixpence on a packet of Poppets. A train huffed and puffed onto the northbound platform opposite, screeching and belching, enveloping me in a blanket of warm, coaly fog. The sound of slamming doors clacked noisily up and down the station. A whistle blew, the locomotive chugged away, and everyone was gone. I stood back as the London train steamed in next to me, avoiding the doors which were being carelessly flung open by the alighting passengers. I hopped on board and sat facing forwards, staring out of the window, licking the delicious sticky globs of chocolate and toffee from between my teeth. As town and countryside rattled by, I found myself breathing more heavily, and my palms sweating, and my brow burning up.

"Are you alright, dear?" a woman opposite inquired.

"Just a bit hot," I reassured her.

She smiled, and I focussed on the dirty factory buildings and rows of blackened terraced houses which had replaced the green, open spaces. My world was changing. Gone were the playing fields and the laughter of loyal pals, and the midnight farts and the whispering chatter between beds, and the piping-hot stews with hunks of fresh bread, and the carefree years of experimenting with my paints and brushes. All-in-all, my life had been hunky-dory. Jerking and jolting into Kings Cross, I copied my fellow travellers and leaned through the window to undo the doorhandle on the outside, and dropped down onto the rushing platform.

"Where you going?" my friendly woman asked, as I was washed along in the stream of passengers.

"Victoria," I replied.

"Circle Line. The yeller one," she directed, and she was gone.

The twisty twilit tunnels echoed with guitar strings, and Roy Orbison singing, 'Only the Lonely'. It soon became apparent, however, that the young man in dark glasses who was sitting on a coat and strumming enthusiastically was an imposter. But it didn't stop one or two generous travellers from tossing a coin into his upturned Stetson as they rushed by. The underground trains were packed with busy workers, all tightly crammed into smoky carriages, the gentlemen in their ten guinea suits, and bevvies of beautiful secretaries squashed between them. As we briefly stopped at each station, I peered out at the giant posters advertising James Bond, Lawrence of Arabia, Zulu and Cleopatra. I caught my scheduled train from Victoria and spent the hour to Brighton sketching Elizabeth Taylor/Cleopatra in my mind's eye. By the time her shapely form was captured to my satisfaction, we were slowing down through a cutting into Preston Park station. In a few minutes I would be at home, in Brighton, yet it seemed a million miles from the world I had come to know. The second I set foot on the platform, a pair of unforgettable eyes twinkled at me through the smoky haze. There she stood, waiting for me, my mum.

Her arms wrapped around me, her fingers stroked my cheek, and she whispered softly, "Max, oh Max, me Max, me little boy, me baby." She seemed so tiny.

"Ya right, son?" barked a rugged Irish voice.

My mum's arms un-cuddled me and she fastened herself to the gorilla lurking next to her, knitting her wrist tightly through his.

"This is Patrick," smiled my mum.

The ape clenched his teeth and nodded his head. I nodded back at him and we took a taxi to a house on Holland Road. The street was on a hill, sloping down to the sea at the bottom, and lined with tall, imposing terraced houses which were split into ratty little flats, and punctuated with grimy Victorian warehouses.

"What d'ya think?" asked my mum, opening the door to show me one of the two bedrooms in her poky basement flat. "This is your room."

"Nicer than Buckingham Road," I complimented.

"I've moved three dozen times since then!" she sighed, ruefully.

"Oh, it's okay for ya, is it?" sneered Patrick, sarcastically. "I'm so glad." And then to my mum, "Let's be getting off to the pub."

As they were leaving, my mum glanced back at me and smiled. Then she was gone. I explored each measly room, the bedrooms, the parlour and the scullery. I noted the neatly made double bed in my mum's bedroom, and Patrick's meticulously pressed shirts and trousers, tatty and cheap, hanging on the window frame. I lay down for a moment.

"Havin' a nice kip on ma bed there?" Patrick's beer-sodden voice boomed, waking me with a start. "Get out, and give ya poor mother a hand!"

In the scullery, my mum was unwrapping fish and chips, and dishing them out onto dinner plates.

"It's alright," she told me. "I can manage." And then, calling out to him, "Patrick! We're outta brown sauce, but I've pickled onions." Then, as she was dashing out of the room with their suppers, "Are ya hungry, Max? There's bread and dripping in the larder."

Waking at first light, I was greeted by the gangs of seagulls which scavenged the streets and sat squawking on the rooftops. I lay in bed and stared up at the fraying tassels of the lampshade as they fluttered gently in the breeze.

"Let 'im be, Patrick!" I heard my mum protesting outside my door. "Just… Please..?"

The Irishman's gruff retorts continued for some moments, fading into the background until finally ceasing when the front door slammed shut. I listened intently, only relaxing when I was satisfied that they had gone off to work. After a period of contemplation, I got up and stepped around the abode, but the closeness of the walls made me feel a little uneasy and claustrophobic. Eager to spread my wings, and not relishing a breakfast of stale bread and crusty dripping, I wandered down the road to a seafront café and bought myself a generous fry-up. The sun was shining, I had money in my pocket, and time was mine to enjoy. I had a crack at sharp shooting on Palace Pier, then sat and grinned at the flirty holiday girls as they were being dragged up and down the prom by their clucking mums and dads. I was amusing myself, watching fat old ladies getting wedged in deckchairs, and children getting smothered in sticky candyfloss, and some mods and rockers taking the mickey out of each other, when Dave appeared. Dave and I were about the same age, and the last time I had seen him was when we were just wee boys.

"Alwight, Max!" he beamed. "What yer been doin' wiv yerself?"

We walked up to Western Road and I blew most of my cash on a red jacket with skinny lapels, and a pair of drainpipe trousers.

"You 'ungry?" asked Dave, gesturing at the Wimpy Bar across the street.

I got us both burger-and-chips and a milkshake.

"Where ya livin'?" he asked, his mouth stuffed to the cheeks.

I took him down to Holland Road, and my mum welcomed him with open arms, and some meat-paste sandwiches.

"You don't 'ave to go out," my mum told me. "Patrick's not comin' tonight."

I spent most of my days and evenings with Dave, often mucking about in town, but desperately trying to steer clear of Patrick whenever he'd show up for a hot dinner and a session with my mum.

"He'll eat ya outta house 'n' home, Dot!" Patrick would complain to my mum, just because I happened to be lucky enough to scrounge a rock of bread or some leftovers. "How old are ya?" he'd nag me.

"Fifteen," I'd answer, then wisecrack, "same as I was yesterday."

"Ah, ya cheeky little shit!" he'd growl, tapping the thick leather strap which encircled his bulging vest. "He needs to get himself a job, Dot. Doodlin' bloody pictures all day!"

I got a job washing up plates in a café. It didn't pay much, but I did get free grub, and the girls were nice.

"That fella yer mum's goin' wiv," Dave announced one day, when he dropped by the cafe for a free cuppa. "He lives in 'angleton. Got a wife, and free kids! Straight up!"

My mum loved to sing, and she would spend the evenings boozing in the Wick Inn with Patrick and their chums Rosie and Jimmy, before returning home sozzled for a singsong in our parlour.

"Come on, Max, giz a tune," my mum cajoled, as I sat in the corner observing. "Oo, he's got a champion voice," she boasted to the company.

"Is that right?" goaded Patrick. "Come on then, son. Let's hear ya. Come on now."

"No, really, I'm not…" I gulped shyly.

"You're full o' shit! That's what you are!" he snarled, clenching his fists and staggering to get up from his chair.

My mum hopped onto his lap and began singing, 'On the Street Where You Live'. Her high notes made me cringe, but as she finished, Rosie and Jimmy cheered and clapped enthusiastically.

The surly Irishman glared at me and threatened, "You wanna watch yourself. You're fuckin' for it. Now put a tanner in that fuckin' meter, ya good-for-nuttin' scrounger!"

It was worth sixpence to get away from him.

The next time Patrick was due to call, I knew as much because my mum rushed straight in from her afternoon job and set about chopping up vegetables and a hefty chunk of chuck steak. Passing by her in the tiny scullery as she was frying off the meat, I complimented her on how delicious it smelt.

"Ee, you're a good lad," she cooed.

"Just off for some air," I said.

Outside, squeezed into the back yard, there was a postage stamp of grass and an overgrown patch of weeds which must have been a former tenant's flower bed or vegetable plot. Constantly looking up to make sure that no-one was watching me, I took out my penknife and began to dig into the earth. At first there was nothing and so I started scraping desperately with my fingers. Then, a fat, brown, juicy worm writhed up into the air, and I caught it by the tip. It squirmed in the palm of my hand. I didn't want to hurt it, but I really had no choice. Laying it on a rock, I cut it in two, then four, then kept chopping until it was just a mass of wriggling pieces. Taking the tobacco tin from my pocket, I scooped the meaty morsels into it and closed the lid.

I waited in the parlour for my mum to take herself off to her bedroom to make herself look beautiful for her beloved, and strode boldly into the scullery. There, on the hob, the big stew pot sat gently simmering. I lifted the lid and a mouth-watering puff of steam wafted up into my nostrils. I could see that the lumps of scrumptious beef were moist and tender, braising gently in a thick, rich, bubbling gravy, topped with plump suet dumplings. I emptied my tin into the pot and stirred it well.

"Ya still here, ya little shit?" Patrick greeted me as he walked in, coughing and snuffling, through the front door.

My mum hugged and kissed him, and I disappeared into my bedroom to sketch a fat, hairy ape in a string vest.

Later, I heard his ecstatic cries of, "Aw, dat's beautiful! Dat is absolutely beautiful, Dotty!"

I couldn't resist, and went and stood in the doorway of the scullery, watching him slobbering and chewing his way through his tasty meal, mouthful after mouthful.

"I bet you'd love some o' dis," he sneered, when my mum was safely out of earshot.

I sniggered to myself each time his mountainous fork slid into his huge, gaping mouth. He huffed and puffed, wiping his sweaty brow, chomping through the worms until he had scoffed the lot. He smirked at me, leaned back in his chair, sighed mockingly, and patted his bloated belly. The meal did him no harm, more's the pity.

A lady outside a huge house down the road prodded her friend as I was passing and grinned, "Ooh, here's a smart young man."

"That's a smashing red jacket," said the friend.

"He's almost the spit of Cliff, isn't he?" said the lady.

"Only more handsome," giggled her friend.

Spotting the name 'Esquire Club' engraved on a small gold plaque, I remarked, "My mum cleans this place."

"You're Dorothy's lad, are ya?" asked the first. "Here, you're not looking for a job are ya, lovey?"

Before I knew it, the lady had led me in through the front door and up the stairs to the second floor.

"My name's Bobbie," said the lady. "And this is my bar. Well, what d'ya think?"

It was a lovely place, cosy but stylish, and Bobbie was a lovely lady. She was about my mum's age, and glamorous and kind. She had ambition, and had just sweet-talked the local magistrate into granting her a licence to convert a downstairs room into a supper club, permitting the premises to stay open until the early hours. In my new jacket and a bow tie, I would greet the guests with a smile and serve them sausages or a bowl of crisps, just to satisfy the spirit of the licence. It was a happy place and I felt wanted there. Bobbie looked after me well, and the guests were friendly and generous with their tips. However, there was one great big fly in the ointment.

I heard the kerfuffle at the door, the booming Irish rant, "He's only fifteen! He shouldn't be working here! I'll get the police onto ya, Mrs! You see if I don't!"

Bobbie shrugged and told me she was sorry to lose me. Patrick was still kicking off as he dragged me up Holland Road by the throat, "Now get yourself a proper job and do some graftin', you fuckin' little scrounger!"

Dave and I both needed jobs, although neither of us saw 'grafting' as a desirable career choice. I saw painting as my future. I didn't really know what Dave saw as his future, but he was musical and taught me how to play guitar. Sometimes we'd muck about on the pier, or boot a ball around on Hove Lawns, or hang out at my mum's flat if Patrick wasn't there. However, any hint of 'the ape' arriving and we'd scarper double-quick. One evening I walked in through the front door and Patrick was waiting for me in the hallway. His eyes were as black as hell and his cheeks were as red as fire. I turned to escape, but he shoved the door shut and I was trapped.

"Right, where is it?" he hissed, stretching out his massive hairy palm under my nose. "Hand it over."

"What? I don't know what you're on about," I protested.

He was about to punch me in the face when my mum appeared and screamed, "Pat no!" She gripped my arms and stared deep into my eyes and demanded, "Have tha nicked brass outta meter? Have tha?"

"I ain't touched it, mum. Honest," I shivered.

Sure enough, the padlock on the meter was bent and snapped, and the pile of tanners from inside the coin box had gone.

"It wasn't me, mum," I assured her again and again.

"Well, I dunno who else has been in da house, do *you*?" glared Patrick, his bushy eyebrows heaving with anger.

As my mum was leading him away to the parlour, he shook his fist at me, and she asked him, "What'll ya have for ya tea, love? I'll make ya summit nice. Now what d'ya fancy? I gotta nice lamb chop…"

I went into my bedroom and lay on my bed, staring up into the darkness. Life at 'home' was unbearable.

"Now…" Patrick's putrid breath panted in my face. My eyes opened in a daze, shaken from my slumber. His rough, calloused palm smothered my mouth. "…it's just you and me."

I went spinning through the air. My skull hit the wall with a blinding crack. He rammed me backwards and winded me. His fists pounded into my belly, pummelling me like a punchbag. In the morning, I sheepishly lifted my vest, and my ribs and stomach were black-and-blue with bruises. I knew then what I had to do. I didn't get a chance to say goodbye to my mum, or to tell her that I loved her, but I knew that I had to leave. Although Bobbie had slipped me a little extra cash when I had abruptly and unceremoniously left her employ, it was hardly enough to fund an escape plan.

Every step of the way to Brighton station, I kept angrily looking over my shoulder. The gloomy rain drizzled down my face and I kicked my way through the piles of golden elm leaves which littered the pavement. Had the cowardly Irish ape given me a fair chance, then I would certainly have kicked *him,* right where it hurts.

"Platform ticket," I stated at the ticket window.

"So what's with the haversack then, son?" quizzed the ticket seller. "Come on, where ya goin'?"

"Victoria single," I sighed, adding quickly, "A child fare. I'm fifteen."

He cast his beady eye over me, then demanded, "Five-and-six. Departing platform seven."

The train was fairly empty, but when I handed in my ticket at the barrier in London, the place was alive with bustling commuters, all charging around, bumping and swerving past each other, with nobody pausing for a moment. I managed to squeeze my way outside, fighting against the unrelenting torrent. There was a smell of hotdogs and diesel, and the noise of bibbing taxis and newspaper sellers yelling, "Eenen Sannow! Eeenen Sannow!" All the traffic lurched a yard or two at a time, then stopped, before starting again, then stopped, then started, progressing at the pace of a wounded snail. I wandered around, marvelling at the chaos and the buzz of big city life. Although it was dark, I suddenly realised that it was always perfectly light. A small shop with flashing bulbs above its boarded window seemed to attract a number of sweaty gentlemen in raincoats.

"You got the time, love?" a friendly girl asked me. "You busy?"

Before I could answer her, she had gone to ask a sweaty gentleman in a raincoat the same questions. People gathered around a man with thickly Brylcreemed hair as he flipped a trio of playing cards over on a table and called out, "Chase the lady." An argument broke out over some money, and as a policeman approached, the man ran off up the road.

When the underground station had quietened down, I decided to make my way towards Paddington. I had the idea that Paddington was a popular area with tourists, and would, therefore, have tourist hotels, and could, therefore, be an area where I might, therefore, possibly find a live-in job. The streets of Paddington were, indeed, full of small B&B type places, one after the other along the rows of big old flaking houses. I went into a couple to inquire about work, but they were too busy serving evening meals to even talk to me. The rain was tipping down and I was shivering and skint, and my tummy and ribs were bruised and sore. I feared the prospect of sleeping outside on a windswept park bench where I might get attacked, or worse. I didn't know anyone and I was hungry. I spent sixpence on chips and stood sheltering in a doorway. I desperately needed somewhere to stay. Padding the streets in search of comfort and safety, I was struck by a barrage of 'No Vacancy' signs.

"You lookin' for a room, son?" called a man on the doorstep of a guesthouse, as he was putting out his milk-bottles. "You'll catch yer deff out there. I've got a little single if yer wannit."

"Yeah, thanks," I gratefully accepted, and followed him inside.

The place was a bit grim and tatty, but it was warm and dry.

"Ten bob," said the man, licking his thumb and flicking open his guestbook.

"I'm sorry, I haven't got any money," I whimpered.

"What?" he frowned, obviously taken aback.

"I'm an orphan. I was supposed to be collected you see, at the station, but they haven't come yet, and they should be here in the morning. I'm sure they'll be here in the morning. They'll pay you when they get here," I assured him.

"Who? Who was supposed to collect yer?" he questioned.

"Nuns," I said. "The nuns. They're coming from Paris and they're taking me back to France with them."

"Nuns?" he smirked.

"Yeah, from Paris. Please?" I pleaded sweetly.

He sighed deeply, "Alright, sign yer name dan there, son." Then, shaking his head, "Reckon I've 'eard it all nah! Breakfast is six till nine, and you pay for yer electric in the room. First floor, number sixteen."

Sinking thankfully into the mattress, and pulling the blanket up to my nose, I broke into a chuckle, pondering on what could be achieved by innocence and charm and youthful good looks. I slept the night away and awoke to a glorious sunlit morning. But as the cogs began to tick, it dawned on me that I was penniless, jobless, and trapped upstairs in a hotel bedroom.

After a prolonged period of contemplation, I shrieked triumphantly to myself, "That's it!"

Launching from my bed, I rushed to the door and crouched down. Next to the door was the electric meter; the electric meter which I assumed would be full of money. Twisting my penknife to-and-fro, I prised off the paltry padlock and tipped the cash box upside down. A pile of sixpenny pieces tinkled out, and I spread them across the lino, rapidly estimating that there were forty or fifty of them. Then, as I scooped them up, it suddenly occurred to me that I could get more. On my landing there were seven more rooms, and seven more meters! I heard the sound of rattling water-pipes, and people brushing their teeth, and the yawning chatter as the guests left their rooms. Fortuitously, I was at the far end of the corridor, where nobody came, right next to the fire escape. I got dressed and bided my time, peeking out along the row of bedroom doors, waiting for my moment. I watched the guests coming out, some going down to breakfast, some with baggage and obviously leaving for good. When the coast was clear, I nipped along into the open rooms, popped the meters and snuck away down the fire escape, then disappeared into the hustle-and-bustle of everyday life.

My pockets were bulging with sixpences. I lay low in the Edgware Road, hiding out in a busy Turkish café until the banks opened. I exchanged the tanners into pound notes, a pound in each bank so as not to arouse suspicion with the tellers. Although I had made more than ten quid in profit, I still had no job, and a face which might just get me nabbed by the police. The cries of "Eenen Sannow! Eeenen Sannow!" which rang out on every street corner were, I discovered, the places where you could buy a copy of the 'Evening Standard', even at eleven in the morning. I scanned through the employment pages, discounting anything to do with 'manual' or 'office' or 'printing'. One small advert caught my eye and I kept going back to it, even though all I knew about it was that Chipperfield's wanted 'Men for Circus' at their winter quarters in a place called Chipping Norton.

"Chippin' where?" shrugged everyone on the Edgware Road when I asked them. "Is it in London?"

A cabby suggested he could take me to, "Chippin' Barnet, over the uvver side of Cockfosters."

"Excuse me, could I have a word?" inquired a deep voice from over my shoulder. I nervously turned around and tried to withhold any evidence of shock as I was confronted by the steely glare of a lanky copper. "If you'd care to accompany me, sir." My stomach churned and I thought about running away, but he looked like an athletic type. There was no escape. "If you'd like to follow me to the police box, I'll find out where Chipping Norton is for you," he smiled. Then, when he'd made the call, he advised me, "Apparently it's in the Cotswolds. Beautiful part of the country. You can get a train from Paddington."

I was relieved to get out of town, and excited to be heading for a job in the circus.

Three hours later, a yokel man leaning up against a Beardmore Taxi grinned at me and asked, "Ar, now where is it you be lookin' for?"

"King's Ride?" I answered. "Chipper…"

"Chipperfield's!" he yelped, joyfully. "Jump in, boy. You gonna join the circus?"

He dropped me off at the end of the lane, refusing to accept the fare, insisting that the trip was too short. As I sauntered in the sunshine, the birds merrily twittered in the hedgerows and the glorious sight of a circus big top came into view, its ship-like masts rising up high above the trees. A wide set of gates opened out onto a field. Dozens of trucks and caravans and tents and corrugated Nissen huts encircled the huge main tent. It was like a village.

"What can I do for you?" asked a man on the gate.

"I'm looking for a job," I said, showing him the ad. in the paper.

The man whistled with ear-splitting vigour, and bawled, "Louis! Someone to see you!" then stood, looking me up and down.

Presently, a tiny Indian gentleman in a leather blouson and baggy turned-up jeans approached. He was around fifty and, as he adjusted the sailor-type cap on his head, he started at me with a quizzical expression as if to say, "Who are you? What do you want here?"

"I'm looking for a job," I told him.

I saw the two men glance at each other and smirk.

"Sorry," Louis said. "We need good strong blokes. This is heavy work. You're too young. Sorry."

He turned to walk away and I called out, "I can do heavy work."

He turned back and felt my biceps, and shoved my shoulder to see if he could move me. Apparently, he wasn't unimpressed, but warned, "You wouldn't be swanning around with the stars and living in five-star luxury. It's hard graft, seven days a week. You'll get stomped on, bitten, farted at and covered in shit, but otherwise it's a good life. Plenty of travel. Are you still interested?"

Leading me across the field, he acknowledged various characters on the way: a pair of sparring unicyclists; a couple of beautifully built girls in spangled leotards; a midget; a clown; a lady feeding some yapping dogs; and a couple of burly blokes with buckets and shovels.

"Here..." said Louis, pulling open the flaps of a sizeable tent so that I could see inside. "This is where you would be sleeping." Three tall camels, munching in a pen, looked up at me from their feeding trough. "You would sleep over there in the corner. You would have a camp bed of course. Come…" And as we walked further around behind the row of huts and trucks, he said, "*This is what your job would be.*" A herd of fidgeting elephants, each with a short chain around its leg, trampled up and down, rubbing and scratching, and playfully swinging their trunks in and out of a water butt. There was a giant fart, followed by a tumbling mountain of poo. "They do a lot of that. Look out!" I was suddenly hit in the face with a trumpet-blast of cold water. "Naughty Leila!" he yelled at the giant beast. And then to me, with a dazzling, toothy grin, "Have you ever worked with elephants before?"

Almost immediately I was put to work, crawling around under the giant's bellies, between their great plodding feet, shovelling up their shit into dustbins. It was a miracle that I wasn't trampled to death. The loaded dustbins weighed a ton and I struggled to carry them, two at a time, to a dung heap some way downwind of the caravans. Then I fed them with bales of hay, which I had to split into slices as they bashed and barged me with their trunks. I bent down to pick up the hose and found myself flying through the air and crashing down onto my face in the dirt. I scrambled away on all fours, lucky that I was only spitting out muck and not my own teeth.

"Did she head-butt you?" Louis asked, staring at me on the ground, and chuckled, "Sally's a bugger for that."

After I had catered for the animals, I was fed and watered myself and, as Louis had promised, I was supplied with a camp bed to sleep on, right next to the camels. It was a cold night and I appreciated the warmth which radiated from them, although the smell of their breath was truly awful. In the middle of the night, I was woken up by lions roaring nearby, although they may have been tigers.

Louis was the head groom and I called him 'sir'. He knew all about elephants and, crucially, the peculiarities of each of our girls, which ones were smart and which ones were stupid, which ones were laid back and which ones were uptight, which ones were funny and which ones were serious, which ones were naughty and which ones were nasty. Louis taught me to respect and recognise them individually, Leila, Mary, Camella, Suzy, Dayla, Dana, Rhani, Seeta, May, Mabel, Janie and Sally, and throughout the winter months I got to know them quite intimately. Each day, I would release their shackles and march them, linked together trunk-to-tail, over to the main tent for training. Upon arrival, the canvas would be flapped open, and then smartly shut as the last one disappeared inside. It was the same for all the animals. Nobody except the trainers was allowed inside.

My years at Barnardo's proved to be good training for the gruelling work and icy hosepipe showers. I always tried to be cheerful, friendly and conscientious. I think it's what gained me the respect of my new family, the circus characters who had taken me in. The job paid eleven quid a week, plus plenty of good grub, and I loved the sense of freedom. Whenever I had any spare time, after my duties were done, I would sit and draw or paint.

"That's good," commented Dickie, as he looked over my shoulder at the collage of wild animals which I was painting in oils. "Can you do signwriting, too?"

"Yeah, I expect so," I shrugged.

"Right," he said. "I'm gonna have a word with my dad."

The Chipperfields had been running the circus for near on three hundred years, and Dickie, who was a couple of years older than me, belonged to something like the eighth generation of the family business. His grandparents and parents, brothers and sisters, uncles and aunties, nephews and nieces, were all performing artists, and Dickie was principally a lion tamer and elephant trainer. We got on well together, and the whole family seemed to like me, although the stars of the show lived in luxurious caravans, drove around in swanky cars, and didn't really mix. Signwriting came easily to me and I was happy to paint anything, whether it be lettering on kiosks or giant jungle scenes on hoardings. Of course, any artistic duties had to fit in with the elephants and camels. It seemed that the big boss was pleased with my creative efforts and I was promoted from sharing my quarters with the beasts, to bedding down in my own comfy little caravan.

As spring approached, we all mucked in to help with dropping the big top, folding tents, washing the fleet of trucks, trailers, caravans and horseboxes, before loading up in anticipation of shipping out. One bright morning at the beginning of April, all species of wild animal were walked, dragged, pulled and pushed into their travelling cages, hissing and spitting, snarling and snapping, until they were all safely loaded and locked on board their trailers. I looked on as the column of diesel engines roared into life, sending up a giant black smoke signal over the skies of Chipping Norton, announcing that Chipperfield's Circus was hitting the road on its grand summer tour.

"Come on, this way," said Dickie, leading Louis and I down the lane in the direction of the railway station with twelve trumping elephants.

"Keep up," called out Louis, as my string of six started to play up and fall behind his.

I felt proud as all manner of townsfolk came out of their houses, shops and pubs to cheer us on and wave us goodbye. In the siding of the goods yard stood a chain of three freight wagons.

"Nice and calm," urged Louis, gently guiding the herd along, with Dickie waving his stick and slapping the first pair into the first carriage.

"Right Max, in you go," directed Dickie. "Get down underneath them. Don't hang about."

I hesitated for a moment before crouching down and cautiously crawling between their legs. They were standing side-by-side at the end of the coach, getting quite agitated, shuffling around and stomping so hard that I thought they might smash through the wooden floor.

"Go on! Get in there! Get them chains on!" Dickie yelled impatiently.

"Be careful, Max!" warned Louis.

I don't think Leila and Mary even knew that I was down there, and they clumsily barged me between them and kicked me, simultaneously peeing and pooing. I scrambled towards one of the giant leg-irons which was attached to a chain and a metal bolt in the corner. Nervously lifting the shackle, I opened it out and fastened it as quickly as I could around Leila's massive front ankle. She stamped her disapproval. I dodged out of the way and manoeuvred myself beneath Mary, kneeling on her foot, then lifted up her manacle and attached it. Before I had even had the chance to secure it properly, Dickie was already goading in the next pair of aggravated elephants.

"Whoa Camella! Whoa there Suzy!" sang out Louis, in a calming tone. "You okay, Max?"

It was a frightening experience, and one which I had to repeat many, many times. With our dozen elephants loaded into their two tailor-made carriages, it just remained for me to put the camels into the brake van at the rear, then load the hay and give the girls a drink before the journey. I stacked the bales in the brake van, before dashing up the platform to fill my mobile water trough (a dustbin on wheels). When I flipped open the side shutters of the elephant carriages, the elephants leaned out and dipped their trunks into the water, spraying me because they felt happy and hydrated. The camels, of course, didn't need to drink. We were hitched up to the billowing steam locomotive and set off up-country.

"See you in Dudley," Dickie grinned from the platform, leaving me to travel up in the hay wagon and look after the animals en route.

When we arrived, I had to brave crawling into the wagons again to release the elephant's chains, then manoeuvre each one out backwards by the tail. We dressed the elephants in glittering show harnesses, then paraded them from the railway station to the circus site. Girls in sparkly leotards rode aboard them, waving at the crowds. And it didn't escape my attention that some of the pretty, local girls smiled and waved at *me* as we went marching by. The circus site was bustling with activity. Riggers and crew were unloading and bolting together sections of the ring and kiosks and stalls, many of which were decorated with my vibrant illustrations. Small convoys of familiar red and blue Chipperfield lorries and trailers kept on arriving, followed by the bosses and artistes in their cars and caravans. I oversaw the elephants as they lifted and shifted some of the heavy equipment around, and hoisted up the heavy masts of the big top. Constructing a circus was hard and dangerous work, but my loyal elephants always did whatever I asked of them. At the end of the day, when we had finished, I got dressed up and Dickie took me out for a slap-up meal at the Mirabelle Café.

"Hay's mine!" I heard a dull and unfamiliar accent spout from a table full of saucy girls. "I love yower hat," pouted another at me. "I doh love a man with a big Stetson!" And they all fell about giggling.

We were seen as celebrities, and all snazzed-up in my new cowboy hat I was never short of kisses and cuddles.

Early in the morning there was a flurry of activity as the handlers washed and dressed the animals and, accompanied by jugglers, dwarves and clowns, at 9 A.M. sharp, we set off on a noisy advertising extravaganza around the town. And our efforts proved fruitful, as later the crowds flocked in to see 'Europe's Largest Circus and Menagerie'. The scale of the show was out of this world, with an audience of 6,000, and scores of spectacular acts, such as flying acrobats, high wire daredevils, bouncing trampolinists, knife-throwers and crazy clowns, all of the acts boasting exotic family names: The Cimarros; The Primlettis; The Biasinis; The Rosaires; The Bedinis; The Nicolodis and many more. And when the performance began, the air was filled with excited gasps and cheers and laughter, then long, drawn out silences which made my heart pound as I wondered what was happening inside.

"Time to rake out, Max," smiled Louis, as I was drying off my girls.

I cringed and sighed, rolling up my sleeves in readiness. 'Raking out' was an unpleasant task, but one which was totally necessary. I started with Leila. Forming my hand into a fist, I pressed it against the wrinkly ring of flesh between her back legs. Then, as I pressed more firmly, her anus opened up into a gaping cavern and I slid my arm up inside her until it had almost disappeared. Unclenching my hand and forming a scoop with my fingers, I began to drag the poo from her bowels. Obligingly, she started to defecate and urinate, and I dodged to one side to try and avoid the worst of the gushing waterfall. When she was empty, I moved on to do Mary, until all twelve had been relieved and were ready to perform without the fear of causing unnecessary embarrassment in the ring.

I quickly washed myself down and got ready for my next task, which was altogether more pleasant. A glamorous and bewitching young lady who went by the name of Zira used a giant glass aquarium to perform her act. It weighed a couple of tons when it was full of water and it was my job to have one of the elephants wheel it into the big top. As the lights were dimmed, I was given my cue to move. The flaps were opened, I patted Leila on the rump, and we marched out into the centre of the ring. I stepped back into the shadows, with the audience murmuring in anticipation. The dazzling spotlights suddenly flared up and the crowd applauded. As the cover was slowly raised from the tank, there was a collective gasp of horror. A genuine, man-sized crocodile was splashing about inside, wriggling and writhing. A cheer went up as Zira was revealed in a leopard-skin bikini, with a huge python curled around her neck. A fish was tossed into the tank, and the crocodile thrashed around, snapping its terrifying jaws open and shut, instantly devouring it. Silence fell and Zira was dropped into the water with the wild, scaly beast. There was a ferocious commotion of swirling water and flailing limbs, then Zira wrestled with it, clasping it tightly around the mouth so that it couldn't chew off an arm or a leg, or eat her. Minutes later, she was lifted out and the astonished punters got to their feet, clapping and whistling as she smiled and waved at them. It was a truly astonishing act; probably the most audacious and bizarre of all circus acts.

However, the animals were the real stars of the show, performing whatever clever and unnatural acts were demanded of them. Each morning and on Sunday afternoons, the general public was invited to visit the on-site Menagerie and see over 200 animals at close quarters. We had almost every creature imaginable: horses; ponies; poodles; camels; giraffes; llamas; grizzly bears; polar bears; panthers; lions; tigers; zebras; hippos; rhinos; elephants; monkeys; chimpanzees; pelicans; ostriches; pigeons; crocodiles; alligators; snakes and pretty much everything else. The punters were even allowed to stroke, cuddle, feed and ride upon the safer ones. It was a wonderful and educational attraction, especially for the children, and at a shilling a ticket it was a real money-spinner, especially as the animals were just lying around on site and doing nothing anyway. Apart from painting giant colourful animals around the enclosures, I kept an eye on the kids who came to see the elephants, making sure that no-one crossed the safety rope which separated the humans from the beasts.

I knew the personalities of all my girls and I knew that Leila could be a bit of a bugger. If she was in a strop, she'd grab a dustbin and toss it thirty feet into the air, or grab my rake from me and whack me with it. And she was a damned good shot! But generally the herd would pretty much let me do anything with them, and Leila would lift me up on her knee and let me climb aboard her. From there I would step from one elephant to the other, walking across the fatty part of their backs as I gave them a final dusting-off before they went into the ring to perform.

"Dickie! No!" I shouted one day, as he nonchalantly went to step over the safety rope. "Watch Leila. She's in a bad mood."

"I train the bloody things," sneered Dickie, disregarding my warning.

The three-ton monster suddenly lunged at him, shaking her head, and barged him backwards onto the ground. I managed to grab Dickie's arm and pull him away, just as Leila brought her giant foot crashing down, trumpeting wildly into the air. It was a close call and, fortunately, after Louis had calmed the situation down, both of them lived to see another day.

We didn't like 'gaff boys' much; they were the lads who worked on the fairground. The funfairs were nothing to do with us. They just followed us around wherever we went, setting up on the same field as us, leeching off our customers as our evening shows were ending. The 'gaff boys' would hop around on the howling waltzer, jumping from car to car and spinning the girls as fast as they could to make them scream, then try to steal them away at the end of the night. It would annoy us if we'd taken a shine to a particular young lady, then see her stolen away by our rivals, and it would sometimes lead to punch-ups. Luckily, I would nearly always win the fights, and the girls.

I enjoyed dressing up in well-fitted suits, and some said that on a night out I looked like I could be the fifth Beatle. To make a bit of extra clothes money, so that I could buy good, classy gear, I sold manure on the side. It was ironic that to look 'cool' I had to do something so 'uncool'. My mum had once told me that in Yorkshire they had a saying, "Where there's muck there's brass," and I found it to be true. Wherever the circus went, there was always a long queue of eager gardeners who wanted what I was able to supply. Myself and another groom called Steve would shovel up the elephant droppings into sacks and flog them for three bob a go. By all accounts it was the most dynamic fertilizer known to man. However, on occasions we would have a problem, and demand would outstrip supply. Desperate measures would be called for and I would tell the customers to wait for a few minutes, then have a quiet word with my girls, roll up my sleeve and 'rake out'.

"We need more!" Steve demanded one morning, as we sold the last bag.

"I've got all I can out of them," I shrugged.

"Ladies and gentlemen, if you'd care to come back," he told

the queue of disgruntled gardeners, "we will be taking delivery of a fresh supply in an hour."

The throng of customers chuckled and drifted away.

I looked at Steve and asked, somewhat puzzled, "What d'ya tell 'em that for?"

"Leave it to me," he grinned, tapping his nose.

He returned fifteen minutes later with a plain white paper bag. Despite my objections, he took out several boxes of Senokot and popped the laxative tablets into the mouths of the greedy elephants. Within minutes, the poor creatures were farting and shitting all over the place. On the plus side we managed to fulfil our orders, but on the minus side we had no way of stopping the deluge. The performance that night didn't go without a hiccup, and Steve was sacked in the morning.

As the circus moved on, I loaded my elephants and camels onto their train every few days, and unloaded them again at various towns across the country. I would parade the elephants through the streets, prepare them for the shows, feed and water them, kiss and cuddle with a few local girls, before marching back to the station and moving on. It all became routine. There were always rumours sweeping around the site about people leaving to join this-circus-or-that. As an experienced groom, I was aware that new possibilities could open up for me, and when I heard that a rival circus was hiring for some big shows in London, I felt an overwhelming attraction.

"I just want some time off," I told Dickie.

"Okay," he sighed. "But you will be coming back, wont' you, Max?"

I found my way to the Olympia Grand Exhibition Hall in Kensington, London.

"Camping and Outdoor Life Exhibition, this way," said a man in a smart grey jacket as he ushered me into a snaking queue which led up the steps to the front entrance.

"I'm here for the circus," I explained, pointing up at an illuminated sign which read: 'Bertram Mills Circus'.

"You're a bit early for that! Come back at the weekend," the man laughed.

I clarified that I had come to work at the circus, and he directed round to the back of the building where boards and timber were being lugged inside by an army of workmen. Carpenters and riggers were busily nailing and bolting the show together, and when I told them I was looking for a job they just chuckled and puffed on their cigarettes.

"What d'ya know?" asked a suited gentleman who seemed to be in charge.

"I can groom elephants," I boasted. "Or anything else you've got."

"Can you tame a lion, son?" he asked. Then after a short pause he grinned, "Only joking. But you're a good-looking lad…"

I followed him into a maze of corridors, assuring him that I knew the ropes and I was a hard worker.

"Here, try this on," said the chap, selecting a costume from a long rail. It comprised of a fancy red and gold braided coat, white breeches and gloves. He looked me up and down, straightened a powdered wig onto my head, then nodded, "Yep, you'll do."

I was hired principally as a ring groom, which entailed assisting any of the acts with their props and so forth during performances. But my duties also extended outside the ring, acting as a personal flunky (assistant) to a couple of the show's big stars. The first star I had to look after was Coco the Clown, probably the most famous of all the circus slapstick funnymen in the world. He was quite a poorly man and hardly able to perform at all. He looked old and tired, although he still had a twinkle in his eye, and was easy to look after. Whenever I approached him to ask, "Is there anything I can get you, sir?" he would simply reply in his soft Russian accent, "Brandy." And as long as I kept him constantly topped-up with bottles of the hard stuff, he was happy.

My second star was called Rogana, a stunningly attractive German lady, sleek and slim, with silky black hair which flowed seductively halfway down her back. Adopting a Native American theme, she would appear in a lavish feather robe and headdress, underneath which she would reveal a spangly silver leotard. She was a remarkable woman and her performance involved various acts of balancing. She would roll into the ring, tiptoeing on top of a large shiny globe, then with a patter of her dainty feet she would propel herself up and down ramps and across a series of high bridges. To finish the act, she would balance on top of two globes which were standing on top of each other, and with another globe balancing on her head. But that was only the first part of her routine. Her main act was totally incredible and death-defying. I would have thought it unbelievable and impossible, had I not learnt how it was done.

As the orchestra played and the drums rolled, Rogana appeared and I passed her a thin-bladed sword, about three feet long. She popped a large balloon with the point, to prove that it was sharper than a pin. With a long dagger jutting straight out from between her teeth, she balanced the point of the sword on the point of the dagger, so the sword was vertical and pointing directly downwards. On top of the sword, she balanced a circular drinks tray, complete with four full wine glasses. Then, tilting her head backwards so the sword-point was aimed directly into her face, she proceeded to climb the rungs of a twenty-foot ladder. One slip and the sword would drop straight into her eyeball or through her cheek. My palms sweated and my body shivered. Once she was perched at the top, the ladder started to rock, swaying backwards and forwards several feet as if it were made of rubber. Rogana arched her body and leaned backwards, aligning the dagger and the sword so they were both upright, balancing precariously tip-on-tip, the sword poised to pierce her heart if it slipped. The drums rolled and a fanfare of trumpets blasted out, and the audience gasped and broke into rapturous applause. As she climbed down and stepped off the ladder, I took the tray and dagger from her. She danced about triumphantly, tossing the wine from a glass into the air, before stabbing the sword into a block of wood, leaving it wobbling as she exited the ring. A cacophony of admiring claps and cheers followed her as she left.

"Vell Max, did you like vot you saw?" she asked me as I went into her dressing room.

"Yeah, it was… amazing!" I gushed. "I've never seen anything like it!"

"Good," she smiled, stretching open her costume and sliding it down to her waist. "Vud you pour me some vorter, please?" When I turned back to hand her the glass, she was slipping the leotard over her thighs, and a moment later it was around her ankles. "Zo, you have never seen anything like it?" she tittered, pursing her lips around the glass, totally naked.

"No, nothing quite that wonderful," I said.

"Oh Max," she sighed, "you are such a handsome young man. If you ver only ten years older, then…"

As I lay upstairs in the circus workers' dormitory, I pondered on what might have been. She was thirty and I was sixteen. However, there were other fish in the sea. The enormous grand hall of Olympia, with its tall arched ceiling of glass, had been split into two to accommodate our six-thousand-seater circus ring at one end and the Camping Exhibition at the other. The only barrier between us and them were some canvas screens which were tied shut with pieces of string. Curiosity was a strong urge in young men, and it was easy enough to untie a few knots and wriggle through to the other side. It came as a wonderful surprise to myself and the other circus grooms that in order to sell outdoor equipment it was necessary to employ a bevy of pretty models. Inside every tent, draped across every camp-bed, pegging out every groundsheet, cooking on every primus stove, pumping up every lilo, showering under every shower, and demonstrating every item of camping paraphernalia, young ladies were frolicking about in shorts or swimsuits. Naturally, us circus lads helped ourselves to the ones we fancied, along with any equipment which the stallholders had been stupid enough to leave out overnight.

Close to where I was standing backstage, a couple of famous faces caught my eye, not in the rows of seats for the general public, but in one of the small private boxes. Hattie Jacques and her husband John Le Mesurier and their two boys were settling into their seats, in readiness for the show. I smiled at them and they smiled back. The show began and I helped, as always, with bringing on the props and shifting them off when the acts had finished. It was pretty straightforward. But this night a new act appeared. A six-foot diameter wooden target on a frame was rolled into the wings, as a troupe of crazy Mexicans ran into the ring amid a riotous flurry of gunfire and deafening explosions. They chased around in a bedlam of gunpowder smoke and flashes, jumping and tumbling, until finally running off to a roar of approval.

The lights dimmed and I was called upon to help shift the target into the ring. A small Mexican man in an ornate tuxedo, and his young lady assistant in a similarly elaborate swimming costume, appeared beside me. He handed me a metal pot and a bundle of knives to hold onto as he strapped his assistant to the wheel. After a dramatic build-up, shouting incomprehensibly into the audience and spinning the lady round-and-round, he took the knives from me, muttering about something in what I assumed to be Spanish. The only word I understood was the last one: "Okay?" As he started his act, it all seemed clear. He opened the pot, dipped the tip of a knife into it and set it on fire. He threw the knife at the girl, missing her by a whisker, then repeated with each of the knives until she was surrounded by a Catherine Wheel of swirling flames. Her smile never faltered, but she looked relieved when finally he released her and she stepped down to take a bow. As he held her hand aloft to acknowledge the admiring applause, he glanced over at me and gesticulated at the array of flaming daggers which were still stuck in the target.

Rushing forwards, I quickly began plucking the knives out, but in a flash I was burning! My wig and coat flared up and I was engulfed in flame. As I dropped the blazing knives onto the sawdust and tore off my melting headpiece, I could see Hattie and John and the children all laughing hysterically. I writhed on the ground, the sawdust catching alight around me, struggling to rip the jacket from my body. Then there was water all over me, then relief. The bells of the ambulance clanged in my head as soothing lotion was massaged onto my stinging flesh. I was taken to Hammersmith Hospital and kept in for treatment.

A nurse strode up the ward with a copious vase of flowers, and I joked with her, "Wow! Someone's popular."

She sniffed the blooms and smiled, "They're for you," and put them next to my bed. "And there's chocolates too. Black Magic. And a note."

I opened the envelope and read the heavily perfumed note: 'Dear Max, I hope you're well and didn't lose any hair! Sorry we laughed, but it did look frightfully amusing and we thought it must be part of the act. Wishing you a speedy recovery. With very best wishes, Hattie Jacques and John Le Mesurier'. I was touched. Three days later I returned to work, slightly singed and costumeless, but undaunted.

A couple of weeks later, when the Olympia shows were over, I took the train from Euston to Wigan and rejoined the Chipperfield's tour. Reunited with my girls, I patted them and hugged them around their trunks. They danced about and trumpeted excitedly and, according to Louis, they had missed me. As there was a new lad helping out with the elephants, Dickie insisted that he and I should hit the town. We went to a lively café he'd discovered, called the Green Parrot Café. Armed with an acoustic guitar, I managed to woo the local ladies, and it was as if I had never been away. And so, none-the-worse for my adventure, life went back almost to the way it had been, shepherding the elephants on and off their train, saying "goodbye" to one town and "hello" to new ones. However, after my trip away, it seemed as though I was appreciated more and my workload wasn't quite so strenuous. But I still had to wash in cold water, except when I could find a public bathhouse wherever we were. It certainly wasn't five star living. When our successful summer tour came to end and we returned to the winter quarters in Chipping Norton, my life went up a gear. I was invited to eat in better company, and it felt as if I had been accepted into the fold.

The new lad screamed. I dashed to see what had happened. He was lying in the straw, curled up, clutching his belly. I had warned him a few times, "The elephants are clumsy, but watch out for the giraffes. Giraffes kick!" And he had taken a hell of a kick. He threw up blood and retired from the job with a ruptured gut. The circus was a dangerous place, as I knew from my own experience, and accidents occurred quite frequently. One of the trapeze artists fell forty feet. She missed the safety net and smashed her skull on the ground. It was fatal. And amongst the general hands, it wasn't unusual to see a missing finger, a mangled limb, or a scar, but it was more likely to have been caused by human error or a mechanical mishap than the act of a wild animal.

The person whose job it was to move the dangerous animals during performances was known as the 'Beast Man'. Throughout the show he would have to persuade more than a hundred lions, tigers, panthers, leopards, etc. out of their cages, into a holding cage, then through a network of tunnels, and into a large performance cage inside the ring. One evening, as was normal, the signal was given to release the lions. As the 'Beast Man' jostled eight lions into the tunnel, his assistants opened and shut the partitions to ensure that they ran obediently straight into the ring cage. Upon their arrival, a gasp erupted from the excited audience, and the lions went on to perform perfectly, jumping through hoops of fire whilst roaring viciously throughout. However, as the beasts left the ring, and the mums and dads and children sat in innocent bliss, a mistake occurred, a howling cockup of monumental proportions. Somehow, as sections of the ring cage were being dismantled, the lions turned about and began to run back down the tunnel and into the ring. For a moment we were all stunned. Two lions got through before the partitions could be shut off. The pair growled and started to pad towards the crowd. People were screaming and scrambling across the rows of seats to get out. I was powerless to do anything. The 'Beast Man' and the trainer and the handlers tried to get the animals under control, but I think the pandemonium made the lions more confused and they prowled around looking angry and agitated. Gunshots rang out, loud and final. The lions lay dead, even though we all knew that they probably couldn't have killed a soul, not without claws or teeth.

One morning in Sheffield, after two years or so of touring, I turned to Dickie and told him that I wanted to move on.

"You wanna go off again for a couple weeks?" he smiled. "Well if you have to. But just you hurry back. It's not just us that needs you. What about the elephants? You know, Max, I really think they love…"

"No," I interrupted. "I want to move on - for good."

Dickie and his family gave me a hundred quid as a leaving present and wished me all the luck in the world, in whatever it was I was going to do. And *that* I didn't know. I had my clothes, my paints, and my money, and I was happy to feel free again, free to go anywhere, and do anything I wanted.

CHAPTER 3:
GIBLETS AND SONGSTERS

London somehow seemed an obvious choice. Heading in the direction of Olympia, I thought it would be best to catch a direct train on the underground to Shepherd's Bush and walk from there. Despite the underground actually going overground, I found myself at Shepherd's Bush Green, which was like a large field with a racetrack of traffic whizzing around its perimeter, and bordered on all sides by rows of shops. A theatre stood prominently on one side, its impressive illuminated signs boasting: 'BBC TV Theatre. Pete Murray. Juke Box Jury'. Around the corner was a long street, full of market stalls and scruffy shops and cafes, and further down were scrap dealers' yards and second-hand car lots. People rushed busily about, and cars and buses tooted them as they stepped off the overcrowded pavement and into the road. In a newsagent's window was a postcard advertising 'Rooms to Let', and I decided that Shepherd's Bush was a good place to be.

Four quid bought me a small room with a bed and a battered Baby Belling cooker. There was a plate and a bowl and a pair of charred saucepans, and a bathroom down the hall with gas hot water. I did glance at the meters, but they were well secured, and it seemed unnecessary to cause a stink in what was now my own back yard. On the lookout for new opportunities, I wandered up Holland Park Avenue from my digs and found myself in Hyde Park. At the top end of the park was a broad street with a row of lofty trees and houses, and a skyscraper. Following the concrete pedestrian tunnels, I found myself at Marble Arch, and then on Park Lane. It was a wonderful feeling to be standing on the most famous and most expensive street on a Monopoly board. As I walked past the Grosvenor House Hotel, a fleet of doormen in top hats was rushing to open the doors of Rolls Royces and Aston Martins for cigar-smoking gents in sprucely cut camelhair coats, accompanied by their glamorous fur-coated companions. The same at the Dorchester, and at the towering building which I discovered was the Hilton. I could smell the money.

"Excuse me," I ventured, to a dismal looking man who was rushing out of the shabby tradesman's entrance at the rear of the Dorchester. He ignored me. I asked another man who flitted by in a white blood-stained jacket, "Any jobs going?" But he was too busy to answer. I waited and asked a man who locked his bicycle to a lamppost, but he disappeared inside with a grunt. A rambling tramp groaned from a nearby doorway.

It seemed crazy. Everyone was too busy to even talk to me, to even address my simple inquiry. And so, I decided that I may as well go in and take a look around. The kitchens were huge and awash with activity. In a haze of sweat and steam, the din of clanging saucepans and clinking plates was almost deafening. I breezed through, as cool as a cucumber, and into some service corridors which led to the storerooms and lifts and backdoors which fed the hotel. Dozens of soda syphons, all empty, were dumped on a trolley, just waiting to be requisitioned, and I slipped a couple under my jacket and walked out. The man in the off-licence near my flat unquestioningly refunded my deposit of seven-and-six, per bottle.

As I tucked into a steaming steak-and-kidney pudding, surrounded by tables of gobbling workmen, I heard a familiar and dreary accent, "Have yow got any faggots?" I looked up and saw a young man at the counter. He was trying to visually describe what a faggot looked like. "Sit down, dearie, over there. The waitress'll be over presently," he was told.

He sat down at my small table, opposite me, took a hearty slurp of stewed tea and sighed, "Nice cuppa tay. I do like a nice cuppa tay."

"Yeah," I agreed.

"I'm Taffy by the way," he yawned.

"Taffy?" I questioned. "You sound more Black Country."

"Stourbridge," he slothfully reported. "Do yow know it?"

I told him that I'd been in Dudley, and he droned on for some time about West Bromwich Albion.

"Where are you staying?" I asked him.

"I'm not toe sure," he said, scratching his head. "I got a bit lost. I think it's opposite a pub somewhere."

"What's it called?" I asked him.

"Called?" he asked me. "The summit summit bed and breakfast, or summit. I think"

"I'll help you look for it, if you like," I told him.

I don't know why I wanted to help him. It was almost as if I felt duty bound to look after him. We did find Taffy's B&B, but his limited cash supply meant that he would only be able to stay there for a few days. Taffy had come to London for the same reason as me, and together we asked around at some cheap hotels which we thought may have wanted to employ us. Ideally, we wanted jobs with live-in accommodation, but whenever we went and inquired as a pair we were told, "We've no jobs at all." I fared better on my own, but Taffy wasn't so successful.

"Try wearing a tie," I suggested. "And smile."

"Hello. My name's Taffy. Do yow 'ave a job for me plaise?" I overheard him mope to the manager on the doorstep of a two-star hotel.

He got thrown out of his bed and breakfast and I let him sleep on the floor at my place. But money was getting tight and I was worried that the landlord might put up the rent if he got wind that two of us were living there.

"There's nothing else for it," I told Taffy. "We'll go to the Dorchester."

Taffy looked characteristically mystified as we walked up through Hyde Park. I left him sitting on a bench, watching squirrels and 'wenches' (as he called them), while I went round to the back entrance of the Dorchester and returned a few minutes later with a pair of soda syphons tucked under a white jacket which

I'd managed to procure. I gave him the jacket and explained everything to him. He came back a few minutes later, syphonless, saying that a housekeeper had caught him wandering about in the corridors and had sent him back to the kitchens. Over the next few days, I did manage to sneak back in and relieve the Dorchester of a few more syphons, and Taffy also managed to nab a couple.

"So where are you getting all these syphons from then, son?" demanded the man in the off-licence, as he paid me out another thirty bob.

"My mum," I chirped. "She loves a good party, does my mum."

"Oh yeah?" he scowled.

"Yeah, she's always having them," I grinned. "I'll get you an invite if you like. See yer."

Taffy and I were lubricating our brain cells with a greasy breakfast, and trying to think up a plan of action. "How about," he suddenly gasped, struck by a thunderbolt between shovelfuls, "we take the syphons to a different offy?"

"I think we've done the syphons to death," I sighed. "No, we need to do something more drastic, more exciting."

"Like what?" he groaned, staring blankly at his empty plate.

"Hayling," I said, with an air of decisiveness and conviction.

As we sat on the train bound for Chichester and heard the customary cry of, "Tickets please… Tickets please…" we got up and legged it.

We were scurrying away along the carriages, when Taffy suddenly stopped outside a toilet cubicle. "It's engaged," I shrugged, somewhat impatiently, pointing out that the indicator clearly said: 'Engaged'.

He knocked on the toilet door and announced authoritatively, "Ticket collector…" The occupant objected to being so rudely interrupted, but Taffy simply demanded, "Put your ticket under the door please, sir?"

It was an act of unexpected genius, and one which we successfully repeated further up the train.

The bus from Chichester to Hayling Island was full of cheery tourists. As the sea came into view, we were still chuckling about the poor swines who we'd left trying to explain to the officious ticket collector why they were unable to produce a valid train ticket. Our bus flitted across the narrow bridge onto the island and drifted along the country lanes where cows and horses stood lazily grazing in the sunshine.

"Coronation Holiday Camp!" cried the bus conductor, a few minutes later.

I gave Taffy a nudge, and an excited bunch of holidaymakers bustled off the bus, laden with bags, and buckets and spades. We followed them, and I couldn't help but notice that amongst the excited families there were teenaged daughters and granddaughters. There were also small parties of playful young ladies, away from home for the first time and looking for fun. Hayling Island was going to be my oyster, I decided, just as long as I could get a job.

"Can I help you?" asked a pair of receptionists in the front office.

I went up to one and Taffy went up to the other.

"So what can you do?" asked mine.

"Oh, I can do a lot of things?" I grinned.

She smiled and said, "We're looking for commis chefs. Can you do that?" I told her I could. "Go in the kitchen and ask for Dick," she smirked.

Dick, a hefty forty-something bloke who towered seven-foot-six in his chef's hat, demanded, "You say you've been a commis chef. Where?"

"In the Dorchester," I said.

"In London? The Dorchester in London?" he questioned.

"That's right. In Park Lane," I said.

His starchy eyebrows raised sharply at an angle and he said, "Right, well get your billet sorted out and report for duty at seven A-M sharp."

I was over the moon as I swaggered off towards the allotted

staff chalet, with Taffy trundling along behind. "So what did they give you?" I asked him.

"Clayning. Bogs."

"Don't worry," I encouraged. "We're in. And we'll soon be *in* with some of this crumpet!"

The deal was that members of staff were allowed to socialise in the ballroom in the evenings, but on condition that they were always courteous and friendly towards the holidaymakers. On our first night, I dressed up in my best bib and tucker, and Taffy wore a tatty old suit which looked like it must have belonged to his granddad. We hurried excitedly to check out the social scene, only to find the dancefloor spinning with boring old mums and dads. I spotted a couple of good-looking girls sitting on their own and we bought them a Babycham. That led to a fumble in the bushes and a promise of things to come. Taffy's alarm clock woke me at twenty-past-five and he left to go and clean the latrines. At 6.55 A.M. on the dot I reported for duty in the kitchens.

"Excellent timekeeping," praised Dick. "Now get your whites on. We need fried eggs."

"How many?" I asked.

"Three hundred," he said. "Frying pans are there, eggs over there, and your lard's in the fridge."

I put on my uniform, got a tray of eggs, lit one of the giant gas rings and started melting fat in a massive frying pan.

"More eggs, more fat, and two more frying pans," he instructed, leaning over my shoulder and plonking a chef's hat on my head. "Go on then, get the first ones in, or we'll be servin' 'em up for dinner! Go on, crack your eggs. Not like that! One 'and! One 'and!"

I tried my best with one hand, but the eggs kept breaking, and when I dropped them into the bubbling oil, shards of jagged shell fell in with them. Dick quickly whipped his spatula into the pan and flicked the eggy mess into the bin.

"So," he barked, "how long did you work in the Dorchester? Eh? How fuckin' long? Two years you told me!"

"Okay," I shrugged, "so I exaggerated."

He kept an eagle-eye on me, swore at me a lot, and it wasn't long before I mastered the secret of cracking open eggs and getting them in and out of the frying pan without breaking the yolks. I got through breakfast, and for lunch he told me to prepare the chicken soup. There were three vast vats, like upside down kettle drums, and he told me to boil up some water and stir in some big packets of soup mix. I stirred each of the pots in turn with a sturdy wooden paddle, and as the soup thickened, I thought it looked delicious. Then he told me to get three chicken giblets from the fridge and add one to each of the pots. I mixed them in and stirred them round and round in the bubbling broth.

"Is it good?" Dick asked me, just as he was about to start serving up my creation to the horde of hungry holidaymakers.

"Cordon bleu," I beamed. "Fit for a prince."

"Excellent," he praised. Dipping his ladle into the first batch, his jaw dropped and he turned to me and bawled, "What the fuckin' 'ell!" He told me to disappear and come back after lunch was finished. When I returned, he scratched his head, looking bemused, but he couldn't hide a hint of a smile as he asked, "What was the name of this chef you said you trained under?"

"Francois? Renoir?" I shrugged. "Something French. I can't remember."

He shrieked, "Well it's a pity that Francois Renoir didn't tell ya to take the fuckin' giblets out the bag before you put 'em in the fuckin' soup!"

"Oh," I said. "Maybe the French prefer to leave 'em in?"

A grin washed across his ruddy face and he sighed, "Max, tell me honestly, have you ever worked in a kitchen?"

"Yeah! I'm a bloody good pearl-diver!" I insisted.

"So you can wash dishes?" he queried. "You're a kitchen porter?"

"Yeah," I assured him. "I'm the best. But, also, I'm an artist, a painter. And I'll tell you what I'll do, I'll paint your picture for ya, for nothing. You can stick it on your bedroom wall. How's that?"

He sniggered, snatching the hat from my head and sent me over to do a giant pile of washing up at the sinks.

On his day off, Taffy took my advice and went on the bus to Portsmouth to spend his pay-packet on buying some decent clobber. My heart sank when he came back and I saw what he'd bought. I marched him back to the gentleman's outfitters in Charlotte Street.

Taffy stood in silence in his new shirt and suit and tie, as I gave the weasel-faced assistant a dressing down. "You could get *him* and Fred Emney in this thing!" I complained. "You've pinched the back in when he's tried it on! And I've seen better cloth on the back of an 'orse!"

Although the ballroom was a sure place for picking up girls, I would always keep my eyes peeled around the camp for those who especially took my fancy. Wherever I saw one, I would make a point of catching her eye and smiling. Then, if I saw her later in the bar or at the swimming pool, it would mean that the ice was already broken. Valerie was a pretty brunette, and I had spotted her ample assets bursting forth from a tight bikini as she and her friend cycled past on one of the camp's twin-seater trikes. We had exchanged a smile, and the next evening I spotted her twisting and twirling on the dancefloor to a rock-and-roll group called the Cruisers. Taffy agreed with me that I should pursue Valerie and he would be better off trying to pull her skinny, mousy-haired pal Janet. However, each time we danced towards the pair, they seemed to spin off deliberately in the opposite direction.

"What yow gonna do?" challenged Taffy. "She ain't 'ardly even looked at yer."

"Yeah?" I countered indignantly. "Well we'll see about that." The band finished their song and I strode up to the stage and proposed, "Okay if I sing a number with you?"

I belted out my rendition of the Elvis classic 'All Shook Up', complete with hip-thrusts, and Valerie was right there, cheering me on. In the pale moonlight, I walked her to the football pitch and kissed her under the goalposts. She could hardly keep her hands off me, and before I knew it, we were lying on the top bunk in her chalet. Down below us, similarly entertaining themselves, were Taffy and Janet. The ladies were squealing and squirming, and the bedframe was creaking and cracking.

"You will pull out?" Valerie implored. "I don't wanna end up…"

"Valerie!" called a man's voice, along with an urgent knocking at the door. "Valerie! Are you awake?"

"Yes Dad," she sighed, "I'm awake."

"Dad!" I mouthed to Valerie. "You never..!"

"What's going on in there?" demanded the dad. "What were those noises?"

"Get under the bed!" Valerie gasped at me in a whisper, pushing me off her. Then she called out in an overstated tone, "We were just listening to the radio, dad."

"Me and your mother just came to say goodnight," he said.

"Just a minute, dad," said Valerie.

I heard the door open and a lot of idle chinwagging. Taffy and I lay motionless, squashed together, peeking out from under the bed at a pair of sharply pressed turn-ups and a couple of stout female ankles.

"I know what these scallywags are like," huffed dad.

"There's nobody here," Janet's innocent little voice insisted.

I squeezed Taffy's bicep as we both desperately tried not to snigger.

Eventually, the mum and dad said, "Alright then. Night-night, sleep tight."

"We will," said Valerie and Janet.

The door shut and Taffy and I burst out laughing.

On the Sunday morning, by the dustbins behind the kitchens, Valerie stared deeply into my eyes, kissed me passionately on the lips and asked imploringly, "You will write to me, won't you? And come and see me?"

"Yeah, course I will," I told her, "straight up."

"I don't want a fast alley-cat," she warned. "So you make sure you write to me, Max."

A new influx of tourists arrived on Sunday afternoons, and I'd say to Taffy, "There's a nice looking blonde came in today. Good hips! Lovely legs!" or some-such thing. Apart from the guests, there were dozens of young desirables working at the camp. I caught my first glimpse of Sammy's reflection in the steamy tea urn as she served me a cuppa in the canteen. The steam cleared and she looked at me and smiled. She was a vision of exotic beauty, dark and Spanishy with an hourglass figure and sexy brown eyes. "Your hair's beautiful," I complimented. She came and sat with me and we chatted for some time. Sammy was from Winchester, a student teacher, just working for a few weeks to fill in during the holidays. But we did manage to meet up from time-to-time, when our shifts allowed. The staff chalets were flimsier than the guest chalets, and quite often I'd think that ours would take off with all the bouncing up and down that went on.

On Saturday nights the Cruisers would play, and I would get up and sing a couple of numbers, more often than not Eddie Cochran's 'Summertime Blues' or one by Buddy Holly. The group turned up one night and asked, "Max, how d'ya fancy doing the whole set with us? Reckon you'd look fab with a silver jacket and black hair."

They blacked my hair and dressed me up, and I went on stage and sang. After the gig they counted out seven-pound notes into my hand and offered me the same every week. It was good fun and I enjoyed the attention it attracted. However, in the midst of a steamy kiss with a redheaded fan, she suddenly shrank back and shrieked with terror. She held up her hands, all smothered in black, and flinched at the stench of the smelly boot polish which was dripping down my neck. For the rest of the season's gigs, Dick's girlfriend got me some proper hair dye to use.

I was good to my word about painting Dick's portrait and he stuck the caricature on the wall in his office. The camp's comedian looked at it admiringly and beamed, "That's a work of art that is," as he filled his fat old face with a giant cream horn. He took it away and showed it to one of the bigwigs, and it was suggested that I set up an easel by the reception and do cartoons of the guests, as long as Dick could spare me. I loved doing the caricatures, drawn in crayon and sealed with fixative, and I'd sell dozens of them for five bob apiece. But, apart from the cash, I also gained a number of admiring fans who would come to watch and giggle as I created an amusing display of bulbous noses and sticky-out ears, pointy chins and goofy teeth. Although life was good, it was almost too easy.

As I lay snoozing alone on my bunk, Carol, a pretty waitress, came knocking on the door, which she did quite often. She called out for me, softly at first, but building to an eager crescendo, "Max? Let me in. Max? I know you're in there. Max? Max! Let me in! Max! Come on, Max! Max! Open the door! Max!"

As finally I gave in and opened the door, I yawned, "I was sleeping."

Although it was between the lunchtime and teatime shift, she was dolled up to the nines, her mane of glossy hair styled high above her forehead, and a fashionable chequered dress which barely covered her perky bum cheeks.

"I just wanna lie down, Max," she moaned. "I'm shattered, serving all them greedy so-and-sos! Bloody pests they are! Can I just lie down with you? Just for a minute, eh? Please?"

She smelt divine, her hair, her face, her body…

To escape the routine of the camp, I would hang around with Dick and his girlfriend. He'd just bought a brand-new Morris 1100 and we would drive over the busy bridge and across the short splinter of water which separated Hayling Island from the mainland. We would go where the fancy took us, often to the hippest shopping streets in Portsmouth. I would buy the latest gear, and we'd go to a lively café for a meal which Dick didn't have to cook, and which I didn't have to wash up after. Whenever we were driving back, I would notice the route signs, and I felt them almost calling out to me: 'London 72 Miles'.

Taffy and I stayed on until the end of the summer in order to collect our end of season bonus. He was going off to learn a trade in the merchant navy and I was going off in search of adventure. We stood at the front gates and said our goodbyes and wished each other luck. He went one way and I went the other.

"Beep-beep-beep-beep!" I pushed button 'A' and the beeping stopped as my penny dropped into the telephone coin box. "Sammy?" I uttered excitedly into the mouthpiece. "Guess who?"

She gave me directions, and within a couple of hours I was giving her a cuddle on the front step of her mum's pleasant semi-detached in Winchester.

After dinner, I watched Sammy's mum as she gazed at the ceiling and rocked lazily backwards and forwards in her chair. She took a long, deep drag on her cigarette, blew out an ethereal plume of smoke and asked, "Do you ever think of death, Max?"

"No," I sputtered, somewhat suspiciously.

"I once saw a hand," she murmured. "It came out from over there, behind the curtains. And on it…" she stopped to draw on her cigarette, before slowly exhaling, "…was the date of my death. Funny, isn't it?"

We stayed for a few days with Sammy's mum and sister, and a guy who seemed to be some sort of lodger. Sammy already had a guitar, and I decided to buy one too; it was a lovely Harmony Sovereign acoustic. One morning we got up, went to the Post Office, got our passports, then found ourselves transported by thumb and ferry across the channel, and then in the medieval city of Rouen. We busked on the streets and found sanctuary in a convent, ate fish paste and cheese with crusty baguettes, and refreshed ourselves with carafes of wine and curvaceous bottles of Orangina. After a couple of weeks of hitching around from town to town, bedding down in hostels and frittering away our funds, we decided to head for Cornwall, in search of gainful employment. Travelling with Sammy was easy. She was cheerful and friendly, but all the blinkered motorists saw was her revealing miniskirt and a tight top, and we were never short of lifts.

Pleasure Haven holiday camp was a couple of miles outside Newquay and, because of their heated pool and the legendary Cornish Riviera sunshine, they enjoyed an extended season. Sammy got a job doing cream teas and the likes, and I found myself waiting on tables. Newquay was known as a surfer's paradise, and Crantock and Fistral beaches were bubbling with energy. The silky harmonies of the Beach Boys' 'I Get Around' and 'Surfin' USA' breezed across the silver sands, where great parties of surfers and sunworshippers spent their days chilling out and cocking a snook at normal society. It was free-and-easy living, and Sammy and I fitted right in. Sometimes we'd discover deserted beaches and rip off our clothes and frolic in the crashing waves. I'd take photographs of her posing playfully on a slippery rock, or sketch her perfect form against the shadows and fading clouds.

As the holiday camp closed its gates, we left with a bit of cash and a plan to travel to Land's End, at the end of the land. However, we were happy to go wherever the wheels of fortune took us.

"Praze-an-Beeble?" called out a chap from a funny looking little frog-green car which was pulling up. As we drove away with him, having no idea what he was talking about, he explained above the buzz of his noisy engine, "Praze-an-Beeble is a village. I'm a travelling salesman you see. I go all over. How do you like the motor? It's new. It's called a Hillman Imp."

Still chuckling, we jumped aboard a local bus, and the driver recommended that we should get off at Saint Michael's Mount, as apparently it was a place of great interest. We did as he suggested, and stood on the beach and looked across at the Mount; a small, circular island with a castle on the top and a few small houses near the shoreline.

"How can we get across to the island?" I asked a man in the café.

"You could swim," he told me. Then looking at Sammy, "The causeway be open tomorrow, Miss, if you wan' wait till then?"

"Is there anywhere we can stay tonight?" Sammy asked him.

"Hotel," he said. Then, just as we were leaving, he suggested, "Farmer's got a caravan."

The caravan was old but cosy, and we found a way of making up a passable double bed out of sofa cushions. It stood alone on a green field full of broccoli, just yards from the village and the sea. And it was cheap, and available to us for as long as we wanted to stay. Although we did paddle across to take a look at Saint Michael's Mount, it wasn't really that interesting, and once was enough. On our side of the water, in Marazion village, we quickly managed to turn our artistic skills into cash. I painted a few local scenes, and Sammy collected pebbles which she polished and decorated, and made into pendants or paperweights, in the popular style of the local Troika pottery.

Sitting cross-legged on the pavement, strumming our guitars, we would sell our pictures and trinkets to passing strangers. In the tiny confines of our steamy caravan, we would cook up a stodgy concoction of cheese and broccoli with bread. Seizing the opportunity to extend our business, we hauled an old door over to the lane which ran past the field, and set it up on bricks and cloaked it with a large colourful cloth, and laid our creations across it, like a pretty market stall. Cars pulled in to look and buy, and we managed to make enough to supplement our dreary diet with egg and chips at the café.

"Come back anytime you like, Max," the farmer invited, shaking my hand vigorously, as Sammy and I hung our possessions round our necks in readiness to hit the road again.

Just as we started trekking up towards the main road, the driver of a fish van recognised us and stopped. "You going near Land's End?" I asked.

"No, I ain'," he said, scratching his head. "But why you wanna go most western most point in Britain, when I can take ye to most southern?"

We unquestioningly accepted his Cornish logic and he delivered us, none the worse for sharing our journey with a basket of smelly pilchards, to the small and simple village of Cadgwith Cove, where he was collecting lobsters. A track ran straight down to a rugged harbour which was enclosed by a rim of low, steep cliffs. A dozen tiny, single-masted fishing luggers stood on the beach, and men with seafaring faces were busily weaving their willow lobster pots. We settled into a room at the hotel and flopped out to enjoy the pleasures of a plush, springy mattress.

"Don't shave," appealed Sammy, as I stood at the basin, working up a lather. "Grow a beard. It's really sexy, especially with your long, gorgeous locks," she purred, kissing my neck.

"I'm not a flippin' hillbilly!" I protested, but she worked her magic on me and the argument was lost.

Music wafted up through the floorboards, emanating from the bar below. It was a sweet chorus of cheery male harmonies, *"Come fill up your glasses and let us be merry, For to rob bags of plunder it is our intent, As we roam through the valleys, Where the lilies and roses, And the beauty of Kashmir lay drooping his head..."*

The snug bar was filled with warmth and hearty seamen in thick blue sweaters and mariners' caps. We took the recommended tipple of fruity 'Rum and Shrub' and stood to one side to listen as the men delivered their rousing repertoire of sea shanties, sung a-cappella. As Sammy and I tapped our feet in time and joined in with the choruses, a cheery voice rang out, "You wanna join in?" And we did. The following day, I painted a couple of nice watercolours of the cove and the fishing boats, and the locals loved them, although I felt compelled to flatter the efforts of the village postman whose artist's crown I'd inadvertently stolen. The regulars asked us to bring our guitars down to the bar, and I obliged them with a performance of the only songs that I really knew, 'I Can't Help But Wonder Where I'm Bound' and 'The Last Thing On My Mind', a pair of my favourite folk songs by Tom Paxton. Sammy's playing wasn't brilliant, but they cheered her enthusiastically and bought her drinks anyway.

Sharkey was a central character in the community. He was a fisherman and a songster, and we were chuffed to bits when he invited us to stay with him at his quaint old cottage on top of the hill. While he was out braving the perils of the wild ocean, Sammy and I would snuggle up and enjoy the intimacy of just being alone together. We sort of settled down with each other and began to fit in. The postie had a studio room in his house and he let me go there to paint while he was out doing his rounds. It made life easier because he had an easel, and it was a place where I could relax and make a mess with paints, as artists do. Around the area there were a number of pubs and cafes which put on live musicians, and I got myself a few gigs, performing my pair of passable ballads and playing a bit of rhythm guitar with some musical mates I'd made. Sammy would recite some of her poetry and sell a bit of jewellery. She was, as always, wonderful, and ever-popular with everyone.

Franklin Engelmann and an entourage of BBC technicians and assistants arrived at the hotel one day. He was a well-known radio broadcaster who presented a popular show called 'Down Your Way', in which he would introduce his listeners to local communities to learn about their way of life, culture and music. The pub singers congregated in the bar to perform their shanties, and Englemann, who had the style and looks of a Hollywood film star and a voice as smooth as malt whisky, interviewed Sharkey. It was interesting to watch the broadcasters at work, setting up microphones and tape recorders and twiddling their dials, as Sharkey explained how he made traditional lobster pots, like his ancestors before him, and sailed through hell and hurricanes in his tiny vessel to bring home the catch each day.

A local gallery owner saw us painting on the clifftop one day and liked my choppy seascapes so much that he paid me twenty-five quid to paint a couple for him. Sammy did four smaller pictures and he paid her the same for those, although I suspect that he was just trying to impress her by the size of his wad. Despite having made enough cash to tide us over for quite a while, Sammy and I both knew that life in Cornwall had to come to an end.

It was a familiar routine, Sammy standing at the edge of the road, her tight stripy T-shirt bulging, and her leather miniskirt riding a full twelve inches above her knees to reveal an ample display of thigh to any passing motorist, whilst I lurked away in the background. Her thumb was hardly above her tiny waist when I heard the squeal of eager brakes. She trotted ahead to engage the driver, as I edged along behind her.

"I'm only going as far as Exeter I'm afraid," panted the sweaty man at the wheel, loosening his tie. "But I'm more 'an 'appy to take yer, love." Then, "Oh! Hello. I never saw you there!" he groaned, when I appeared. It was a white van, but at least we could smell immediately that it wasn't a fish van. "You can ride up front wiv me if yer like," he offered Sammy excitedly. "Okay, both go in the back then," he sighed, as we clambered in through the back doors. "Sit on the box there. Make yourselves at 'ome."

The shiny wooden crate was long and sturdy, and it served as a reasonable seat. As we drove along, our driver grinned at us in his rear-view mirror and asked whether we were married, and told us that he was not, "unfortunately." He was chatty, probably about forty, slightly thinning and a bit wheezy, and he wanted to know where had we been, where were we going, and what our plans were.

And then Sammy asked him, almost playfully, "So what's in the box?"

He glanced at us for a moment, mopped his brow and chuckled, "Tis a coffin."

"Wow!" shrieked Sammy. "Is there anyone in it?"

The man looked somewhat amused, and bemused, and mumbled, "Well yeah, tis an old lady, but..."

"Can we have a look?" blurted Sammy. "Please? If it's not too much trouble."

"Well, I mean if you really..." he shrugged.

"No!" I shrieked. "I don't wanna see a bloody stiff!"

At the next roadside café we pulled into the car park and I leapt out. Sammy stepped down, then turned and smoothed her palm across the top of the brightly polished casket. "Isn't it lovely?" she beamed, her fingers gently fiddling with the ornate brass handles and fastenings.

"Tis top quality," the ghoul assured her. "Bain't screwed down," he announced, sliding the lid away.

"Come on, Max," urged Sammy. "Come and have a look. She won't bite."

The old lady was shrouded in black. Her skin was grey and she looked hard, as though she was made of brittle plastic.

"You're a lucky man, Max," our new friend insisted. "If I was just a few years younger…" he sniggered, gawping hungrily at Sammy's bum as she leaned inside the coffin to stroke the cadaver's cheek.

I knew I was a lucky man to have Sammy, but we had plans, plans which were separate, and plans which didn't include each other. And so, we rode the trail together one last time, until she headed off to pursue the world of higher education, and I headed back to the buzz and the banter of London.

She told me, "You'll be a great painter one day, Max," and then she was gone.

CHAPTER 4:
INJECTING DONUTS AND SWAYING PALM TREES

Shepherd's Bush was the same place which I'd left: cars racing around the green like fairground dodgems; the saucy yells of the market traders; the confused old ladies dragging around their shopping trolleys full of old newspapers and millet; the drunken beggars trying to fight with everyone, but falling over; and the huddles of weary workmen waiting for a job. But up West, there was still the pop of Champagne corks and the sharp suits, the mink coats and the diamond rings. London was full of money, yet somehow I was almost skint.

I shared a mouse-sized flat with a snoring Irishman, but the landlord was a philistine and he threw me out because he hated the smell of my paints and objected to the odd stain on his manky ten-bob furniture. Money was tight, but they had put up a warning notice on the back doors of the Dorchester: 'Keep Closed at All Times'. I sat on my eiderdown on Shepherd's Bush Green, busking and observing the tramps, trying to work out where would be a good place to sleep. Along the meandering pathways were a number of park benches, and as dusk descended, I watched the dossers preparing for bed, staking their claim on their preordained pitches and chasing off any unwanted predators. The prime benches under the trees were soon occupied, and I opted to set up camp a distance away from the thieving hoi polloi. Laying down my cover across the bum-buffed planks, I got on top and rolled myself and my guitar snugly inside it, and used my haversack as a pillow. Despite the fact that I felt perfectly at home, I couldn't ignore the constant tooting of horns and flashes of light which penetrated my holey bedding. At daybreak, the roar and the rattle of the lorries and buses vibrated through my bones. Domestic ladies, much like my mum, and working men, rushed to meet the needs of their masters.

"Okay?" a sunny voice called from the next-door bench. I poked my head out like a turtle. A beaming black face and a set of dazzling gnashers greeted me. "You wanna cuppa coffee or summat? I'm Charlie. Come, the café is open."

With a mug of steaming hot tea warming my belly, Charlie told me that he was from a small island in the Caribbean called Curacao. Due to a financial crisis at home, he'd stowed away on an oil tanker and had been sent to prison when he arrived in England. We shared a bit of bread together and he assured me quite exuberantly that he had a pal who could help us. I trusted him, and as we strolled along through Brook Green he recounted tales of when he'd been a cocktail waiter on the Queen Mary in the nineteen-thirties, inventing exotic tipples for the likes of Marlene Dietrich, and Laurel and Hardy. Spotting a copper in the distance, Charlie grabbed my arm and yanked me away down a side street, wiping the sweat from his brow.

He took me to Olympia, a place I knew well. Just around the corner from the exhibition hall was a massive old building, a big brown lump of a place, a hundred yards long and a hundred feet high, called Cadby Hall. We hiked around to the sunless rear yard, where blocks of multi-storey offices and factories had been added on over the years, covering acres and acres. As Charlie made inquiries about his pal, I observed the fleet of impressive royal blue lorries scuttling about, collecting and delivering trays and sacks in a never-ending stream. It was a buzzing industrial plant, yet there was no pong of pungent chemicals or boiled bones, just a sweet smell of pastry and icing. The following morning at six o'clock, Charlie and I stood in a murky line-up of thirty desperate men, and waited for his chum to appear from the back shutters of the warehouse.

"You, you, you, you..." beckoned Charlie's mate, marching briskly along the row with his clipboard.

He led ten of us, including myself and Charlie, through the halls of whirring, clattering production lines and steaming ovens. Kitted out in a regulation Lyons Bakery jacket, I was stationed on a conveyor belt and spent twelve hours picking off bread rolls and depositing them into baskets. In various departments across the site, there were thousands of workers making every conceivable type of loaf, roll, scone, cake, tart, pie, pudding and donut. Working on the donut injection machine was one of the easier jobs, and the boss always joked that I got a thrill from pulling my lever and squirting sticky jam into mounds of squidgy dough. I buttered up the boss with a flattering portrait and my days of vagrancy were over. But bread was boring, unless it came in rolls of green notes.

Somebody told me that Portobello Market was the 'happening' place for artists, and as I wandered amongst the countless antique shops and stalls, examining the modern pictures on offer, I knew that I could do better. Holed-up in some grotty digs, I bought some cheap canvases and second-hand reference books, and spent my days and nights painting portraits of Nelson, Napoleon and Washington, and a collection of dramatic sea battles. The following Saturday, I found what looked like a convenient space on the side of Portobello Road and unfurled the blanket which contained my pictures. Suddenly there was a shout of "Oi! Oi! You can't put 'em there!" Undeterred, I shifted further down the road and tried again, and once again I was told to "hoppit" in no uncertain terms.

"These pitches are like gold dust," explained a wise, old Irish voice, as I was packing up again. "People wait years and years…"

"I haven't got years," I told the wee chap, whose oversized suit jacket partly concealed an off-white vest, and who was carrying a heavy sack. "I'm skint. I need to sell these paintings today."

His name was Bill and he took me to a cafe, and explained the form regarding the traders and the market inspectors. "Here, come with me," he beckoned, and I followed him back up Portobello Road towards the junction with Westbourne Grove. Clasping the iron railings, he told me, "Here, set your blanket on the pavement.

Go on." A couple of antique dealers turned round from their stalls on the roadside and glared at me threateningly. Bill glared back at them and nodded, then directed me, "Go on, Max, you just set your paintings out here."

After a while, and with no buyers for my paintings, I strapped on my guitar and started strumming and singing one of my Tom Paxton numbers, broadcasting to the punters and traders how I was travelling a long and dusty road, with a hot and heavy load, and wondering where I was bound.

"Marvellous," applauded Bill, who had been discreetly circling around me like a mother hen. A few shillings bounced onto my blanket, but it wasn't enough to buy me a meal or pay my rent. "Don't worry," said Bill, "things'll get better, you'll see. Here, come and give me a hand. Your stuff'll be safe here," he assured me, indicating to the nearby stallholders that nothing of mine would be touched. Glancing back nervously at my abandoned possessions, I put my trust in Bill and strode along with him, twenty or thirty yards up the road.

"Ladies and gentlemen! Ladies and gentlemen! Stand aside!" boomed Bill, scooping the mass of tourists out of the way with his arms and clearing a broad spot between two stalls. "I am the Great Ramondo, and the act which you are about to witness, I have performed for kings, queens and celebrities across the globe. Gather round. Gather round, my friends." He stood on the pavement and directed the curious sightseers into an amphitheatre around him. Stripping off his jacket, he tightened his giant belt buckle and stooped to delve into his hessian bag. A hundred or more heads craned to see what he was doing.

"Max here will be assisting me in this feat of death-defying strength and courage," he told them, as he beckoned me over and started unravelling a sturdy metal chain from his sack into my hands. "Max here, who is the most talented artist in the world today, will bind and lock me in these chains so that there is no hope of me escaping. Max..?"

Under his instruction, I wrapped the chain round and round

his wiry torso and stringy arms and legs. Then yanking it as tight as I could, until it was biting into his bones, I secured it with a meaty padlock. Members of the audience were asked to check and verify my handiwork. I helped Bill hop into the sack and tied it shut. He fell onto the tarmac, and the bag began to shake about and wriggle furiously. When, some five minutes later, he emerged unshackled and triumphant, he hurriedly hustled the crowd into giving him money, before they could escape.

Returning to my pitch, half expecting to see empty spaces where my paintings and guitar had once been, one of the neighbouring traders thrust a tenner into my hand and told me that Admiral Lord Nelson had been sold to a Jewish gentleman.

When, later, I assisted Bill with his act again, I must have been overzealous or something. After several minutes of squirming and grunting and groaning, he fell motionless and his voice hissed from inside the sack, "Pssst! Max! Max!" Bemused onlookers mumbled amongst themselves as I knelt down and lay my ear on the hessian. "The key is here…" Bill whispered. "There's a little hole. Can you see it? Put your fingers through the cloth and hand it to me."

I lay over him so that nobody could see, and took the key from its hiding place in his belt, and slipped it into his icy fingers. Then, as I stood back, he jiggled about for a few moments, before emerging once again triumphant. "Thank you very much, ladies and gentlemen," he hollered. And as he thrust himself at them and snatched their donations, he called out, "And don't forget, Max Brandrett the world-famous artist and musician will be selling a collection of his paintings, just down there, on the pavement. Works of art, ladies and gentlemen! Works of art!"

Bill's advertisement was widely ignored and I stood playing 'I Can't Help But Wonder Where I'm Bound' and 'The Last Thing On My Mind' until my own fingers were turning blue.

"Don't you know any other fickin' songs?" grumbled Bill.

"No. Just those two," I sighed.

"Give me a hand will yer? I can feel a performance coming on," he said, rolling his bony shoulder-blades and tensing his muscles.

I tried to avoid the landlord at my digs, but he banged on my door and extorted half the rent from me, with a warning that he would evict me if I couldn't settle up with him by the following weekend. I had no food and no means of buying any. And then, a bright idea struck me. Sauntering through the staff entrance of the Lyons factory at 5 A.M., I nodded at several of the unfamiliar nightshift workers as they rattled by with their trays of bread and buns. Once in the changing room, I grabbed a brown work-coat and slipped it on.

"Oi! Son! Where ya goin'?" demanded one of the nightshift foremen, passing me in a corridor.

"To the mixing room, sir," I replied, looking as sweet and innocent as an angel cake.

He sighed deeply and groaned, "It's not that way! It's that way!"

I roamed freely, nipping in and out of the various departments, stuffing myself with delicious sandwiches and fancies, and taking a bagful with me. I snuck out before six o'clock when the familiar dayshift was due, and spent the week chomping on snacks and pastries as I completed some more paintings.

"Oi! Not so fast!" snapped the landlord, as I was leaving early for Portobello. "And take all your crap with yer!"

There was no point in arguing, although I was a bit annoyed with myself that I hadn't robbed his electric meter.

"Any luck?" asked Bill, when he came to visit me halfway through the morning. "Don't sweat, you're the best fickin' artist for miles. Now, will ya come and give us a hand?"

Although he didn't pay me anything, I was happy to help Bill, as he'd helped *me*. Mostly his act went to plan, but if it didn't and I had to give him a hand out of his chains he would pacify his disappointed audience by telling them, "Sorry ladies and gentlemen, but my performance this morning/afternoon was hampered by undue metal shrinkage, due to the atmospheric conditions."

Having failed to hit my daily sales target at Portobello, and with the sky looking warm and clear, I headed for another night out under the stars on Shepherd's Bush Green. Charlie wasn't about, and I had no idea what had happened to him. In the early hours of the morning, I hid my stuff away in the bushes and went out on a humanitarian mission to supply food for the hungry - namely *me*, and my fellow nomads. I breezed into the bakery and went foraging, giving my name as 'Tony Williams' when challenged by a suspicious supervisor. However, when I arrived to help myself to some sandwiches, I saw the last trolley-load of cheese rolls being wheeled away into the despatch bay. And there were no meringues or sponge-cakes either. Then, in one of the icing rooms, I came across a tall, three-tiered cake. There was nothing else there, and so I lifted off the top layer, slid it into a bag and hid it under my coat.

"Which department you in?" called a voice, just as I was heading for freedom. "What's yer name, son?"

"Tony Williams," I smiled. "I've just been working on the 'travelling oven' and I'm just on my way over to the 'winkling machine' to see if they need an extra pair of hands."

"Okay, on yer way," said the bloke.

I hightailed it out of the building and kept on going until I was a safe distance away. I leaned back against a wall and sighed deeply, then peered into my bag and pulled out my prize, a big, thick, creamy, circular wodge of iced heaven. Tossing away the little figurine couple from the top of it, I greedily stuffed the thing into my mouth and took a massive bite of the sweet, sickly marzipan and moist, tasty fruit. It was divine, and I dished it out to my chums, until every last raisin had been devoured. Apart from feeling a bit sick, I didn't give the cake a second thought. Sitting with Bill in the café off Portobello Road, he rustled the Evening Standard which I'd buried my head into and demanded, "What's that you're reading? You've hardly said a word."

"Oh, it's nothing," I sighed. "Just a couple had their wedding day ruined. Somebody stole their wedding cake."

"That's not nice," he frowned.

"Only the top tier of it," I stressed. "There *were* two others. And Lyons are gonna bake 'em a whole new cake, a better one, so…"

"Oh, well that's alright then," he confirmed.

Things were going a bit better and I was making a bit more money for my pictures. Dougie was a dealer who had a proper shop in the Portobello Road. In the league table of Portobello dealers, having an antique shop or an art gallery generally meant that you were first division and could get away with charging a lot more for your merchandise. The 'antique dealers' on Portobello Road often specialised in what they sold, whether it be paintings, collectibles or furniture, although many would sell anything which turned them a quick profit, genuine antique or not. Dougie's main business was in paintings.

"Not bad," he muttered, casting his roguish eye over my work. "Where d'ya get 'em from?"

"I paint them," I told him.

"You mean old ones, touched up?" he assumed.

"No, I paint them," I reiterated.

"Looks a bit Flemish," he noted, poring over a scene of windswept galleons in a squall. "Got a bit of the young Van de Velde's about it. And this race'orse one, very nice. A bit like an 'Erring."

"Herring Senior," I elaborated.

"Ain't got his signature o' course," he grinned. "You know what primitives are? And I don't mean Zulus," he chuckled. "Portraits of people's prize bulls and pigs and that."

"Popular in the early eighteen-hundreds," I interjected. "A lot of amateurs used to paint 'em."

"Yeah, well they're very popular round these parts," he enthused. "The Yanks love 'em!" Then turning to my pictures hanging on the railings, he inquired, "So how much d'ya want for these?"

"Which ones?" I asked.

All of 'em," he said.

"All five? Thirty quid," I shrugged

"Give yer twenty-five," he said. "Bring 'em up to the shop. Oh, and wrap 'em in yer blanket will yer? Know what I mean?"

I packed up for the day and took my paintings along to Dougie's gallery. He nervously scooted me through into the back room and pushed the door ajar. "Now," he whispered, peering shiftily out into the shop, "if you did some more of them marine oils, and one or two 'appened to 'ave a signature on 'em… Know what I mean?"

"How much?" I asked.

"Don't worry, I'll see you right," he said. "Now, you'd better get off."

"Haven't you forgotten something?" I asked. He looked puzzled, until I jogged his ailing memory and prompted, "My money?"

"Oh yeah!" he chortled. "Silly old me!" As he opened his bulging wallet and counted out my remuneration in grubby pound notes, he delved, "Not looking for a flat are yer? It's just I've got this lovely little apartment in Cricklewood, ideal for an artist." He took me there, and when I agreed to rent it he held out his hand and smirked, "Fifteen notes a week okay?"

It was a tiny, scruffy little room on the top floor of an old house which he owned, and hanging on every wall were dozens of old and precious pictures. "I know these are safe with you, Max," he said. And they were.

Dogs in cages and crates were yapping all around as I flipped through the stacks of grubby old paintings on Club Row Market in the East End. Little girls and boys yanked the sleeves of their reluctant parents as they eyed-up puppies which they yearned to take home with them. Broken men, and women, fought to sell you the clothes off their back, and they would have sold their souls for the price of a drink. Digging under the piles of bric-a-brac, I managed to hoick out a good supply of worthless and weather-beaten frames and canvases suitable for my purpose.

"They're mine," suddenly announced a deep, velvety voice from behind me. I turned to be confronted by an older gentleman with a white Father Christmas beard and cheeks of claret. "Sorry, they're mine," he smiled, stretching out his paint-stained fingers in eagerness to rob me of my spoils. "You don't really want a load of old 'potboilers', do you?"

"I do," I told him.

"What do you want them for?" he questioned.

"What do *you* want them for?" I countered, sensing something dodgy about him.

"Come on, Tom," urged the glamorous young hippie chick on his arm. Then, quite warmly to me, she smiled, "Sorry."

I paid a quid for each of the scabby old paintings and headed home on the tube with a good armful of them. Although ostensibly junk, to me they were gold dust. Using paint stripper, I removed the weary efforts of bygone amateur artists, and rubbed the canvases down and coated them with primer, then produced ten good paintings, some in oils and some watercolours, some shipping scenes and some small portraits of prized farmyard beasts with overblown genitalia. I washed the paint colours out a bit, before remounting my new-old pictures back in their antique frames, and fastening the woodwormed backs on with the original nails. They looked a treat, as if they had *real* age, and under glass I would've hardly been able to tell how old they were, unless I hadn't painted them myself in North West London in nineteen-sixty-six.

"Lovely work, Max! Lovely!" Dougie praised, as he stood admiring the new batch of pictures which I'd taken down to Portobello Road. "But with me shop, I've gotta be careful. Can't have too many Van de Velde's turning up at once, can we! Listen, I'll take that naval battle, two fat pigs and the prize bull. Shall we say fifty quid for cash?"

I took his money, knowing full well that he would be selling my work on for ten times what he had paid me. But it didn't bother me; it was a lot more lucrative than making holes in donuts. When he had time, between his dubious business pursuits, Dougie would squeeze into my over-stuffed bedsit with his young girlfriend and ask me to supply him with one or two iffy works of art. We'd catch up for a yarn and a drink, but otherwise I hardly ever saw him. He never hassled me for the rent money and seemed more than happy to have somebody honest to look after his stash of pictures. However, living downstairs was a Polish guy who, for whatever reason, had taken a dislike to me and used to try and wind-up Dougie against me. I think he was jealous that Dougie and I had a common interest in art and got along so well.

Business was picking up and I was selling a few scenes of sailing ships, in the style of Clarkson Stanfield. In the early eighteen-hundreds, Stanfield had served in the navy, before turning his artistic skills to painting theatre sets, and then to painting seascapes and landscapes. He was highly accomplished, prolific and successful, which made his work desirable to replicate. I found no difficulty in following his technique, and I seemed to have a natural ability to look at any colour on a painting and mix up an almost identical match, as if it had been mixed by the artist himself. It was all quite simple, except for one major factor; the oil paints which I used would ordinarily take around six weeks to dry properly; and I needed to eat more often than that, and sell pictures on a quick turnover basis.

'Which Paint Would a Professional Use?' the press adverts asked, adding that, 'It dries in one to two hours…' I bought a tin and took it back to the flat, eager to give it a go. I mixed it in with my usual oil paints, recreating the colour I required, and began brushing it onto the canvas. It worked a treat. A whole range of colours was available, and it was cheap, and it was oil based, which made it ideal. Decorators all across the nation used Brolac to prime wooden doors and skirting boards; I used it to paint masterpieces. After a couple of hours, the picture would become tacky, whereupon I would waft it over the electric fire and let the glowing heater elements dry it off and bake it until the paint began to crack. A wipe over the surface with white polish subdued the brightness of the colours, and a wipe around the edges with turps produced a clean, neat border which looked to an inquisitive 'expert' as if the painting had been securely ensconced in its frame for centuries. Under glass, it became almost indistinguishable from a genuine old work of art. And with the addition of the artist's signature...

I could sell my Clarkson Stanfield's all day long for fifty quid, mainly to a couple of dealers who were turning a handsome profit on them. But the market superintendent gave me a tipoff that whispers had been circulating about me flogging counterfeit pictures. As a council official, he told me, his job would be on the line if the 'Old Bill' came sniffing around and nicked me on *his* manor. He was a nice guy, he'd been good to me, and we'd actually become quite chummy. The same weekend, my brother Joey came up to visit me. He'd got married and lived close to mum and our other brother Kenny, and he painted a rosy picture of how life could be if I moved back to Brighton.

Treading carefully down the steps with my bags of clothes and paints, I was greeted at the front door by my family. My brothers looked on with beaming faces as I hugged my mum. It was a two-bedroomed flat, in the basement of an old terraced house in Lansdowne Road, just around the corner from the flat where I had last seen her. We all ate and drank and chatted, and had a pleasant afternoon. I stayed overnight, but by morning I was itching to get out-and-about and see what was going on. Nothing much had changed. I instinctively headed for the shops in The Lanes and rummaged through all the junk and antiques, in search of old 'potboilers'. There were plenty there, in the rougher shops, although I did have to haggle quite hard to buy a few for a decent price. Whilst mum was out at work, or in the pub with friends and fanciers, I got stuck into working on some seascapes and primitives.

A week later, I revisited The Lanes in the expectation of getting a decent price for my work. I had seen what some of the more upmarket dealers were charging for similar pictures, but their offers to me were paltry and their attitude was very much, "Take it or leave it." I decided that, considering my circumstances, I would begrudgingly take whatever I could get.

"Do you have any qualifications?" asked one of the three seated gentlemen who represented the Arts Funding Council.

"None, Sir," I replied. They muttered amongst themselves. "But I do have some pictures which I could show you. You see, sir, I learnt to paint when I was a Barnardo's Boy."

I showed them some of my contemporary works, portraits and Brighton beach scenes, omitting any of my antique shipping scenes, and they seemed particularly impressed by my caricatures.

"Mum," I said, quite excitedly when she arrived home from work, "I've been accepted into art school. The council are gonna give me a grant. A thousand quid a year!"

"Whew! That's not bad!" she gasped, taking off her coat and pinny. "So tha'll be staying here for a while then, son?"

I paused awkwardly and she hesitated from hanging up her apron.

"No," I sighed. "It's the college - it's in Southend."

"Aye, well you make sure you send your mam a postcard," she warned, turning at me with a wag of her sharp finger, and a gentle smile.

I found digs in Southend with a lovely, middle-aged landlady. The other students on the course were a bit younger than me and readily took guidance from the lecturers. I, on the other hand, had started my career early and didn't feel that the college was teaching me anything. They had a leaning towards design, rather than what I considered to be *real* art, and I had little interest in learning about graphics and layouts for the advertising industry. For that reason, they hardly bothered me and let me pursue whatever artistic projects took my fancy. And when I did a few amusing caricatures and some large oil paintings of blazing galleons fighting each other in wild seas, and some local pastoral scenes with cheerful cows grazing in sunny meadows beneath crooked church spires, I think they were rendered almost speechless.

"The museum in Southend have asked us to provide some illustrations of Roman Britain," my tutor told me. "And we wondered if you would be interested?"

I accepted little jobs which the college set up for me, and I soon became known as the 'Phantom Illustrator'.

My landlady decided that she was going to sell her house, and gave me notice on my room. She had a sister called Dorothy, who kindly offered me board and lodgings with her, not far away in Glenwood Avenue. It was a spacious and not unattractive Edwardian terraced house, and she lived there alone.

"This is your room," said Dorothy, stretching to open the velvet curtains, her ample figure silhouetted against the tall window.

"The light'll be good for painting," I observed. "That's if you don't mind?"

"Max, you can do anything you like," she smiled. "Now, you get settled in and I'll make us a nice bit of tea."

"There's no need to go to any trouble," I said.

"No trouble at all," she grinned. "And afterwards, maybe you could play me a tune?"

We sat and chatted over a chicken casserole and vegetables, followed by syrup pudding, and she seemed fascinated by my opinions on art.

"Oh, do go and get your guitar," she insisted.

I sat on the sofa and she watched me from her armchair as I played her my brace of Tom Paxton songs. When I yawned and told her that I was heading to bed, she took my hands and drew me to my feet. "Right then, Dorothy," I said, "I'll see you in the morning."

There was a competition at the college to design a poster for a national safety campaign. The students were buzzing at the prospect of having their work displayed across the country, plus the chance to win a cash prize and secure a job at an advertising agency. And, of course, there was always the fame and glory. My fellow students set about drawing pictures of sizzling clothes irons, jolting electric plugs, falling ladders, sinking boats, tumbling rocks, speeding motorcycles, speeding cars, speeding buses, speeding lorries, speeding trains, and every conceivable type of accident imaginable. I wasn't particularly interested and turned my interest towards painting some life studies, and asked a fellow student if she would pose for me in the local park, topless. Tucked away, sitting on a blanket under the trees, Jill was more than happy to accommodate me in my work. Then, up in my room, she continued to satisfy my artistic needs.

"That girl who was here yesterday..?" inquired Dorothy. "Was she..? I mean *is* she..?"

"Just a girl from college," I shrugged. "She's been modelling for me."

"Oh," chirped Dorothy. "Well that's alright then? Here, what would you say to a bit of steak and kidney?"

"Yeah, alright," I agreed. "I wouldn't say no to some of that."

"Just a thought," she said, twisting on her shapely hips and facing me as she reached the door, "if you do ever need a model… I know I'm not as young as your friend, but I think I've still got quite a nice figure."

"Very nice," I agreed. "But I'm doing nudes at the moment, so…"

"There's no shame in the human body," she declared. "Perhaps we could do it when the steak and kidney's gone down?"

Dorothy ate eagerly, and I noticed that occasionally her shoulders would quiver. She told me that she had worked as a hostess in a club, dining with malcontented married gentlemen whose wives misunderstood them, offering them a sympathetic ear and a shoulder to cry on. However, in the everyday world, she confessed somewhat sadly, that she had never met the man of her dreams, the man who would sweep her off her feet and hold her and protect her and love her as she desired.

"Where do you want me?" she asked, as she returned to the sitting room in a silk robe.

"How about, reposing on the sofa?" I suggested. "Like a Greek goddess."

She slipped off the gown and tossed it to one side, standing as tall as her structure would allow, flattening her tummy and displaying her magnificent breasts. Even as she struck a restful pose, lounging on cushions, her voluptuous bosoms remained quite buoyant and resolute, not unlike Goya's 'The Nude Maja'.

As I sketched her, she asked, "Is it okay to talk?" I nodded and she continued, with a slight breathlessness, "You're not like other young men, Max. Your expensive style and clothes, that sort of regal, Regency look, it's really quite…"

"Why be like the others?" I vaunted. "And besides, I don't really drink, so I have to spend my grant on something."

"A fool and his money are soon parted," she joked. "Not that you're a fool, Max. Far from it."

I presented my spontaneous idea for a safety poster to the college. The lecturers stared at it, then mutteringly discussed it, commenting on the layout, and the Letraset font which I had used, and finally the actual slogan, which was the thing of most importance: 'A Fool And His Life Are Soon Parted'.

Although Dorothy extended an open invitation to model for me, I did have other offers, and Jill was always more than keen to make herself available. As I lay in my bed, rolling a cigarette in the calm hiatus, with Jill's warm breath wafting gently across my chest, I heard the muffled howls of pitiful sobbing from along the landing. It was quite profound, and something which I had never had to listen to before.

"Well Max," said the principal of the art college, "I suppose now you'll be leaving us early to join the world of advertising?"

"I will be leaving," I told him. "But not for advertising." However, I was more than happy to accept the hundred quid prize money.

Dorothy insisted that she wanted to buy me a parting gift. I told her that I was thinking of buying a new guitar, and before I knew it, we were on a train bound for London. We took a taxi from Liverpool Street to Soho and I played acoustic six-strings in all the shops up and down Denmark Street and the Charing Cross Road, until finally I plumped for a sexy Gibson Jumbo, which set Dorothy back the princely sum of a hundred-and-fifty quid. We returned to Southend and embarked upon a long and beautiful night of passion.

The next evening was to be our last, and we both dressed to

the nines and headed out for a swanky meal at the best restaurant in Southend. There, misty-eyed with Champagne, she squeezed my hands across the linen tablecloth and breathed her heartfelt confession to me: "I love you, Max. And when you leave me, my candle will be a long time burning out. A long, long time."

I was excited to be meeting up with Sammy again. She was studying at a teacher training college in Canterbury. I hadn't seen her for ages, although she used to send me little poems occasionally. I'd acquired an ageing Mini, and when I arrived to pick her up from the halls of residence, she hopped in, we kissed, and sped away.

After a couple of minutes, she happened to glance around onto the back seat, and asked, "Max, why do you have a skeleton in your car?"

"No reason," I shrugged. "It was hanging around in our art society room at college, and…"

"Max! You're incorrigible!" she shrieked.

"Is that the same as irresistible?" I grinned, and she smacked me playfully on the shoulder.

We drove out a couple of miles from Sammy's campus, and as we came into the high street of a small village, I said, "Why don't we live here?"

"Alright," agreed Sammy. "Why not? Sturry it is."

We found a small cottage which was comfy and cheap to rent. I set about painting and she took herself off to college each day. Sometimes I would paint her, literally, daubing and caressing watercolours or foodstuffs all over her delicious, naked flesh. I sold my pictures in a few galleries in Canterbury, on a sale-or-return basis, and because I didn't have any returns, we were soon in a position to rent a much nicer and quaint old cottage. Everything was okay, except, as time went by, Sammy and I saw less and less of each other, until it became obvious that we were both satisfying our desires in pastures new.

There was a dilapidated pub in Canterbury called the George. As I pulled back one of the wooden boards which covered the windowpanes, I peered inside and could see a few sticks of upturned furniture, bar stools and benches, covered in cobwebs and dust. I don't know why, but it had a certain appeal, perhaps because I thought it would provide a wild and far-out space which I could comfortably occupy. I telephoned directory inquiries and got the number for the brewery which had its name above the door. In turn, a manager who represented the owners told me that the pub would, at some point be demolished, but until that time they would be happy to rent it to me. He came down, showed me around, and we shook on a rent of ten pounds a week for the entire premises, which included the bar and several bedrooms.

I had ripped most of the planks off the windows and was adding the final brushstrokes to a landscape, a Norfolk creek and windmill in the style of Jonathan Crome, when I became aware of a lady calling out and tapping on the glass outside. I let her into the saloon and she said, "I'm looking for some rooms to let, and I happened to notice that you'd moved in here. I'm from the Marlowe Theatre, just up the road. It's just that some of our actors are looking for… What a beautiful painting!"

Before I knew it, I was sharing my pub with a trio of talented and rising young thespians, Chris Ellison, Nick Brimble and Joanna David, who were putting on a production of Chekhov's 'The Seagull'. I charged them the reasonable rent of four quid a week per room and found myself with a small profit. I already had a couple of young ladies who would regularly call by to keep me company, and as long as people entertained *me*, I was happy to entertain *them*.

One of my new lodgers wandered into my bedroom as I was working, and announced, "Hello mate, I'm Chris. Nice picture." He sat on the bed and watched me paint, although it seemed obvious that he was somewhat distracted by my cleaning lady as she jiggled around, sweeping and dusting. When she had left, he asked, quite deadpan, "How come that girl was topless?"

"Her jumper's hazardous," I explained. "The fibres get into my paint, so I always ask her to take it off when she comes."

"Oh," he said, "I see," nodding his head reflectively as he mulled over my explanation.

"Well, she believes it," I shrugged.

The big-breasted girl in question was called 'Thunderboots' because of her penchant for wearing huge 'bovver boots'. But despite her less than flattering nickname, she was attractive, intelligent and creative. One of her ornamental projects involved the use of a Navajo Indian's head, and it fitted quite neatly on top of the skeleton which I had liberated from my art college. We dressed him up in a toga and stood him in the corner. Rose was another saucy friend/cleaning lady, and she was quite game to pose naked for me, or join in with any of my silly games. With a roaring log fire burning in the hearth, a whole bunch of us would muck about and play music and dress up in silly costumes.

My brother Joey came to visit. In the name of live entertainment, I proposed one night that we create a piece of animated, erotic art. Rose obligingly whisked off her top and I dabbed green and brown emulsion on her boobs, and splodges of blue on her belly. Then, as she danced, her torso became a heavenly mirage of swaying palm trees over a rippling oasis. I dared her to parade her body art all the way up Burgate to the Olive Branch pub. She set off without a qualm or a stitch on top, proudly thrusting out her coconuts and wobbling them at anyone who passed by. Fortuitously for me, despite my enthusiastic rubbing and massaging with soapy water, it was a week before the dazzling desert faded away into the sands of time. Joey was quite enamoured of Canterbury's charms, and wanted to stay for longer, and also wanted to take me back to Brighton with him, but life was just too good.

I walked into a local gallery, and a man with a grey pointy beard was asking the owner, "Excuse me, dose pictures on de vall? Who is dee artist?" The proprietor pointed at me. "Deez pictures are very good," the foreigner told me. "I am Freddie van Dijk. I am an art dealer, from dee Nederlands."

Freddie looked like a sort of older version of what Vincent van Goch might have looked like if he had survived for a couple of decades beyond his thirty-seven years. He was warm and pleasant and cultured, and I took an instant liking to him, and he to me. We left and I took him to see some more of my work.

"Your paintings I thought, at first they must be expensive reproductions of original artists," he said, marvelling at one of my Napoleonic battle scenes. "How much would dat dealer in de gallery pay you for one of deez? A hundred? Two hundred pounds? And he is selling dem for what? Ten times dat!"

Freddie was spot on. He told me that he knew a gallery owner called Timothy in Royal Tunbridge Wells, and he drove me there to meet him. Between them, they assured me that they could shift as many old Dutch Masters as the market could reasonably soak up, and pay me three or four times what I was being paid by the Canterbury dealers. It was a thrill to think that I had now gone international; my paintings were being sold in galleries in Holland and beyond. I got a letter from the brewery and it seemed that the bulldozers would soon be moving in to flatten the pub.

CHAPTER 5:
FLIRTING AND FLANNEL

Mum was pleased to see me again, although I decided quite quickly that I needed my own space, and rented a large, high-ceilinged bedsit in Springfield Road, a ten-minute drive from her flat. Apart from selling seascapes and Dutch barges to Freddie and Tim, I discovered a dealer called Jack Powell with a shop in nearby Portslade who was particularly keen on my 'primitive' paintings of farm animals. Although eighteenth and nineteenth century artists like John Boultbee were renowned for their portraits of prize pigs, bulls, sheep and horses, even unsigned pictures of subjects like the 'Craven Heifer' or the 'Durham Ox' were collectible and achieved good prices. This was especially true if a painting was deftly produced in oils and had the style, the finish, the colours, the canvas and the frame of a genuine antique original.

"Albert! Albert!" I called out, tapping on the windowpane of Jack's shop, trying as discreetly as I could to attract the attention of the little old man who was Hoovering inside. Eventually he looked up, pulled the soggy dog-end from his mouth and shuffled over to let me in. The bell jangled above my head and he quickly locked the door behind me. I skirted into the back with my bundle of small pictures, manoeuvring my way round the piles of wobbly furniture and 'antique' odds-and-sods.

"Jack's still up in the land of nod," Albert coughed. "Can I have a look?" I unwound the towel from around my pictures and laid them out across the desk. "Phwoar! That's bloody marvellous that is!"

A hairy hand squeezed my shoulder. I flicked round and Jack's toothpasty voice hit me in the face, "Good stuff, Max. Even better than the last lot." He picked up the three paintings in turn, slanting each one against the dusty lightbulb and peering at them through his giant magnifying glass. Then, pulling out a wad of notes and beaming up at me, said, "Shall we say..?" Then, glowering down at Albert, "You finished yer sweeping 'ave yer, Mister Derby?"

Against the deafening din of the roaring vacuum cleaner, Jack and I agreed a deal, then made our way towards the shopfront. Albert stopped his machine and yanked the front door open for me.

"Albert Derby," I inquired, "is that really your name?"

Albert scratched his head and snapped indignantly, "Yeah, what of it?"

"Nothing," I grinned. "It's just a good name. See ya."

Downstairs from me in Springfield Road, in the basement flat, lived a guy called Tony. He was a young guy, about the same age as me, and we both had a common interest in gigs and girls. There was a funky music club and coffee bar opposite Brighton station where I'd get up and sing a couple of songs with one of the regular bands, and it would often lead to young ladies wanting to come over and sit with me. The form was, that I would start flirting with whichever girl I fancied and leave Tony to chat up one of her friends. Tony was chuffed to bits to have a ready-made supply of desirable females on tap, whereas I was more blasé, and there were occasions when I would, to my shame, arrange a date with a girl, but leave her waiting at the clock-tower or outside the Curzon cinema. However, I did get my comeuppance when my brother Kenny just happened to date one of my castoffs, and brought her home to meet my mum while I was visiting. I was confronted by the young lady and given a right earbashing in front of my mum, whereupon my mum waded in and gave me an even worse earbashing.

"It's Sat'day. We goin' to the club tonight?" asked Tony, buzzing with enthusiasm.

"Not me," I said. He looked downhearted and so I told him, "It's just... Sammy said she might come up from Canterbury." It wasn't a total lie, Sammy and I did still get together on odd occasions, if the fancy took us.

"Oh, okay," he sighed. "Might see yer later then?"

"Yeah, maybe," I said.

At about eleven o'clock I was crazing a Lord Nelson portrait, watching his pale skin gently cracking as I floated him from side to side across the orange glare of the electric fire, when I heard fingernails drumming on my door. I froze for second.

"Max! Are you in?" appealed Tony, in a half whisper.

"Yes," I answered.

"Is Sammy wiv yer?" he inquired, with a hint of caution.

"No," I called back.

"Good," he said. "I've got these two birds with me. Absolute crackers! You'll love 'em!"

I thought about it, then sighed, "Yeah, alright. I'll be down in a minute."

"Bring yer guitar will yer?" he said. "And a bottle o' wine."

I freshened up, put on a neckerchief and velvety frock coat, and trotted downstairs. As I breezed into Tony's flat, I was greeted by the warm smiles of two alluring young ladies who were sitting side-by-side on his ruffled bedclothes, their knees pricked up and their miniskirts retreating down their thighs.

"This is me mate Max," bragged Tony. "Like I said, he's an artist and 'e sings."

"I'm Linda," announced the perky brunette, "and this is Pam," she added, indicating her blonde friend.

"Very nice to make your acquaintance," I said, hailing them with a bow.

"Hmm, not often one meets a gentleman," complimented Linda. "And you play too!"

"I do indeed," I grinned, slinging my foot up onto a chair and bursting into my song about the long and dusty road, and the hot and heavy load.

They applauded so energetically when my two songs were done, that their tight, pointy jumpers were jiggling almost to bursting point.

Linda and I sat together with glasses of sweet wine, and she asked, "So Max, what sort of things do you like to paint?"

"Why don't you come and have a look?" I suggested.

We left Tony lecturing Pam on the genius of England's World Cup-winning squad, grabbed some wine and beat a hasty retreat upstairs.

"Did you do all of these!" gasped Linda. And after I had revealed and demonstrated to her some of the secrets of my artistic techniques, such as 'scumbling' and 'impasto' as used by the great masters, she implored, "So how did you learn all this? I want to know all about it, and I want to know all about *you*."

I indulged her with some snippets about my life, then we lay down, fully clothed, snoozing on the bed, spooning and sometimes gently kissing each other on the face and neck, until finally we both drifted off into a world of sweet dreams. In the morning, we called round at Pam's flat, just a stone's throw away, and the four of us had a jazzy Sunday lunch in Preston Circus. Linda and I chatted and laughed our way through the afternoon, oblivious of the trickling grains of sand which were slipping through our fingers. And then, suddenly, it was time for her to go.

"Okay then," she said, pecking me on the cheek and picking up her bag as the train chuffed and squealed along the platform beside us.

"Portsmouth! This is the Portsmouth Harbour train," yelled the station porter. "She'll be stopping at Hove, Aldrington, Portslade, Fishergate…"

Just as Linda was about to step aboard, she turned and gave me a big kiss on the lips, and giggled, "That's to keep you going." And as her train disappeared into the evening grey, I could still feel a trace of her warm breath on my face.

It was two days later, in the evening, when there was an unexpected knock on my door. I was packing up a parcel of pictures which I had just finished. "Hang on, Tony," I called out, with no great urgency to find out what he wanted. "Just a sec… Just coming…" Then, casually opening the door, I blurted, "Come in, mate, I was just about to… Oh! Hi! Sorry, I was just… Come in, come in."

"I was passing and I thought…" shrugged Pam. "And as we're practically neighbours…"

Pam was slightly shorter and more buxom than Linda, and she had the most beautiful straight blonde hair which flowed almost down to her waist. She admired my paintings and we talked about what a smashing girl Linda was, and about how long they had known each other, and about what good friends they were, and about how she loved the fact that I was an artist and a musician. And when I noticed that it was getting late, and mentioned that I had to catch a train in the morning to Tunbridge Wells, she insisted that she would drive me there in her car. At 10 A.M. she picked me up, and by 11 A.M. we were well on our way to Timothy's gallery, meandering through the pretty lanes of the Weald with my bundle of paintings carefully stowed in the back of her Mini Countryman. The deal with Tim was that he would estimate what he thought he could sell my pictures for and we would split the profits when they were sold. Tunbridge Wells was an upmarket town with royal status. It had an international reputation for its art and antique shops which attracted thousands of wealthy visitors, and I was more than happy to have my paintings exhibited in a posh gallery there.

When Pam called round to see me again, I showed her some of my sketches and she cooed, "Ooh, how wonderful. I've always dreamed of being sketched. Please will you draw me? Please?"

She was a good-looking girl and I didn't have the heart to spoil her dream. I made a few suggestions and before I knew it she was unhooking her bra and striking poses in the style of classical Greek statues. Her portrayal of Aphrodite was quite satisfying. However, my real interest lay with Linda. We had spoken on the phone a few times, and I felt a shiver when I saw her striding down the platform towards me in a red plastic mac and boots, flaunting a copy of 'Revolver' and brandishing a ravishing smile. Although we did venture out briefly, to socialise and see a folk group, we spent the weekend amusing ourselves in my room, laughing at nothing and listening to raindrops.

Linda's suggestion that I should visit her parents came as a bit of a surprise. They lived in an area of Cosham which she had described as "quite posh" and her parents as "old school." In the thick of a blizzard, I held onto Linda's warmly gloved hand as we teetered cautiously along the deserted suburban street. The trees which ran along the pavements on either side looked like scrawny skeletons with long, spiky fingernails. The houses were pre-war and sizeable, and amongst the tightly shut curtains we could see the occasional twinkle of coloured fairy lights. We arrived at her parents' house, one of the larger style properties, with its own garage and a fair-sized garden front and back.

Linda's mother Zena opened the front door as we arrived and dragged us in out of the cold. She was a warm and sunny soul with a bright smile, and when she had relieved us of our snowy coats we went through to the lounge where a wingback chair sat before a blazing fire. An older gentleman, upon hearing us, turned and got up and greeted me with a firm handshake. Eric was, as Linda had described her father, a kindly man who, appropriately, exuded the authority of a retired naval captain. On every shelf and cabinet stood a display of ornaments, photos and mementoes, and between the leafy patterns of the flock wallpaper were paintings; old paintings; large ones and small ones; mainly shipping scenes. As Eric welcomed me into their home, I couldn't help but focus on the pictures behind him, looking to see what techniques the artists had used, and hoping that I wouldn't spot any familiar brushstrokes!

"You like my little collection?" inquired Eric. "I have quite a few around the place, some of them quite valuable. Would you like to see them?" Zena looked at me, rolled her eyes and smiled, and a parrot in the corner started squawking. As I followed Eric from room to room, he puffed on his pipe and told me what he knew about the artist of each painting, and the subject matter, and details of where he had acquired each one. "This one is a great favourite on mine," he chuckled, staring gleefully at a party of exaggerated, portly Georgian diners glutting out on a tableful of food and wine. "I believe it's called 'Good Living'. Very old, and paid a pretty penny for it, too! Artist unknown, unfortunately."

"Shame," I said. "But I'm sure it's worth every penny."

"Exactly what the dealer said," he beamed.

As I scrupulously examined the quality of my composition, I felt a wonderful warm glow of satisfaction and pride. And it was only when I was alone in the loo and flushed, that I allowed myself a subdued titter. Linda and her mum and shy little sister Christine prepared a tasty meal and rounds of drinks, and I made a point of joining them in the kitchen to lend a hand and raise a smile. Eric and I nattered by the fireside about naval matters, racehorses, the World Cup and the fall of the British Empire. Linda's father was a bit old-fashioned, and I was sentenced by him, and the family guard dog, to a night of solitary confinement in the spare room. However, I did manage to escape across the landing in the wee small hours for a muffled romp in Linda's bed.

Over the next few weeks, Linda would tell her parents that she was getting the train up to Brighton to stay with Pam, then stay with me in Springfield Road. Or sometimes, I would go down to Portsmouth and sleep in the spare room. It was a buzzing city with vibrant cafes and music pubs and clubs, and Linda and I would hang out in all the cool places, like the Manhattan, the Keyhole, Del Monico, the Podmore, Kimbells and the Railway Hotel, listening to music until the early hours. Linda was at hairdressing college in Portsmouth during the week, and I was in Brighton, painting my pictures and selling them, mainly through dealers and auction houses around Sussex.

"Max," groaned Linda, in an ominous tone, "some of these wheeler-dealers and places that Pam takes you in her car, are they... well are they dodgy?"

"No," I chuffled, quite indignantly.

Then, after a wary pause, she ventured, "You're not doing anything illegal are you, Max?"

"Me!" I objected. Then kissing her on the neck, "Of course not, darling."

It was just a bit of luck that I happened to be in the right place at the right time. 'Ray's of Hove' was a jammed little car lot which had been flogging second-hand cars for years. It was quite close to my mum's flat, and occasionally I would drop in to see if he had anything like an MGB, or something special, parked on the front. As I stared at its bewitching beauty, its sheer audacity, its divine perfection, its sexy body and pretty face, I knew that I must have it - *it* was totally irresistible!

"How much for the Sunbeam Tiger?" I asked.

"You serious?" asked Ray. "Hold on a sec," he insisted, darting back to his office, before returning a moment later with a genteel young blonde in a faux leopard-skin coat. "This is the lady who's selling it." And to her, "This is the gentleman who wants to buy it."

"Pleased to meet you," I smiled, "I'm Max Brandrett."

"Tonia Campbell," she replied.

"Beautiful car," I gushed.

"It was my late husband's," she said. "Donald Campbell?"

"Oh!" I blurted. "I'm sorry, I didn't…"

"Enjoy it," she said, smiling warmly, and Ray courteously escorted her away to a chauffeur-driven motor.

Donald Campbell had died just a few weeks before, as he was trying to break the world speed record on water.

When Ray came back, I said, "Ray, you're a man who looks like he appreciates a nice picture…"

It turned out that Ray was a man who appreciated a nice coaching scene. John Maggs, an artist who was around in the eighteen-hundreds, was noted for his coaching scenes, and the massive painting which I did sat nicely on Ray's office wall. The Sunbeam was rare and valuable, and I did have to pay a few quid on top of the painting, but I was more than happy with the deal. It had a big V8 engine, and it was blindingly fast.

"Well, what d'ya think?" I asked Linda, pulling up outside her house and blipping the throttle.

Eric and Zena emerged from the house, beaming for

ear-to-ear, and Linda's sister Christine followed, covering her ears with her hands and wincing. I switched off and noticed the twitching curtains.

"Oh! What a super car, Max!" shrieked Zena.

"It's called a Tiger," I grinned, holding up my claws and roaring.

"That's some motor, Max!" gasped Eric.

When the family had gone back indoors, I said to Linda, "I thought we'd take a spin down to the West Country."

"But what about my course?" questioned Linda. "And what about my mum and dad!"

A week later we were blasting down the A303, the wind screaming through our hair at a hundred miles an hour as I fought to keep the beautiful blue beast on the tarmac. Linda had told her parents that the college was closed and that she was nipping off with Pam for a few days. We got a self-catering apartment in North Devon, and as we explored the coastline, we came upon a small village called Bucks Mill where, according to the locals, a galleon from the Spanish Armada was once shipwrecked and seven Spaniards came ashore and married local girls, which accounted for the swarthy look of the villagers. It was a funny story, and one which might well have been true, judging by what we observed.

Driving up above Brighton, near the village of Ditchling on the South Downs, we spotted a board which was advertising: 'Puppies For Sale'. Almost in perfect harmony, Linda and I turned to each other and asked, "Shall we?" There didn't seem to be any reason not to. After all, surely it was innocent enough just to go and look at some puppies? It wasn't as if we were seriously going to buy one.

On the journey home, Bonnie, a big bundle of fluff, fidgeted excitedly on Linda's lap. Standing up, she plonked her giant front paws onto Linda's shoulders and licked her face, as I held onto the steering wheel with one hand and ruffled her big soppy ears with the other. It was love at first sight. There was no way that we could not take Bonnie with us. She grew and grew, and was soon huge and full of playful energy, as was the norm for Old English Sheepdogs. I kept her at my flat sometimes, and sometimes I would drive her down to stay with Linda's family. There, she would romp around the back garden with Shane, their massive German Shepherd.

Dropping off some pictures one day, I screeched to a halt outside Jack Powell's shop in Portslade. I was just getting the paintings out of the boot when Jack suddenly appeared and closed the lid down. "Leave em!" He snapped. "You better come inside, Max." He locked the door behind us and yanked down the shutter. "I've 'ad a visit from the 'Old Bill'. They searched the place and found some of yer paintin's under me bed. I never told 'em you done 'em, Max. I'd never do that."

"Thanks Jack," I said.

"They're after my blood though," he sighed. "Frettened to fit me up for somefin' else if I didn't give 'em yer name. Watch out they don't fit *you* up an' all, Max! Bent fuckers!"

A couple of the other local dealers told me that they too had received a visit from the constabulary's Fraud Squad. And it seemed that word was going around that a lot of fakes were popping up in the area, and several of my regular contacts said they wouldn't risk selling my pictures, at least not for the foreseeable.

I had been to pick up Linda from Cosham and was cruising along the A27 towards Brighton, when a squad car shot up my rear end and started flashing me. To let him by, I dutifully veered in towards the left. Despite my impeccable road manners, he continued to sit on my tail and flash his lights. Naturally, I accelerated, and contemplated leaving him in the dust. However, when he put on his siren and blue flashing light, Linda thought I'd better pull over and see what his problem was. As he got out of his motor, I quickly snatched the tax disk out of my windscreen and ate it. It wasn't actually a tax disc, but a Guinness label which I'd painted red and pink to pretend that the car was taxed until the following year.

"Afternoon," said the fat copper. "Belting it a bit, weren't ya?"
"Not in trouble am I, sir?" I fawned.

"*You* should know," he said. Then, after looking around the car, he demanded, "Where's yer tax disc, driving licence, insurance and logbook?"

I tapped my pockets and sighed, "Not on me, I'm afraid, officer."

"You've got seven days to produce 'em at the police station," he advised, pulling out his notebook. "Name and address? And don't give me any flannel."

"Max Brandrett, Forty-Two Springfield Road," I said. "You can ask *her* if you don't believe me, officer," I suggested, nodding at Linda.

Linda fluttered her eyelashes and simpered, "That is right, officer."

I was relieved when the cop had gone, and thankful that he wasn't from the Fraud Squad. A few days later, I politely told the constable at the police station that my documents were with my lawyer, who was on vacation, and that I was flying imminently to the U.S.A. where I had been commissioned to paint some portraits. I asked him if it would be alright to produce my documents when I returned to England the following year. Obligingly, he made an official entry in his traffic book that I had been excused and the matter had been dropped. Some more art dealers blanked me, and I got pulled over again, and used the same scam again, but I'd started to get paranoid that the cops were watching me. I stood out like sore thumb; there was only one long-haired and bearded young bloke around Brighton who wore a Victorian-style frock coat and bright silk scarves, and whizzed around in a Mediterranean-blue Sunbeam Tiger.

A few miles outside Portsmouth was a paint sprayer in a place called Denmead. He came highly recommended by Linda's father. "But why change her colour?" inquired Eric, scratching his head and looking quite bemused.

"Just fancy a change," I told him. "I was thinking of orange."

And orange it was. But changing the colour of the car to bright orange didn't exactly make me invisible!

Bonnie and Shane got on well together, but the stress of trying to control two large dogs became too much for Linda and her mum. My landlord was never too keen on Bonnie, despite the fact that she was quiet and well-behaved, but it was obvious that a difficult decision had to be made.

Bonnie jumped into the car and sat herself down on the passenger seat, and I shut the door. "Well, this is it then," I said to Linda. "Time to say goodbye."

Linda leaned into the car and hugged Bonnie's neck, and kissed her again and again. "You be a good girl," she sniffled, her eyes misting over. "And you be a good boy," she sniffled to me, hugging my neck and kissing me again and again.

I watched Linda in the Sunbeam's mirrors, waving and disappearing behind us. Bonnie tilted her head back and squinted as the warm wind fluttered across her face. She had come to love going out on car journeys and was a perfect passenger. I just prayed that she would love this journey too.

Portobello Market was just I'd left it, buzzing with tourists and traders, vagrants and vagabonds, everyone looking for a jackpot and a jolly. Brighton had been okay, but London was the place to be. My mum and my brothers had been disappointed when I told them I was leaving, but the capital seduced me like a passionate lover. We had unfinished business. And Dougie, my old landlord, was more than pleased to see me back again. He had never re-rented my ramshackle room in Cricklewood, which came as no surprise to me considering its size and condition, and the fact he had his haul of dodgy art treasures hanging all over the walls. I forgot to mention to him that I had acquired a furry flatmate, but I knew that the nasty Polish guy who rented the room downstairs would grass me up as soon as look at me. Luckily, the toerag was away when I moved back in. Whenever Linda came up to visit, we had to breathe in, what with Bonnie, my easel and all my painting stuff. But my little hideaway in Cricklewood suited me just fine.

A middle-aged Jewish man in a plush, velvet-collared overcoat stopped to look at the paintings on my stall in Portobello. I was entertaining myself, singing and playing guitar at the time, but I desisted when I realised that he wanted to talk to me.

"Nice dog," he complimented, looking at Bonnie who was half asleep at my feet.

"She's not for sale," I said. "She's a special, performing dog."

"Yeah? What does she do then?" he demanded.

"Look into her eyes," I said. Bonnie sat up and stared back into *his* eyes. "Blimey!" he exclaimed, maintaining his gaze. "She's got one brown eye and one blue!"

"Yeah, Bonnie's wall-eyed," I said. "That's cos she's a special, hypnotic dog."

"What d'ya mean, hypnotic?" he frowned.

"Can't ya feel her reading yer mind?" I asked. "Ya should be feeling it by now. Keep staring."

After a minute or two, the man sniggered, "Fuck off! You had me going there!" Lifting the spectacles from his nose, he gawped at my paintings and challenged, "Are these originals?"

He introduced himself, saying that his name was Sam Cohen, an art dealer, but I wasn't sure about him. He said that he might be interested in buying a few of them, so I made a point of emphasising that my paintings were all definitely 'after' Samuel Palmer or 'in the style of' Bonaventura Peeters the Elder, and I definitely wasn't claiming that any of them were painted by anyone but me.

A few minutes after he had gone, I looked up from strumming my guitar and smiled at a baby-faced young guy who was looking thoughtfully at my portraits. He was exceptionally dressed in a sharp grey serge suit with slim lapels, and a flashy Caribbean-blue swirl waistcoat. The outfit was quality, bespoke, and just smelt of money.

"Here mate, these smudges, are they real or are they printed?" he asked.

"They're genuine oil paintings," I said.

"And you done 'em, yeah?" he asked. I nodded and he continued, "And can yer paint anyone?"

"Anyone you like," I said.

"Well, I'd like yer to paint 'er," he said, slipping a photograph out of his pocket and handing it to me. "Can yer do it?"

It wasn't a difficult task. The lady was quite average, sixtyish, smiling, blonde, with a plain updo hairstyle. I painted a good-sized portrait, and I took my time to do a nice job, then mounted it in a smart, elegant frame. I was pleased with it, but when the lad came back to Portobello Market and I showed it to him, I wasn't so sure that *he* was.

"Is it okay?" I asked him. "It *is* what you wanted?"

"It ain't for me," he said. "It's a present for a couple o' geezers I know. They'll tell yer if it's the business or not. You bring it up to the Earl O'Lonsdale bar, right? We'll be waiting for ya."

I'd already done the picture, and obviously it was of no use to me, and he hadn't paid me for it, so I didn't really have much choice. The pub was only up the road, a short hoof up the hill. Walking in from the street, there was a large public bar with big windows on two sides. It was busy, mainly with visitors to the market, but there was also a collection of colourful dealers who were either drowning their sorrows or celebrating their luck. Scanning around, I couldn't spot the delicate features of my youthful patron. Clutching the picture under my arm, I wandered into the saloon bar, my eyes gradually adjusting to the murky gloom. The room was thick with cigarette and cigar smoke, and the only sound was the mumble and chuckle of private men. Through the haze, the young man spotted me and approached with a beaming smile.

"Alright mate?" he chirped. "Over 'ere." As I followed him to a bench in the corner, I was aware that half-a-dozen pairs of piercing eyes were watching my every move. "This is the geezer," he told a pair of suave, identically suited gents who were sitting bolt upright, shoulder-to-shoulder.

"Alright son?" one of them rumbled. "What yer got for us?"

I handed him my offering, which I had wrapped in a sheet of brown paper, tied with string. All went quiet as his manicured fingernails fastidiously undid each of the little knots and he carefully peeled away the wrapper. Ronnie and Reggie Kray sat staring, and staring, and staring at my picture. I knew immediately who they were; everyone did.

After what seemed an age, Ronnie cried, "Holy shit!"

Then Reggie gasped and shook his head and blurted, "That's 'er! That is 'er!"

"Buy the man a drink," someone called out, and suddenly everyone was smiling and celebrating.

"Sit dan 'ere, son," beamed the giant gentlemen, as they parted and squashed me in between them.

"The eyes!" marvelled Ronnie. "I can't believe ha you done that!"

"That expression is mint!" gushed Reggie. "She's gonna love it!"

I sat with a glass of wine, answering all the twins' questions about who I was, where I came from, and how I had come to be an artist.

Then one of them had a lightbulb moment and insisted, "Tell yer what, why don't yer come back and meet 'er? She'll love yer!"

"I would," I told them, "but I've left my dog with someone, and she'll be fussing. Women!"

Ronnie ordered another man to, "Bung 'im two."

"Two quid!" I silently blurted. "For all that work!"

Then a gargantuan wad of crumpled banknotes appeared, and two-hundred quid was counted out into my hand.

Bonnie and I lay side-by-side on my bed, and I splayed the banknotes out like a deck of playing cards and fanned my face with them. I chuckled and kissed Bonnie on the face and started to sing: *"We're in the money, we're in the money..."* when suddenly her ears pricked up. There were voices downstairs. It was Dougie and the Polishman. I heard the word "dog" mentioned, then footsteps approaching up the stairs.

"Bonnie! Quick!" I hissed, jolting to my feet and lifting the skirt of the bedclothes aloft. Bonnie understood immediately, and shrank down onto her belly and sidled underneath the bed.

The door knocked, and Dougie's voice rang out, "Max? Are you there?"

Bonnie stared out at me as I flapped the blankets down over her face. "Shhh!"

"Alright Dougie?" I cheerfully greeted, opening the door.

"Bitta lumbago, but can't complain," he said, squeezing into the room with the toes of his shoes brushing the hem of the bedclothes. "Thing is, Max, Stan reckons you got a dog up 'ere."

"A dog!" I huffed. "I couldn't even fit a bleedin' hamster in 'ere, could I?"

Dougie glanced at my four tiny walls and shrugged, with a tinge of guilt, "Point taken, Max. It's just a health and hygiene thing."

"Tell 'im to worry about his own health and hygiene," I warned.

We sat down on the bed and had a drink, and a long discussion about life and love and the price of art; how the popularity of old paintings was growing and their value was escalating. When finally he left, I peeked between the curtains and made sure that he had driven away, before lifting the bedclothes and giving Bonnie permission to come out from under the bed. My giant friend bounced up-and-down on her giant paws, excitedly wagging her tail and whimpering. I couldn't stop her, and I was sure that my nasty neighbour downstairs would hear her, or wonder why his lampshade was jigging up and down on its flex. It was obvious that poor Bonnie was desperate to pee. I opened my door and she fled, her claws slipping and sliding on the lino, her legs flailing around in all directions, like a drunk on ice-skates. As I passed Stan's door, it opened a fraction. He peeped out and I told him to "F' off." Bonnie scampered away downstairs to the kitchen door, and when I let her out, she released a gushing waterfall which I thought would flood the garden. Luckily, Dougie never did believe that I had a dog living in my room.

As Bill wriggled around on the frosty tarmac in Portobello Road, desperately trying to unchain himself for the delectation of cackling crowd, Sam Cohen came back and patted Bonnie enthusiastically on the head and asked me, "I wondered if you was gonna sell me some of yer paintings? It's alright, I'm not the fuzz or anything, I'm a respectable businessman."

Bonnie liked Sam, and I considered her to be a pretty good judge of character. We went to the caff for a nosh-up, and Bonnie had sausages under the table. Sam gave me a good price for a couple of primitives, a landscape and a pair of armada paintings, and I gave him a hand to lug them up to his car. The pictures disappeared into the vast boot of his ice-blue Mark Ten Jag.

The following week, having tested the market, Sam was quite buoyant and beamed, "Max, I've got a proposition for you. How about you and me go into business together? I've seen a lot of artists and a lot of fakes in my time, but what you got is a god-given talent. I'm telling ya, with your smudges and my chutzpah, the schmocks at the auction houses'll be crawling all over each-other to get their grubby mitts on 'em! What d'ya say, Max, eh, *you* and *me*?"

"Okay," I agreed. "You're on."

"We'll split the profits sixty-forty," he said.

"Is that sixty for me and forty for you?" I questioned.

"Of course," he smiled. "What do you take me for? I'm an honourable man."

We cruised along the Kings Road in Sam's Jag, admiring all the fashionable women in their macs and minis. Around the corner in Lots Road, on the borders of Chelsea and Fulham, it was a different story. A row of dilapidated terraced houses was begrimed with years of soot from the power station which loomed bleakly at the end of the street. There were docks and dockers, and greasy factories and warehouses. Hiding away, behind closed doors, was an auction house, not as swanky as those in Mayfair, but nevertheless a thriving hub of commerce where shrewd businessmen ventured into the lucrative occupation of buying and selling art and antiques.

We went inside and a toff at the desk with an Eton or Harrow plum in his mouth inquired, "May I help you?"

"We'd like a catalogue, please?" requested Sam.

"May I inquire," pressed the man, "are you gentlemen interested in buying, or selling?"

"Definitely," Sam confirmed, and I could see the gent almost cringing as he handed over a brochure.

Sam and I wandered all around the saleroom, referring to the sales catalogue as we paused to admire a Chippendale chest or a Hepplewhite dining chair, and nodding discreetly at one another when we spotted a painting which was apparently from the eighteenth or nineteenth century.

When we came outside to the car, I said to him, "Did you see that primitive of the pig? That was never eighteen-hundreds! More like a week-last-Thursday!"

The streets of Fulham were bounteous with second-hand shops and downmarket emporiums where, hidden amongst the bric-a-brac of the desperate and the deceased, we found several gloomy paintings of deformed vases and wobbly landscapes, veiled under centuries of dusty glass and candle smoke. Invariably, Sam would knock the barefaced traders down to a half or a quarter of their asking price for the old 'potboilers', or nonchalantly walk away empty-handed.

Returning to my flat with a collection of decrepit paintings, Sam stared at a preliminary sketch of some comical-looking dogs on my easel and commented, "This looks very promising."

"Inspired by Kash Coolidge," I said.

He chipped in, "Poker-playing dogs. Very nice. But what I'm thinking, Max, for our first hit, is perhaps something a bit more mainstream. Maybe a prize pig? Just to dip our toe in the water, so to speak."

"How about a bull?" I suggested. "A big, fat Hereford bull."

"Yeah," he pondered. "That's good. A big, fat Hereford. Yeah, perfect."

I selected a simple frame and canvas from the 'potboilers', not huge, only about twelve by eight, but with a good age. Over the next few days, I stripped back the canvas and primed it, then set about the real work. From the local library, I found a book with a photograph of a suitable painting and copied it, but carefully altered the angle and background and lighting so that my painting looked totally unique.

When Sam returned, he gasped, "Cor blimey, Max! That's some bull you got there!"

"I left it unsigned," I said. "Most of the oldens are."

"Yeah, quite right," he agreed. "But how about a smidge more white polish?"

There was no great rush; we had plenty of time before the next auction to make any alterations and discuss a plan of action.

"So, should I take it into the auction house, or you?" I asked.

"We both go," he said. "And we don't just take this one, we take a few of *them* along too," he stated, pointing at some of the artless efforts which we had picked up on our travels. "We'll clean the glasses and frames up a bit and make 'em look like they've all come from the same place. You know, a job lot."

"And we slip the Hereford in with 'em?" I deduced.

"You got it," he smirked. "We'll need a bubbe meise, a bit of a tall story." He put his head in his hands and fell silent for some time, then clicked his fingers and pointed at me, and blurted, "You're my son!"

"And you're my dad," I grinned.

"Put on a bit of a Landon accent," he chortled. "Go on, give it a go."

"Alwight dad," I said. "What yer doin', dad? You got that paintin', dad?"

"That's it!" he shrieked, almost falling off the edge of the bed with laughter.

I was making him laugh so much that I started to exaggerate more and more, putting on an almost imbecilic accent, like something from a Dudley Moore comedy sketch. "Here daaaad, is it rainin' aertside, daaad? What's a paintin', daaad? Is that what a painter does, daaad?"

When we drove into Lots Road, Sam made a point of parking

the Jag directly outside the auction house, just to show them that although we gave the impression that we weren't the brightest candles in the box, we might be smart enough to turn up with something of value. And we wore trendy leather jackets and polo neck shirts to promote the notion that we were just wannabe antique dealers. Stumbling in through the doors with half-a-dozen paintings clutched to my chest, I followed Sam and we waited our turn to see the man at the desk.

"Yes?" said the man, calling us forward and peering down his spectacles at us.

Sam said, bowing his head and doffing a make-believe cap, "We got some smudges 'ere, sir, and we wondered if you'd be interested?" Then to me, "Come on, son, show the gentleman. He's a very busy man."

"Sorry daaad," I bleated, leaning forwards and dropping the pictures onto the desk.

"Be careful of the gentleman's desk, son!" Sam admonished sharply. And then to the gentleman, "Sorry abat that, sir."

The professional rapidly flicked through our offerings with no more than a desultory glance and sighed, "Well, I'm afraid they're not…" He suddenly fell silent and pulled my Hereford bull from the pack. I glanced at Sam, my lips quite dry. "Now then…" gleamed the chap, "this… this may be more interesting. Hmmm, interesting."

"Do you like the cow, do you, sir?" inquired Sam.

"Hmmm, quite some beast!" shrilled the man. "Where did you say you got these pictures from?"

"Now, where was it, son?" frowned Sam, apparently devoid of any recall.

"That 'ouse clearance in Exeter, weren't it, dad?" I offered.

"That's it, Exeter!" recalled Sam. "An elderly lady who was movin' from a big 'ouse into an 'ome. Lovely 'ouse. Had all these bunged in 'er garage she did."

"No signature," noted the man. "But that's not unusual."

"Didn't them painters used to put their moniker on their pictures then?" queried Sam.

"No, not always," he informed us. "As for age... hmmm... probably early nineteenth-century. Now, as for value... did you have a figure in mind?"

"Not really, sir. You're the expert," toadied Sam.

"We could put a reserve of say, five hundred on it," mused the man. "Possibly up to eight with the right clientele in the room. Would that be acceptable?"

"Whatever you say, sir," shrugged Sam. "You're the one what knows."

The toff took all of the paintings off us, albeit with a caveat that the old 'potboilers' would be lucky to reach a fiver for the lot. Due to the compiling and printing of catalogues, our pictures weren't due to go on sale until the Monday week.

I joshed all the way back to Sam's house, "It's a lotta bull, innit daaad? That man's an expert in bulls, ainy daaad?" as we drove beyond Hampstead Garden Suburb and into neighbouring Finchley. Sam's semi-detached was quite sizeable and in a sleepy residential street. Bonnie jumped out of the Jag and ran straight through the front door, her tail wagging as she bounded down the hallway to greet Sam's wife Mary and daughter Jacqueline. They welcomed us in and insisted on warming our cockles with a chicken supper. It was a spacious and comfy home, with springy wool carpets, a crystal chandelier, a sprawling three-piece suite and gold braided pouffes, and an air of fragrant lavender polish. I sat in the glow of the fire, wrapped up in jovial conversation and sipping malt whisky.

After a pleasant evening, when Sam ran me up the road to Cricklewood, he asked, "You alright for cash?"

"Yeah, I'm alright ta," I answered.

Then, as I was getting out of the Jag, he chuckled, "You and me, father and son, eh Max?"

The auction house was filling up with a steady stream of punters; all sorts, from well-to-do ladies and gents, to a colourful bunch of bohemian sorts who were obviously in the trade. Sam and I stood amongst the latter and blended in with the background.

Various lots of furniture and collectibles went under the hammer, and my heart raced whenever the bidding on an item climbed way beyond its estimate and sold for thousands. One-by-one, the pages of the catalogue turned, until finally our paintings appeared.

"Five paintings, flower vases etcetera, unknown origins," announced the auctioneer. "Five pounds? Four pounds? Three pounds? Sold! Next, a very nice primitive painting of a Hereford bull, circa early eighteen-hundreds. What am I bid? Do I hear five-hundred-pounds?"

A pair of bushy eyebrows twitched. A pretty finger moved.

"Five-twenty," announced the auctioneer.

A monocle flashed, a cap was tugged, an eyelid blinked, a catalogue waved, a chin was rubbed, an ear was brushed, a wrist was wagged, a fag was flicked, a hankie fluttered... I found it hard to keep up, and often I didn't see who had done what or who was in and who was out, but in what seemed like two shakes of a lamb's tail the gavel dropped and the auctioneer declared, "Sold for seven-hundred-and-sixty pounds."

We left immediately and Sam reminded me, "Of course, there'll be commission and tax to pay." And before we had even reached Bonnie, who was peering out from the back seat of the Jag, he grinned, "That's six-sixty net, give or take. Not bad eh, Maxie?"

We returned about a week later to collect our money from the cashier's desk. The cashier skimmed down his register and found our lot number. He peered at us over his half-rimmed spectacles. "I'm afraid there's been a problem, the painting is a fake," I thought he'd say, followed by ringing alarm bells and a chase through the building, then a scuffle and our arrest. I was ready to run. But the man smiled and asked politely, "And what name shall I make the cheque to?"

"Make it out to cash," said Sam, and we went straight to the nearest Midland Bank and exchanged it for a big wad of beautiful banknotes. "So what d'ya fancy doing next?" Sam asked me.

"What about a nice, serene Samuel Palmer? A woodland

shimmering in the moonlight," I envisioned, tucking into a thick slab of Black Forest Gateau in the Aberdeen Steak House.

"Gorgeous," smiled Sam. "We'll take it to Phillips, they're a good, reputable auctioneers."

I fancied getting out of London for a couple of days and drove down to see Linda.

"Where are you taking me?" she giggled, jumping into the passenger seat of the Sunbeam.

Despite her pleas, I refused to tell her, and drove the short distance down to the seafront in Southsea and swung into the car park of the Queens Hotel.

"A sea view is extra," the clerk informed us, as we checked in.

"I'd be disappointed if it wasn't," I quipped. "Send up a bottle of Champagne will yer?"

We gazed out from our room and watched a hovercraft skipping across the murky Solent in a flurry of spray as it charged towards the Isle of Wight. A sedate cross-channel ferry chugged towards us, and a giant oil tanker was voyaging through, on its way out to the ocean beyond. It was a big old hotel, considered to be one of the best in the area, and it certainly beat sleeping in a spare room at Linda's parents. I drew some sketches and we lay on the deep, rich mattress, sipping bubbly and giggling, until the orange glow of evening had faded away. We didn't want to go out. We just wanted to *be*. Linda telephoned home to explain that she wouldn't be back that night. There was obviously a hint of disapproval from her parents, although I guessed that that was more to do with Eric than Zena.

"My dad *does* like you," Linda assured me. "He might be a bit stuffy, but he'd never stand in our way."

The streets of Southsea and Fratton were littered with scruffy pockets of second-hand shops. Linda helped me scrabble through the piles of old pictures, stopping whenever she found one to ask whether it was of any interest to me. Of course, I would look and assess each one on whether I thought it would supply good camouflage for a planted 'masterpiece'. Our 'potboilers' had to have a bit of age, but I thought it would also help if one or two of them fitted in with the subject and style of the hidden gem which we were going to present to the auction houses. With Samuel Palmer in mind, I chose a few pastoral and forest scenes to fit in with the theme. The rest were just a twopenny-halfpenny selection of pictures: flower vases; fruit bowls; churches; old maids; and angelic looking children.

"So many!" Linda proclaimed, as we lugged a couple of dozen or more pictures to the car. "And just to paint over them! And a jar of rusty nails!"

CHAPTER 6: THE GILDED FRAME AND POPPING CHAMPAGNE

I was keen to return to my flat and get on with the job at hand. Sam had told me when the next auction was being held at Phillips, and I was over-the-moon to arrive back in London and get started on a painting. There was a lame landscape amongst my finds, and I wasted no time in removing the canvas from its dull, gilded frame. The glass was slightly imperfect and the thin wooden verso was peppered with tiny wormholes. It had the age and character which indicated that it was about a hundred years old and, therefore, could make somebody believe that it was the original frame of an authentic Samuel Palmer. At around twenty-four by sixteen inches, the size of the picture would also add credibility to the painting which I was endeavouring to create. Having cleaned and primed the canvas, I was ready to begin. I loved to recreate Palmer's dreamlike visions of trees and skies, copying his techniques, and merely twisting everything in his familiar settings, giving the impression that it really was his work and not mine. I often painted night and day, only keeping track of time by Bonnie's need to pee or poo or eat. When the painting was finished, I faded it and polished it and crackled it and stretched it and tacked it in place with corroded nails, until I could almost have conned myself that it was a genuine work by Samuel Palmer.

Phillips Auctioneers was in the West End, a bit more upmarket than where we had previously scored a result at Lots Road, and I could see that Sam was mopping his brow as we drove down Edgware Road and skirted past Marble Arch.

By the time we arrived, he'd cooled down a bit and beckoned me as we entered, "C'mon son, this way. We've gotta wait 'ere for the gentleman."

The toff at the desk was almost the same as the toff at Lots Road, except even more toffee-nosed. "May I?" he demanded, seizing the pile of ropy efforts from my hands and flipping them through his fingers like a pack of vulgar playing cards. He paused immediately at my unreal creation. Another chap appeared and stared, and they stood, mumbling, unintelligibly, about the technique and so forth: "Hmmm... the fssssuss... and the frosssossoss... and the trissscsstriss... and clsssssusss... and the flbbbflbbbflbbb... outstanding! Quite outstanding!"

As soon as I heard those words, I knew that we were in business. The picture sold for nearly three-thousand pounds.

Sifting through some old 'potboilers' in Club Row, Sam suddenly held up a scrappy old painting of some Jack Russel Terriers and showed it to me. The sizeable wood-and-plaster frame had a nice bronze tint. But, even though it was a fair find, it seemed pretty unremarkable. Sam smiled and twisted the picture over. A label stuck on the reverse was slightly moth-eaten and brown with age. An inscription, printed in Old English script, gave the name and address of a London firm which had, at some time, framed the piece. There was no date, and no certainty as to whether it was the original frame for the painting or whether the painting had been reframed at some time, many, many years in the past. From our point-of-view, any ambiguity about a picture at auction was a plus point, and a genuine old label just added to the possibility that the work was authentic.

Wanting to widen our net, Sam and I loaded bundles of pictures into the Jag and drove to auction houses as far away as Birmingham and Manchester, and any sleepy, provincial towns which had a sales room, such as Arundel and Billingshurst. Wherever we travelled, the reaction of the valuer was always the same: a quick and dismissive look through our worthless 'potboilers', followed by a sharply raised eyebrow, then a silence, and a cough, and the question, "May I ask where you got this one?"

Our bumbling, well-rehearsed routine would follow, "Now, where was it, son?"

"Oxford (or anytown) weren't it, daaaad?" I'd reply.

Basking in the sunshine outside the house in Cricklewood, I was sitting on the pavement and gently strumming my guitar, and singing, when a lovely-looking young lady stopped and commented, "That's really beautiful."

"It's a Tom Paxton song," I said. "Do you like him?"

"Oh, I do," she gushed, her friendly smile at odds with her somewhat severe skirt and jacket. "I don't always dress like this. Only at work. I love your dog."

"Her name's Bonnie. And I'm Max," I said.

Bonnie sat up, swishing her tail excitedly, and the pair of them spent the next few minutes hugging and kissing.

"Sorry, I'm Dianne" she said. "So what do you do then, Max, apart from play guitar and own an adorable dog?"

Dianne was good company and she loved to look at my pictures. Occasionally, over the next few weeks, she dropped in to see what I was working on. It was all pretty innocent and I think she saw her visits as a relaxing escape from her routine; a way of letting her hair down. She seemed to find my lifestyle quite exciting, painting pictures and selling them at auction, although, obviously, I kept her in the dark about any unorthodox aspects of our operation.

"I love painting," I said, "but it's the banking and stuff that's the biggest drag."

"Well why don't you let *me* do it?" she proposed, with a deal of enthusiasm. "It'd be no problem, honestly."

Dianne worked in the West End, and in her lunch hour she was happy to pick up our cheques from London auction houses and cash them through her bank, along with any which had arrived in the post. I paid her a sort of commission for her time and trouble, and Sam and I were relieved to be spared the unwanted attentions of any suspicious cashiers or officious bank clerks. And as the cash came rolling in, Sam and I decided that we should push the boundaries a little. Not only would we sell through more upmarket auctioneers, we would also test how gullible they were, and how gullible the art buyers were.

"This is a very nice picture," the plummy-toned expert at the posh auction house advised us, as he stared hungrily at the Yarmouth seascape which I had painted in the style of John Crome.

John Crome was an artist who never signed his pictures and whose work was often emulated, often by me.

"Is that a gooden then, is it, sir?" Sam ignorantly inquired.

"Well… It's signed by…" I glanced at Sam, as the chap peered into the swirling waves at the bottom left-hand corner of the scene, "Albert… Ah! Albert Derby!" he exclaimed triumphantly.

"Is 'e any good, sir?" I squeaked, quite soppily.

"Oh yes," the chap boomed with authority. "One of the Norwich School, if I'm not mistaken."

"Oh! He went to school in Norwich, dad," I said.

The man sighed wearily, "The Norwich School of Painters was a fraternity of talented artists, set up in the county of Norfolk in the early nineteenth century."

"Nineteen-hundred, eh dad!" I yelped.

"This gentleman's an expert, son," said Sam. "Takes years o' learnin' to be that clever, son."

The scholar and another expert conversed for some time, hmmming and nodding, as they pontificated on the skill of the artist and his status within John Crome's Norwich Society of Artists. And when they had finished their highbrow discussion, they concluded quite emphatically that Albert Derby was a talented nineteenth century artist and student of John Crome, and not, as we knew him to be, the sweeper-upper in Jack Powell's second-hand shop in Portslade.

"I'm so pleased to see you!" shrilled Linda, hugging me so tightly that I thought she was going to squeeze the life out of me. "What's been happening? What have you been up to?"

"Just working," I shrugged, when our lips finally separated.

We enjoyed a couple of nights together, staying at the Queens Hotel and mingling in the folk clubs, catching up with a few pals, and with each other. But my heart was back in London, in Portobello Road, and working at my easel, and cashing in at the auction houses with Sam. Money trickled through my fingers like running water, but I loved nice clothes and fancy food, the things which I had never had.

Sam and I had eaten well and, after a walk with Bonnie in Kensington Gardens, we stopped by at one of our regular downmarket antique shops in search of old frames. The moment we stepped through the door, the owner's eyes lit up and he crowed, "Ah, gentlemen, you're always on the lookout for a character frame. What d'ya reckon to this beauty?"

It was big and oval, wood-and-plaster, gilded-and-patterned, old and rare; just perfect for a special painting. The dealer wanted twenty-five quid for it, along with a few other old 'potboilers'. Sam knocked him down to twenty. I could hardly wait to get the painting back to Cricklewood and get the frame dismantled. The moment I eased the back off, I examined the reverse of the linen canvas and ran my fingers over its fine quality weave. The timber stretcher, which held the canvas taut, and the frame itself, were obviously constructed by a master craftsman using top-quality timber. It must have been a hundred years old, yet the glass and the lacquer were flawless and almost perfect. Judging by the lopsided vase of irregular flowers in the picture, it seemed likely that the frame and canvas, and probably a box of extravagant paints, were originally given as a gift to a lady whose artistic aspirations exceeded her talent. I was exhilarated at the thought of painting a picture which would be housed in such a superb frame.

"What have you got in mind?" Sam asked me, as he was rubbing away and meticulously re-cleaning the canvas which I had cleaned the previous night. "How about a nice Dutch shipping scene?"

"Van de Velde?" I mulled.

"Backhuysen?" he countered.

"Vernet?" I shrugged.

"God Max! You can do 'em all, can't yer!" he grinned. "I've never met anyone like ya!"

"What about..." I pondered, "Dutch... but not ships... how

about… a winter scene… skaters… a great big skating scene? Skating on the canal!" Then, grabbing the canvas from him and holding it up to show him my thoughts, I gushed, "The canal running there… Skaters here… with reflections in the ice… and a building over there… red brick…"

"And the artist?" beamed Sam.

"Dommersen!" I blurted. "Pieter Cornelis Dommersen."

"Max," said Sam, "you're a bloody genius! We'll take it to Phillips."

"How about Bonhams?" I said.

"Yeah, or Sotheby's," he said.

"Sam, the world's our bloody oyster!" I laughed.

Although I was fired up, I took my time and concentrated intensely, putting real care and graft into the painting. I copied precisely Dommersen's style and technique from book prints which I'd acquired, and painstakingly went over my brushwork again and again, touching up every minute detail before ageing it. And when, after four days of burning the midnight oil, Sam saw it, his eyes bulged and his jaw dropped. He gazed at it on its easel, at first taking a step back from it, then peering at it up close, then from half a step back, then with his nose pressed to the canvas, then from the far side of my tiny room.

"My, my, my! Max!" gasped Sam. "I can't believe it!

"I was thinking about a touch more glow on the reflection, *there*…" I suggested. "And a touch more contrast on the shadow, *there*…"

"Yes, yes," Sam reflected, staring dreamily at the icy scene, then shivering, "Just a touch. Maybe just a touch."

We picked through the collection of scabby paintings in our junk pile and spent longer than usual agreeing on twenty perfect eyesores with decent frames to take with us to the auction house. I had already traced a well-defined copy of the artist's illiterate looking signature, and Sam lightly scribed the crude, single outlines of each letter 'P.C. Dommersen' at the bottom left of the painting in pencil. I prepared a fine-bristled brush and mixed a reddy-brown paint for him to use. He quite expertly followed the simple lines of the signature with a single, flowing movement, and afterwards he gently rubbed away the end of the inscription so that it read 'P.C. Domm...' before fading away to nothing. We both stared in awe at the finished work on the easel. It was magnificent.

Sam's Mark 10 Jag was so wide that there was enough room to lay the pictures across the back seat and still have enough room for Bonnie to lie down next to them. We had taken reams of pictures to auction houses in the past, but that day we were feeling excited, and more nervous than usual. As we drove towards town from Cricklewood, I kept thinking about whether there was more that I could have done to the picture; another brushstroke, another wipe, another touch. What if the valuer spotted that our Dommersen was fake and called the police?

"Dommersen's not your normal choice for a fake, is he?" Sam pointed out. "Anyway, any trouble and we just stick to our story. How can they prove that *you* painted it?"

Parking up outside the auctioneers, I gave Bonnie a pat, and Sam and I grabbed an armful of pictures each. We bumbled towards the entrance, where a waiting doorman guided us inside, as Sam's witless voice called out, "Be careful there, son! Ya nearly knocked the gentleman over! Sorry sir. Sorry abaat me son, he's a bit..."

"Good afternoon, gentlemen," the gentleman at the desk politely greeted us, with a slight lick of his lips in anticipation. "And what goodies do you bring today?"

"Oh, just the usual house clearance odds-and-sods, sir," said Sam.

We plonked the pictures down in what would appear to be a total jumble, but with our 'ace' carefully planted in the middle of the pack.

A few seconds later, there was a predictable cry of, "Oh, I say! What a beautiful..! Charles! Charles! I'm sure my colleague will be very keen to look at this one! Charles, do come and look!"

Charles appeared and we waited patiently as the two experts conversed, "Do you think..? What year was..? Where do you think..? What about the texture..? What about the craquelure..? What about the signature? Hmmmm…"

Finally, they turned their wary eyes towards us, and Charles demanded, "And where exactly did you say you acquired this?"

"Was it the old lady wiv the bat in the attic?" Sam asked me, scratching his head. "Or was it the one wiv the blue rinse?"

"Blue rinse I fink, dad," I answered moronically.

"I fink it was Hastings," Sam told the gentlemen. "No, no. Or was it Banbury?"

"It was Banbury, dad," I stated. "Where we 'ad the puncture."

"That's right!" snapped Sam. "We 'ad a puncture… Big ass in Exeter wiv an instrumental pond."

"Hmmm," mumbled the gentlemen. "Well, there's every indication that it is a Pieter Cornelis Dommersen. We see more of these winter scenes by Avercamp and Van Goyen, so this is something of a find."

"Is it werf anythin', sir?" I asked.

"Oh yes," said the experts. "Three or four… maybe five thousand."

Sam signed the paperwork, and we strolled calmly outside and climbed into the car. The engine purred into life and we drove steadily up the street in silence. When we were away and around the corner, we suddenly turned to each other and burst out laughing. Bonnie scampered excitedly across the back seat, from one side to the other, wagging her tail and barking.

"Cheers!" smiled Sam, chinking glasses with me at one of our favourite wine bars in West Hampstead, a spit away from Abbey Road where the Beatles had been recording 'Sgt. Pepper's Lonely Hearts Club Band'.

"We'll go to the auction preview," said Sam, "and see what the vibe is."

We stood in the hall, quite close to where my painting was hanging, surrounded by the works of several notable artists. There was a lovely Coolidge painting of dogs playing poker, an Alfred Munnings horse racing picture, and a Gainsborough portrait with an astronomical reserve price. I went hot and cold and my fingers tingled at the sight of my painting alongside them. I wondered what my mum would have made of it! I eagerly flicked through the catalogue and pointed out our entry to Sam: 'Lot 42. Pieter Cornelis Dommersen (Dutch 1834-1908) 'Skating on a Dutch Canal.' Oil Painting on Canvas'.

"Oh, isn't it beautiful, darling!" I overheard a female gasp, and glanced across my shoulder to see a glamourous-looking lady in a fur coat praising my picture to her husband.

The lady sounded American, and the man drawled back to her, "The reflections of the skaters! Exquisite! Quite exquisite!"

I found it hard to sleep for the next three nights and stayed awake, working on my next painting, nipping out occasionally with Bonnie for a breath of fresh air and a stretch, just to escape the staleness and confinement of my cramped garret. Lying on my bed, I played out the scene on auction day. Sam and I had worked out how we would make sure that my 'Dommersen' would achieve its maximum price. It was a simple system, although it wasn't without risk.

I checked my watch as I followed a small shuffle of interested parties towards the front door of the auction house. Just inside, as the prospective buyers arrived, officials were presiding over their registration procedure: "Write your name and address *there*, and your bank account details *there*," they instructed each guest.

I waited in the queue, and when it was my turn, I filled in a false name and address, along with details of the Midland Bank in Finchley and an appropriate-looking bogus account number. "Thank you, sir. Here is your bidding number," advised the man at the desk.

As I turned to walk away, I was shocked to almost bump into Charles, the same expert valuer who had inexpertly appraised my painting a fortnight before. Spinning quickly around to avoid him, I came face-to-face with the man at the desk again. He gave me a quizzical look and asked, "Sorry, was there something else?"

"Yes, there is," I said, shielding my face with my catalogue, whilst trying not to look suspicious. "I wonder if you would be able to advise me..? Whether you would be able to advise me..?"

"Yes?" frowned the man.

"Whether you would be able to advise me what happens to lots which don't reach their reserve price?" I asked.

In a supercilious tone, he advised, "Well, any lots which fail to meet their reserve price are marked as unsold and stored away until such time as we have spoken to the..."

"Thank you," I said brusquely, as soon as I saw Charles trotting off. "That's very helpful." And I rushed away towards the sale room with my head down.

Although Charles had disappeared for the time-being, heaven forbid that he should suddenly reappear during the auction and spot me bidding for my own picture! I made my way into the grand auction room, praying all the time under my breath that he had been called away to some dying relative and would never come back. A healthy flock of eager, chattering punters filled most of the rows of seats. Some looked slightly risible in tweeds and brogues, more suited to the great outdoors, whilst others were definitely suave city-slickers, guffawing and flaunting their Rolex watches and monogrammed cufflinks. Then, leaning around the edges of the room, were the professional chancers/dealers, wearing workaday corduroy and a collection of eccentric hats. I was chuffed to see that the eager American couple from the viewing had turned up. I didn't feel any sympathy for any of them. They were there for the same reason as me - to make money. And most of them had probably been born with a silver spoon in their mouth, or at least a pair of shoes on their feet.

As the minutes on the giant clock ticked towards the starting hour, I was pleased that the room was filling up. The more people who attended, the higher the bidding, and the easier it was for me to blend in with the throng of traders on the fringes. The auctioneer stepped up onto his platform. Only then, did I dare to scan around the room. Over to the left of the room, as we had prearranged, Sam was keeping a low profile, blending in amongst some punters in the corner. As the auctioneer banged his gavel and was making his welcoming speech, I glanced towards Sam and he glanced back. I touched my hair and he scratched his nose, our signals to each other to either bid again or stop bidding. I quickly looked away and couldn't help smiling, my heart booming in anticipation of what was about to happen. The auction began with bidding on the first few lots proceeding at a fairly sedate pace. By about Lot 10, the auctioneer and the bidders were warmed up and becoming more enthusiastic. By Lot 20, the competition between buyers was getting hot, and the auctioneer was baiting them to fight between themselves and outbid one-another.

"Lot forty-two," announced the auctioneer, gesturing at my picture. "A delightful skating scene by acclaimed Dutch artist, Pieter Cornelis Dommersen. I hope you've all had a chance to look at the amazing detail and condition. I have a telephone bid for three-thousand pounds."

Bidders in the room were hungry to muscle in, and the auctioneer announced in rapid succession, "Three-thousand-one-hundred, three-thousand-two-hundred…"

Within a minute or so the auctioneer was calling, "Four-thousand-eight-hundred, four-thousand-nine, five-thousand pounds. Do I hear five-thousand-one-hundred? Five-thousand-one-hundred, thank you, sir," he said, acknowledging Sam's bid.

"Five-thousand-two-hundred? Do I hear five-thousand-two-hundred pounds?"

I nodded.

"Five-thousand-two…"

The American lady swung her eyes in my direction and nudged her husband, nagging him to stick his finger in the air.

"Five-thousand-three-hundred…"

And the bidding started to climb again, without Sam's help, or mine.

"Five-four, five-five, five-six, five-seven, five-eight, five-nine, six-thousand. Any advance on six-thousand pounds?"

Sam caught my eye and scratched his head, and I nodded at the auctioneer.

"Six-thousand-one-hundred…"

Immediately, the Americans went into battle with me.

"Six-thousand-two…"

Sam rubbed his head and I bid again.

"Six-three…"

The Americans bid again.

"Six-four…"

Time stood still and there was silence, and the Americans turned and smiled at me victoriously. My heart was pounding.

"Any advance on six-thousand-four-hundred pounds?"

The eyes of the room suddenly darted to Sam, as he bid again.

"Six-five…"

Several eyebrows were raised, then the Americans continued on their quest.

"Six-six…"

I waited, then Sam wiped his forehead, and I bid again.

"Six-seven…"

Then the Americans paused for an urgent confab.

"Any more bids? I am selling at six-thousand-seven-hundred pounds…"

I was the highest bidder! I held my breath, adrenalin pulsing through my veins. You could hear a pin drop. I waited for the "bang" of the falling gavel. If it did, then we were done for. We would have to raise nearly seven grand to buy our own picture! I watched the American man's finger twitching. His wife nudged him, and his finger shot into the air. Both Sam and I were out, and we were off the hook.

"Six-eight…"

I sighed with relief, and my heart almost stopped. I glanced at Sam. His hand went up to his forehead, the signal for me to bid again. I couldn't. We'd pushed things as far as we possibly could. I scratched my nose, the signal to tell him that we must stop.

"Anyone? Any more bids? Sir..?" the auctioneer asked Sam.

Sam waited a moment, then nodded at him. I couldn't believe it. We had six-thousand-eight-hundred pounds in the bag - and Sam had bid again!

"That's a bid of six-thousand-nine-hundred pounds to the gentleman."

I could have throttled Sam. The Americans were shaking their heads and huffing, obviously dithering and in two minds whether to battle on. We waited. The auctioneer waited. Everyone in the room waited.

"Do I hear seven-thousand pounds?"

The Americans cogitated, then conversed, then conferred, then cogitated some more.

"I'm selling for six-thousand-nine-hundred pounds to the gentleman in the corner. Any more bids?"

Under duress from his wife, the Yank bid again.

"That's seven-thousand-pounds."

Before I could even let out a sigh of relief, Sam jumped right back in and was bidding again. I was scratching my nose at him so vigorously that I thought I would permanently injure myself.

"That's seven-thousand-one-hundred. Any more bids? No? Then I'm selling to…"

The Americans came back.

"Seven-two…"

And despite my desperate signals, Sam just carried on.

"That's seven-three…"

And suddenly, the battle, which I thought was already over, re-erupted into rapid fire between Sam and the Americans.

"Seven-four, seven-five, seven-six, seven-seven. Any more?"

The bidding stopped with Sam's bid. His was the highest. He had committed to buy, and we would have to pay for the painting, plus the auctioneer's commission. I groaned inside.

"I'm selling at seven-thousand-seven-hundred pounds…"

Sam smirked at the scowling Americans with such mockery that he provoked the man into peevishly thrusting his finger into the air again.

"Seven-thousand-eight-hundred pounds I'm bid."

Sam looked forlornly at the Americans and shook his head. They grinned at him with disdain and extreme satisfaction, like a lion which had just mauled a gazelle to death.

"Any more bids? Anywhere? No? Sold for seven-thousand-eight-hundred pounds."

And the gavel came thumping down. And it was all over. I watched as a porter took my picture away. As arranged, Sam left immediately, and I waited until he had gone before I began to make my way out.

"Sorry," grinned the American lady triumphantly as I passed by.

"There'll be plenty more pictures," I shrugged, somehow stifling my overwhelming urge to burst out laughing at her.

I left and quickly trotted off round corner to where Sam was waiting in the car.

"Shit Sam! You almost gave me a bloody heart attack!" I shrieked. "You almost bought the bloody thing!"

"*Almost* isn't the same as actually buying, is it?" he chuckled. "I'm a married man, I knew the schmock would go higher with his wife nagging at him. It's a fact of life."

We went to the Gaslight Club that evening for a quiet celebration, as we did from time-to-time. It was a lively little haunt, quite posh, with oak panelling, leather Chesterfields, exotic drinks and expensive food. The place was probably best known for its infamous gangland clientele who would drop in for steak-and-chips when they were 'up west' collecting their protection money. As well as criminals, celebrities and socialites, there were always plenty of pretty waitresses, and plenty of pretty girls who just sat around waiting.

"I was gonna push the Yanks up to eight grand," said Sam, wiping Champagne bubbles from his beaming chops.

"Well I'm bloody glad ya didn't!" I snapped.

"This is just the start, Max," he chortled, clouting his wine flute against mine. "Come on, cheer up, you've just made over four grand. Some poor sods don't even make that in five years!"

"Yeah, I know," I sighed. "It's just…"

"What? What's up?" he probed, his smile fading. "What is it?"

"It's just… It's silly, but it made me sad to see the painting go," I said.

"I know," he condoled, wrapping his arm across my shoulders. "It must be like saying goodbye to someone ya love."

"Oh well," I shrugged, my spirits quickly returning, "I guess it's just the name of the game."

"Here Max, keep yer head down, that dolly-bird's givin' you the eye," Sam warned, discreetly pointing her out with his eyebrows. "You know who her fella is, don't yer?"

And as he said it, half a dozen big blokes, suited and booted, entered and went up to her and her glamorous friends and kissed them.

"I know who they are," I said.

"You wanna steer well clear," Sam advised, "or you might find yourself without any fingers."

Linda and I hadn't seen each other for a while, but we kept in touch on the phone. She had decided to move out of her parents' house in Portsmouth and move in with Pam, probably thinking that she might see more of me if she lived in Brighton. Although I did occasionally drive down to see my mum and take her presents, I was loving life and loving London.

With a wallet full of cash, I accepted Sam's offer of joining him on a family jaunt to Cornwall. The five of us (including Bonnie) luxuriated in the sprawling comfort of the Jag and enjoyed the three-hundred-mile cruise down to Newlyn. Sam had some hired hands who worked in his car rental business, and they had cleaned and polished his motor like new, although by the time we arrived it was plastered with swarms of splattered insects. We had a couple of luxury holiday villas next door to one another, me and Bonnie in one, and Sam and his wife Mary and their daughter Jacqueline in the other. The accommodation came with all the mod-cons, including a maid who would come and clean and tidy up every day, and bring in the newspaper. On our first morning, as we scoffed freshly buttered croissants and homemade strawberry jam, Sam suddenly turned the front page of his paper towards me and tapped my shin. Across the table, the explosive headline reported that a gang of notorious (and familiar-looking) London mobsters had been arrested for murder.

Cornwall was a county which I loved and which I had come to know pretty well. The five of us motored around together, with me acting as tour guide, eating delicious seafood, fresh from the day's catch, and lounging lazily in golden coves. In the evenings, we would go out for a drink and socialise in the local pubs in Newlyn and Penzance. Every day, I was eager to make some sketches, mainly around the harbour, where an army of oil-skinned fishermen from the trawlers, crabbers and tiny mackerel boats landed their glistening treasure on the ancient quayside. The family was keen to explore the local gallery, and as mum and daughter admired the modern art, myself and Sam were eyeing up the paintings by artists of the renowned 'Newlyn School' and discussing whether any of them were worth forging. The equestrian scenes by Alfred Munnings were the most interesting, and I loved painting horses. All I wanted to do was to see my pictures hanging on the walls of the top auction houses, and experience the cut-and-thrust as seasoned collectors fought to buy them. The buzz of the art business had become the passion of my life. My appetite for drawing and painting was insatiable. I could have happily drawn night-and-day, and missed the passing seasons.

Sam and I breezed into Lots Road and were greeted, as usual, with an enthusiastic, "Ah! Good morning, gentlemen. And what gems do you have for us today?" The man panned through our pile of dross, but was struck by a fine pen-and-ink drawing of Dunstable Priory. "May I inquire as to where you acquired it?"

"D'ya remember, son?" Sam asked.

Turning his steely gaze on me, the man suggested, "Dunstable by any chance?"

"That's it," I agreed, "Dunstable."

He went on, "It's just that we have had a query from the buyer of a Samuel Palmer sketch which you sold through us three months ago. The cottage in Shoreham? Supposedly from around eighteen-thirty?"

"Don't remember that one," Sam sighed, blank-faced.

"It was during his 'Rat Abbey' period," the gentleman glowered. "There's the entry in the book. It was definitely one of yours."

I remembered it. I remembered all my pictures.

"We pick up stuff from all over," said Sam. "Sometimes ten 'ouses in a day. Ain't that right, son?"

"Twenty some days, dad," I chirped.

"The police believe it may be a forgery," said the gent.

"What's a forgery mean, dad?" I gormlessly asked.

"We just pick the stuff up, sir," shrugged Sam, "and *you* tell us what it is."

"If you wouldn't mind confirming your particulars?" demanded the man. "The police will probably need to speak to you."

They had Sam's genuine address in Finchley, but there was nothing incriminating in his house or garden shed. Nobody had my address, but if the police had ever dropped by for a chat, then we would have been right up shit-creek, what with all my painting paraphernalia and Dougie's dodgy art collection. Luckily, the matter never came to anything, but it did serve as a warning that we were always skating on thin ice.

The moment I pulled up outside Pam's flat, I noticed the curtains twitch. The second I got out of the Sunbeam, Linda was there, flinging her arms around me and trapping me in a bear-hug, squashing her lips onto mine as if her life depended on it. She clung to my side for two days, smiling and making me happy.

And when it was almost time for me to leave and drive back to London, she hid her tears from me and sniffed, "Will you be coming back?"

I paused for a split-second, then beamed at her, "Don't be silly, of course I will."

She stared deep into my soul and asked, "Do you love me, Max? Really?"

"Course I do," I smiled. "Come on, what is all this?"

She held me for as long as she could, until the moment I had to leave. That week, we spoke on the phone and she said that if we couldn't be together, then I must tell her.

Then, the next time we were close up, face-to-face, I just blurted out, "How d'ya fancy getting married?"

It was as if an almighty firework display had ignited. Her eyes lit up and before I knew it, she was dancing around with Pam, and on the phone to tell her mother and sister and Eric. Being the traditional old sort that he was, I felt the need to go round and see the father of the bride for a man-to-man chat.

"Well," he pondered, leaning up against his mantelpiece and puffing sedately on his pipe. "Marriage? Hmmm?"

"Yes," I confirmed.

"And what erm… what would you do exactly?" he frowned, his face shrouded in a cloud of grey smog. "I mean, how would you live? How would you keep her? Would you be able to get a job or something?"

"I dunno," I said. "What kind of job?"

"As you know, now I'm retired I work at the car showroom," he said. "Maybe I could ask there?"

"What's the pay like?" I asked.

"As a start," he shrugged, puffing and blowing smoke to buy himself more time, "I suppose you'd be looking at, a thousand pounds?"

"A week?" I jested, maintaining a totally straight face.

"No! Not a week! Of course not!" he spluttered.

"I think I'll stick to the painting then," I grinned. But to soothe his exasperated wrinkles, I assured him earnestly, "It's alright, Eric, I *do* make a good living. And I *will* look after your daughter."

His mood lifted, and as the Champagne corks were still popping, frantic phone calls were being made: a church was chosen; a clergy was contacted; relatives were called; bridesmaids were courted; a venue was chartered; a menu was created; cars were chased up; and the whole grand wedding show was about to hit the road. Linda and I went up to Laura Ashley in Fulham in search of her wedding dress. Clutches of excited young ladies pointed and gasped at the rows and rows of dazzling gowns, desperately trying to attract one of the overworked assistants to bag the dress of their dreams. For Linda and me it was an easy choice. I spotted it, she tried it, and her father's money paid for it. And that was the case with everything to do with the marriage. There was nothing which was too good, or too expensive, for Eric and Zena's eldest daughter.

The afternoon before the big day, I went to collect my mum from Portsmouth and Southsea station. We hugged on the platform and she gently smoothed down my hair where it had blown up into a mess. It was only a five-minute drive to the Queens Hotel on the seafront, but I think she enjoyed the attention from the curious pedestrians who looked up to gawp at the occupants of the loud, orange, open-top sports car. When I pulled up at the front doors of the hotel, she sat for a moment, looking puzzled.

"Come on then," I said. "All out! We're here."

"Ooh," she cooed. "Ooh."

She suddenly shrank back in her seat as a porter appeared from nowhere and swung open the passenger door for her to get out. The porter grabbed our suitcases and jogged up the steps with them.

Mum stood, gazing up at the heady heights of the top-floor windows and said, "Eee, I wain't wanna be cleanin' this place!"

"Don't worry, mum," I grinned, "there'll be none of that. You're the guest of honour."

She stared into my eyes and smiled softly. I took her by the arm and escorted her inside.

"Ah, Mister Brandrett!" greeted the desk clerk. "We've been expecting you. Two top-floor rooms with a sea view."

As the lift ascended to the fourth floor, mum's eagle eyes flitted around, expertly examining the mirrors and brass fittings for careless smudges or fingerprints. When we came to a stop and the doors slid open, she was nodding to herself, apparently quite satisfied with the quality of the hotel's housekeeping. Mum had a lovely room next to mine. I went in with her to check that she was satisfied with it. We stared silently together across the waves, at the bright crests and dark troughs, ebbing and flowing.

"Who'd a thought!" mum suddenly exclaimed with a smile. "Come tomorrow, all me childer'll be wed!"

The lych-gate at the entrance to the pretty, Gothic-style church at Purbrook village had been decorated with scores of white, fragrant blossoms. I stood with my brothers and my mum, welcoming the throng of beaming guests as they passed through on their way into the churchyard. Rays of golden sunlight danced between the trees, and the joy of pealing bells rang out heartily from the tower. It was the most glorious setting, a purely English masterpiece, like a Constable or a Turner. My family, and Linda's, could not have been happier. Zena was so affectionate and effervescent that she could have been mistaken for the bride herself. Pam and Christine were the gorgeous bridesmaids. As the hour approached, I could hardly wait to see my bride-to-be. The expectant multitude filed into the nave, where displays of magnificent flowers adorned the sill of every glowing stained-glass window. And there were more blooms, lots more, around the chancel and altar. I had never experienced such a sweet scent of good fortune.

The congregation settled into the rows of crowded pews, and the coughing and muttering subsided, and the organ softly trilled. My mum was sitting proudly in the front row, her matching dress and hat and makeup looking immaculate. I stood before the altar with my brother, waiting to embark upon the most wonderful voyage of my life. As I stared up at the stained-glass windows, marvelling at the intensity of the colours, it brought back childhood memories of sitting in my cupboard and drawing colourful cartoons of Mickey and Minnie Mouse. The organ suddenly burst into life, and Mendelssohn's Wedding March and a choir of sweet sopranos echoed around the church, heralding the arrival of my bride. I couldn't resist and glanced over my shoulder. She was a vision of beauty, bathed in flickering sunlight and dressed in a flowing Elizabethan gown, gliding gracefully up the aisle, arm-in-arm with her father, he resplendent in his full captain's uniform. As Linda stood beside me, she raised her head, our eyes met, and she smiled softly. My heart was racing and I kissed her tenderly on the lips.

We vowed, "to have and to hold… for better, for worse… for richer, for poorer… in sickness and in health… to love and to cherish, till death do us part."

And as the vicar said, "I now pronounce you husband and wife," the bells rang out and I kissed my bride.

My mum was delicately wiping away a tear with her pristine hankie, and as Linda and I stepped out into the daylight, we were showered with clouds of confetti and cheering voices. We posed for the photographer, laughing and kissing, and totally in love. A vintage Rolls Royce, with an open top, picked us up and drove us through the streets to the yacht club, where Eric was a member of their committee. There, we were greeted and piped 'aboard' as guests of honour. The music played, the Champagne flowed, the people danced, and there was a lavish buffet of meats and savouries and salads and desserts.

As Linda and I were wandering about and chatting to the guests, I overheard someone say, "Oh! He's your son!"

This was followed by an unfamiliar and stuck-up female voice reply, "Oh yes. He is an artist you know. He is frightfully good, and very well known."

When I glanced up, I saw that it was mum!

In the morning, I gazed across the sunny view of the Solent. The ferries and the tankers and the hovercraft were sailing by, going about their business, as if nothing had happened.

I gently tapped on the door of mum's room and it sprang open almost immediately. "Oh! I didn't know if you were up," I said. She *was* up, and all washed and dressed and made-up and hair done. Her case was packed, her bed was made, the towels had been folded, the floor was clean and, I think, the mirrors had been polished. "You could have had a lie-in," I told her. "And you didn't have to clean the place!"

"What'd folk think if I didn't fettle room!" she gasped.

For our honeymoon, I whisked Linda off to spend a few romantic days in sunny North Devon. When we returned, we lived with Bonnie in a property which I had rented. It was a handsome, period farmhouse, late Georgian, set in acres of beautiful Hampshire countryside, in a village called Denmead, just a short drive from where we were married. Tucked out of the way on Edney's Lane, the house had more than enough space for the three of us, plus a few spare rooms for guests. Our only neighbours were cows and horses, yet it was only five or six miles to Linda's parents, and not much further to Portsmouth city centre.

"Oh darling! This is beautiful!" gushed Zena, as she gazed around at the giant fireplaces and ornate cornices. "Linda, you must show me upstairs!"

Eric sat with me in the drawing room, puffing on his pipe and sampling my malt whisky.

"I must admit," he puffed, "it's more than I was expecting. Your paintings are obviously in great demand."

"Yeah, people seem to like them," I shrugged.

Then, hesitantly, he started, "So where exactly do you sell..?"

"Oh my god!" shrieked Zena, as she and Linda burst in on us. "Eric, Linda is going to be so happy here! It's wonderful!"

Although the house came fully equipped, Linda loved to decorate the place with flowers and soft furnishings, transforming it from a house into a home. We invited friends and family to visit, sometimes just for a meal, but often for weekend gatherings, when we'd play music and laze around in the garden. The pub was the focal point of the village, and as we got on well with a few of the more arty types, they would casually drop by for drinks and fun. People knew that I was the longhaired artist who roared around the village in the bright orange sports car, and that Linda was a hairdresser. But I think our unusual and flamboyant lifestyle stirred up a certain amount of curiosity and suspicion amongst the older folk. I also had to reassure my mum and explain to her that we really were legitimate tenants and not illegal squatters.

Linda invited her parents and sister to come and spend Christmas with us. We had put up a big tree, and Linda had decorated the entire house. She cooked, and Zena and Christine helped out, as Eric and I were banished to the drawing room. I somehow managed to deflect any awkward questions and ply him with drinks. The feast was served up on our meaty, oak dining table, and we spread ourselves around it and tucked in, warmed by the heat of a roaring log fire. Afterwards, we relaxed on the sofas, sipping hot punch and dozing off as we watched the snowflakes gently trickling past the windows. Outside was a vision of a winter wonderland, deep and crisp and even. We made a snowman and threw snowballs at each other, larking around and laughing, as Eric snored away the afternoon.

When I went to fetch logs, Zena cornered me, and gently caressed my cheek, and whispered, "Thank you, Max. You have made my daughter, and all of us, so very happy. Thank you."

It was a truly magical Christmas, almost like a fairy-tale, and such a far cry from some of my Christmases past. However, when it was all over, it did have to be paid for.

Linda peered at the painting on my easel and blurted, "Ah! Shrover Hall! That's brilliant, darling! I must fly, I'm doing a perm."

We kissed and she dashed off. As I heard her car start up and drive away down the lane, I slipped the picture off my easel and replaced it with another one, a half completed painting of some comical cats which I was eager to finish. I'd been commissioned by the owners of the neighbouring hall to immortalise their old house in a painting, for which they were going to pay me the princely sum of forty pounds. On the other hand, I knew dealers who would pay me ten times that amount for a signed picture by the popular anthropomorphic artist Louis Wain. I enjoyed painting Louis Wain cats and, similarly, caricature dogs in the manner of Cash Coolidge. My earnings from these pictures paid the rent and the bills, and kept us in the style to which we had become accustomed, whereas the paltry sums offered by galleries for my original works were hardly enough to feed a dog. Being a successful artist was all about having your work endorsed by the experts, and time-and-again they had evaluated paintings like my Samuel Palmers and Van den Veldes as great works of art, so I knew I had the talent, but just lacked the profile.

I kissed Linda and Bonnie goodbye and put three new paintings on the passenger seat next to me, and headed off to see a dodgy art dealer in Arundel. It was freezing cold and there was still a lot of snow about as I chugged gingerly up the single-lane track in the Sunbeam. The roof was shut, but it was freezing in the car, and with such a huge engine it took an age for the heater to warm up. As I peered through the misty windscreen, a police car suddenly appeared from nowhere. I slammed on the brakes, but they had no effect and I found myself sliding straight towards it. Easing my foot off the brake pedal didn't help, and stamping my foot down hard didn't help either. There was nothing I could do, except wait for the bang. It seemed to take an age, and I could clearly see the look of horror on the coppers' faces. But there was no bang, just the tiniest little jolt, and I stopped dead. I stared eyeball to eyeball with the cool-faced officers. Glancing down next to me, I was relieved to see that my pictures were undamaged. When I looked up, the dynamic duo were adjusting their caps and crunching through the snow towards me. I had no way of hiding the paintings.

I wound down the window and they addressed me in a strong Hampshire burr, "Mornin' sir. Reckon you been an' crashed into our Panda."

"Sorry," I gulped. "It was the ice. The brakes didn't work."

"Obviously," they said. "And where you off to exactly, sir?"

"Just into the village," I said.

They peered inside and saw the paintings.

"You're Max the artist, ain't ya," they stated.

"Can't deny it," I said.

"These your pictures are they?" they inquired.

"Might be," I said.

"Have a look can we?" They asked.

"Help yourselves," I said, as they were already having a good old gawp.

"You paint 'em did ya?" they asked.

"What of it?" I asked.

"Bloomin' good, ain't they!" they whooped, grinning. "Them cats is funny! Bloody marvellous! And that one's dogs playing cards! Bloody marvellous!" When the hooting laughter had subsided, they said, "We'll give yer a little push back. Bain't no damage to the vehicles."

They were still chuckling to themselves as they went to the front of the Sunbeam and heaved it backwards off their Panda Car. Then they reversed back up the lane to a passing point to let me drive through, saluting me as I went. I was laughing all the way to Arundel, and all the way back, especially as the paintings fetched a damned good price.

Country life was nice enough, but after a while I was getting bored and missed the buzz of London. Apart from which, the provinces offered only limited financial opportunities to a habitual art forger. Linda, too, wasn't happy just cutting hair anymore and wanted a change. By luck, she heard about some auditions which she hoped might open the door to a whole new career.

"Auditions this way, madam," indicated the doorman of the Metropole Hotel on Brighton seafront, instantly recognising the purpose of Linda's visit.

I followed Linda inside, where dozens of hopeful local ladies, dressed-to-the-nines and made up like Barbie dolls, were queuing to register. The girls ranged considerably in height and shape, and some were clearly beyond the stated age bracket. I stood at the back and watched as a panel of male and female judges scrutinized the swaggering applicants who paraded before them. Some of the ladies were quickly asked to leave. The remaining twenty or so changed into their swimsuits and walked up and down, swinging their hips and thrusting out their boobs, desperate to make a big impression. Linda, however, was just her normal smiley self. "Shall we go?" she asked me, as the girls were given a short break. "I don't think I stand much chance, do you?"

"You're the most beautiful woman here," I assured her.

Then, when the applicants were interviewed, the judges got rid of all the others and kept only Linda. She was asked to pose for a photographer from the Brighton Argus and, seeing me with my long hair and outlandish Victorian garb, they requested that we be photographed as a couple.

"Thee never told me owt about this!" teased my mum, waving the newspaper in my face. "Penthouse Pet! In London! Whatever next!"

We moved with Bonnie into a comfortable second-floor flat on the Finchley Road in Hampstead, an easy commute to Linda's new place of work in Mayfair, and with a suitable room for me to use as a studio. The Penthouse Club was set up by Bob Guccione as a rival to Hugh Hefner's Playboy Club, and the Penthouse Pets were modelled on the essence of the famous Bunny Girls. However, instead of wearing a costume fashioned on a cute-looking rabbit with a fluffy tail, Linda's outfit was more like a saucy chambermaid's uniform, with a short gingham dress, white frilly pinny and cap and pants. The club employed a housemother who would inspect the girls before they went out on duty and keep them in line. All of the girls were good-looking, and it was their job to serve drinks and food to the well-off clientele, enticing them to part with generous tips in return for fleeting glimpses of cleavage and derriere. It was all innocent enough, and Linda was happy and made good money. Also, she would leave home each evening and not return until midnight or later. This was my creative period, a time when I could crack on with producing some quality, high value paintings.

Although I still had the gift-of-the-gab to hit the auction houses and fleece a few unsuspecting punters, I missed doing it with Sam. We had lost touch when I went off and got married and lived in the countryside. And he had other business interests and was busy pursuing them. It was a shame, but life went on. More-often-than-not I would sell through the auctions in London, but sometimes I would drive out further afield and let the provincial dealers appraise and sell my work. It just gave me a kick to paint well and to see the bidders fighting over my pictures. However, working alone wasn't as easy as working the old father-and-son routine which Sam and I had perfected, and 'ringing' pictures at the auctioneers wasn't as fruitful when there was just one of you. Consequently, my profits weren't as healthy as they had previously been.

Occasionally, I would go down to the Penthouse Club for a drink, or just to pick up Linda when she had finished her shift and take her to listen to music, or go for a bite to eat in the West End.

The Penthouse staff knew me and, as I breezed through the lobby one night, Bob Guccione looked up and said, "Hi!" He was easily recognisable, with his pointy-collared shirt half-open to display a jangle of gold chains across his suntanned chest. As we chatted, he remarked, in an accent which wouldn't have been out of place in the Godfather film, "So Linda's your wife. She's a beautiful gal. Great figure. Very cute."

"Yeah, she is," I agreed.

"Does she model?" he asked.

"Only for me," I said.

"We're always lookin' for a beautiful gal to shoot," he said. "Think about it."

I didn't mention it to Linda, but one night when we were snuggled up at home and drinking a good bottle of Taittinger Champagne which she'd been gifted, she giggled, "They've asked me to appear in Penthouse magazine. I wondered what *you* thought? They'd pay me heaps of cash."

"You don't have to worry about cash," I said.

"Some of the models have gone on to do acting," she said.

"Soho acting?" I sniggered.

"No! Proper acting! In films," she protested playfully. "Like, 'There's a Girl in My Soup' and that sort of stuff."

"Penthouse magazine is totally starkers, yeah?" I pointed out.

"It's a stupid idea," she sighed. "Forget it. Anyway, what's money when you've got love?" And she smiled and rolled on top of me and started kissing me all over.

There were only so many rare, authentic masterpieces a 'dealer' could discover amongst the junk in the garages and attics of England, and I was forced to travel further-and-further afield in order to locate unsuspecting sales rooms and experts.

"Hmmm, it's a very nice painting, but I'm not a hundred-percent sure that it really is a genuine…" was becoming an all-too-familiar phrase from the valuers. "As a very good pastiche, I could put it in the auction with a reserve of say, twenty pounds?"

Linda and I had met some interesting new friends, musicians and opera singers and the likes, and we enjoyed having them round for dinner and entertainment. However, entertaining came at a price, and I was finding it a bit of a pressure to keep up with our outgoings. Linda did pretty well out of her pay and tips, but she never had to worry about the cost of buying trendy outfits and jewellery, and living the high life. I was working hard, not only painting, but out-and-abouting to search for suitable frames and canvases in the second-hand shops.

Arriving back at the flat with some old potboilers, I found Linda sitting cross-legged on the sofa, flicking fretfully through the pages of the latest issue of Cosmopolitan magazine. When I kissed her gently on the forehead, she didn't react and I could tell that something was wrong. I took my hotchpotch of old pictures and frames through to my studio. Things had been moved, not in a malicious way, but Linda hadn't hidden the fact that she had been rummaging through my pictures. On my easel, where I had left the colourful and innocuous painting 'Changing of the Guard at Buckingham Palace' by Max Brandrett, I found that it had been replaced by a completed 'Valley of Vision' picture signed by Samuel Palmer. Leaning up against the frame of the easel were a couple of primitive paintings of prize bulls and pigs, which I had aged and framed, all ready for the sale room. I returned to the lounge. Linda made out that she was engrossed in her magazine, although I knew she was only pretending.

"What's up?" I said.

She sighed and tossed back her head, before looking at me quite calmly and asking, "Why Max? Why do you have to keep doing it? You're a talented artist. But it's like you're addicted or something, like an illness. And when the police break our door in and rifle through all our stuff, and take you away to prison, what's left for me, hmmm? Visiting you in Parkhurst Prison every Sunday! Smuggling in cigarettes and toilet paper! Or would you prefer I smuggle in some paints for you? I know," she sneered, "I could bring my mum and dad, and my sister with me! We could have family outings! Maybe *your* mum'd like to come along too! Do you think she'd like to see you in jail, Max? Her favourite son, doing time? What would she make of that then, eh? Make her proud, would it?"

She stood up and left the room. Within a few minutes she was packed and ready to leave me.

"I'm taking Bonnie," she said.

I drove her back to Cosham, and for two hours we said nothing. It was only when we parked in the driveway of her parents' house that I tried to persuade her to change her mind.

"No Max, it's over," she told me sternly.

"Why?" I asked.

She sighed deeply and whispered, "Because... Because I love you, Max."

She burst into tears and fled into the arms of her mother. Bonnie trotted along behind her and disappeared indoors, wagging her tail excitedly. Eric silently approached me. I opened the boot of the car for him and he took away Linda's cases and bags. I watched as the family went inside and closed the door behind them. I waited. The front room curtains were drawn tightly shut, and it was over. I don't really remember driving back to London, but when I pulled up outside our flat, I decided that it was time to move on.

CHAPTER 7:
HARD BEDS AND SOFT BEDS

With little cash and just a few belongings, I went back to my attic in Cricklewood. Nothing had changed, apart from a few extra cobwebs. And Dianne still lived down the road. Life was okay and I struggled on for a while. Then, bored and almost skint, I left. I had no plan and nowhere I needed to be, so I headed back to Brighton. The dealers in The Lanes were just ignorant parasites and they offered me peanuts for my paintings. The traders all around the area were being wary and stingy, and I knew that the police were keeping an eye on me. Mum wanted me to stay in Brighton, but quickly I felt that I'd had enough of the place. And I'd also lost the will to paint. A guy gave me a lousy cash offer for the Sunbeam, but I was happy enough to offload it. It didn't bother me, and everything that had happened was just the opening a new chapter.

I travelled around a bit with my guitar, my life packed into two cases, thumbing lifts and freeloading on trains. Sometimes I'd make a new friend-or-two and grab myself a bed for a few nights. At other times, I'd head off and visit old haunts and seek out old acquaintances. And wherever I ended up, I could always busk, until people got bored of my pair of Tom Paxton songs. Over the years I'd learnt a few tricks, and I wasn't above sneaking into the odd hotel in search of a free bite to eat, or some carelessly abandoned valuables. From my days in Portobello Road, I knew a bit about antiques, and every town had dodgy dealers who were keen to pick up jewellery and timepieces on the cheap.

It was a bitter night on the streets of the old port town of Folkestone, and I tramped around on the lookout for an opportunity to present itself. It was late and most of the townsfolk were already snoring in their beds. A slither of a gap in a window yawned out at me. It was a guesthouse and, being way out of season, the sight of an empty made-up bed with warm sheets and blankets was too much of a temptation. After a sound night's kip and a quick spruce up, I made the bed and crept out the same way I had come in. Although it was still cold, I felt the sun shining down on me. The sight of the choppy-brown waves and passing freighters, and the distant chalk cliffs of France, stirred me to make a sketch. The grand crescents of giant Victorian houses and the row of seafront hotels reminded me of places I knew, and it seemed like a friendly enough place. I went into Stricklands Bakery to ask for a job.

"Have you worked in a bakery before?" asked the manager.

"Yes sir," I told him. "Lyons Bakery at Cadby Hall in London. I worked in all the departments, on the winkling machine, on donuts, cakes, bread, everything."

"Okay," he said. "You live local, do you? Cos it's an early start."

"I know," I said. "I thought of that, and I thought it might help you if I lived in."

"Oh," he frowned. "Well we don't normally…"

"To be honest, I'm not really living anywhere at the moment, so it'd be doing us both a favour, wouldn't it? I wouldn't mind living up there," I said, pointing at the flour store above. "I could sleep on the sacks and you wouldn't even know I was there."

He looked me up-and-down, in my black frock coat, and shrugged, "That's okay with me, but it's a bit dusty up there."

It was comfy enough, and lovely and warm, and a bakery cat scurried about, keeping the place free of mice and rats. In the morning, I got myself ready and went to the canteen for a cuppa. As soon as I walked in, I was fussed over by a bevy of lovely cake-makers, apparently so touched by my circumstances that they felt the need to spoil me rotten with a fry-up and thick slices of buttered bread, followed by a plate of French Fancies. I drew a few caricatures to make them laugh, and I earned a bit of cash, but after a few weeks the novelty of baking wore off. One Friday afternoon, on the spur of the moment, I took my wages and went.

Dorchester was a pretty town, small and quaint, not far from Weymouth and the sea. The locals were friendly and I would busk and earn enough for sandwiches and cigarettes. At night, I would return to the town's main railway station where I had first arrived. Dorchester South was an average little station, with two platforms, a newsagent's kiosk and a cafeteria. Alongside the main lines, the tracks ran into a siding where trains and carriages were parked up overnight, and this became my home. When the railway staff had turned out the lights and gone off to their beds, I would sneak aboard a comfy carriage and snuggle down under my blanket for a cosy night's kip. In the mornings, I would stash my stuff and get washed in the Gents, and look forward to the day's adventures. The ladies who fried the breakfasts would greet me each day with, "Hello lovey! You back again? Play us that song."

It was a cold morning and I woke up freezing at four-thirty. There was no point in trying to get back to sleep and I decided that I may as well go for a scout around, just to see if there was anything worth seeing at that time of the morning. I was familiar with the town and knew my way around. The High Street was still asleep as I wandered along the rows of shops, looking for a prospect. There was a hotel, its illuminated sign shining out invitingly to weary travellers. As I approached, I could see that the front doors were open, and I slowed to a dawdle so that I could peek inside. The reception was in half-light and there was nobody there. Checking to make sure that no coppers or nosy milkmen were about, I darted back and went in to carry out a proper recce. As I crept into the entrance hall and approached the desk, I was struck by the sight of a lovely brass clock which was sitting on a side table. It stood about eighteen inches tall, including the stand. It was an elegant piece and it obviously had some age. Just as I was about to lift it, I was aware of something above me, and looked up. There, hanging above my head, was a large, crystal chandelier which, even unlit, was twinkling alluringly at me.

I peered warily this-way-and-that, silently listening for footsteps or voices, but there was nothing. A single hook was all that kept the impressive light aloft. Grabbing a chair and hopping up, I tore the flex from the ceiling and had the thing down in a few seconds. It was heavy, heavier than I had expected. Spotting a luggage trolley, I loaded the lamp and the clock and sped off into the night. A few yards round the corner, I slowed to a busy walking pace and covered the booty with my jacket, so as not to arouse suspicion, then pushed the hand-truck five minutes up the road to the station. By rearranging my belongings, I managed to pack the glittering chandelier and clock into the larger of my suitcases. I stowed the baggage in "Left Luggage" and went for my breakfast, until the first departing train was due.

"Hello lovey!" chirped the cheery charladies, amid clouds of steam and sizzling lard. "Cuppa tea and the usual?"

As I sat in the corner at my regular table, glancing at a discarded newspaper's offer of a reward for information about property stolen from safety deposit boxes in the 'Baker Street Robbery', my thoughts turned to Weymouth, and my imminent escape to a warm and comfy hotel on the seafront. There was only half an hour to go before the tannoy would announce the departure of my train, but the station clock tortuously ticked away the minutes as if each one was an hour.

"There you go, dearie," said the woman who delivered me my sausages, eggs and bacon. "Be careful, it's very hot."

I had just started tucking in when I noticed a couple of suspicious-looking police officers marching up to the ticket window. The only door out of the cafeteria led straight into their long arms. And the window which overlooked the platforms was locked. I kept my head down and concentrated on the business of spearing my egg yolks with a sausage. From the corner of my eye, looming ever closer, I could see two pairs of size ten boots plodding towards my table. They stopped dead next to me.

"Hello son," boomed a deep and unwelcoming voice, "we'd like a word."

"And I'd like a sausage," I grinned, stuffing one in my mouth.

The coppers grabbed my arms and lifted me out of my seat. A

gang of trackmen and a brood of bleary-eyed shift-workers edged out of the way to let us through.

"What am I supposed to have done?" I protested.

The waitress called after me, as I was being escorted to the booking office, "Should I keep it hot for ya, lovey?"

The yokel booking clerk was quite excited and blurted to the coppers, "He's been hangin' round here for days! I reckon he's come down from London. Bag weighs a ton! Very suspicious I thought, very suspicious."

I lugged my suitcases up onto the desk, and the sergeant demanded, "Open 'em." I did as he said and he lifted out a silk shirt which was lying on the top. Then his eyes lit up and he exclaimed, "Well, well, well! What 'ave we got 'ere then?"

"God! How did they get in there!" I gasped.

Word was quickly received that, despite their dreams of recovering some illustrious stolen property, the clock and chandelier had only been nicked from a hotel in the high street. Also found in my luggage were a wallet and a soda syphon. I was taken to the local nick, charged and locked in the cells, pending an appearance at the local magistrates' court.

There were three magistrates presiding on the bench, two ladies and a gentleman in the middle. Standing with my head bowed, the magistrates listened intently to the evidence submitted by the police, then asked if I had anything to say before sentencing.

I slowly gazed up at the bench, focussing especially on the ladies, and with sad puppy-dog-eyes, did sincerely submit, "Sir, madams, I can only say that I deeply regret my deplorable behaviour, and apologise most profusely. I was brought up by Barnardo's, who taught me right from wrong, and I promise you that after this wake-up call, nothing like this will ever happen again. I'm sorry."

I kept up the orphan act and tried to catch a sympathetic eye as they considered my fate.

"Taking into account the fact that you are just a young man without previous convictions," said the chairman, "We are prepared to give you the benefit of the doubt, and sentence you to two years' on probation."

"Thank you, sir. Thank you, madams," I said, exchanging the most fleeting hint of a smile with one of the women.

I was led away and locked in the cells below the courtroom, then waited patiently until I was called by a guard to stand before the clerk.

Requesting confirmation of his paperwork, the clerk asked me, "You are Maximilian Brandrett?"

"Yes sir," I said.

"Right Max, you'll be issued with a train ticket to Brighton. Sussex police and the probation officer will meet you at the station and escort you home," he informed me. "And if you try and hop-it, you'll have every police force in the country looking for you. What's the address in Brighton?" he asked, his pen poised in readiness.

I pictured the scene: burly coppers waiting on the platform; nosy passengers staring as I handed myself in; everyone gawping at me being led away; the nosy neighbours twitching their curtains; my mum's humiliation and embarrassment at having her youngest son delivered home by the police.

"Sorry sir, I haven't got an address," I shrugged.

"What do you mean?" frowned the clerk.

"Come on," urged the guard, "you have to give an address before we can release you."

"I haven't got an address," I repeated.

They looked at each other, somewhat bewildered, then at me. "Now look here, Max," sighed the clerk, "if you don't provide us with your address, then we can't release you. It's standard practice."

"Haven't got one," I told them. "Sorry."

"Look son, you don't wanna get locked up, do ya?" warned the guard.

"We don't want you to go to prison, Max, but…" sighed the clerk. "Okay, you'll be kept here overnight, give you time to think about it."

Despite their persistence, I refused to supply my mum's address and spent the night in the cell as a result. The next day, at noon, I was hauled up in front of the beaks again. They looked totally bemused as I was brought up and placed in the dock before them.

"Mister Brandrett," said the chief magistrate, "all we ask for is an address! It is a requirement. You must advise us, or we will have no alternative." His response to my silence was, "You leave me no alternative. I sentence you to three months in prison."

It was late afternoon when officers came to transport myself and two other prisoners away. We were led out in handcuffs and locked up in the back of a prison van, in small individual cubicles. The streets of Dorchester flashed by through the tiny porthole: the shops; the pubs; the trees; the gardens; the fresh air; the pretty girls. I sat on my rock-hard pew, wondering where I was going and how long it would take to get there. Shortly, I saw the sight of a morbid Victorian prison looming. We stopped and I pressed my face to the window and peered out at an angle to watch the huge iron gate swing open. We rolled forwards twenty feet and stopped again at another gate. The first gate shut behind us, and our van was trapped in a short and gloomy tunnel. Suddenly, I heard men's voices and doors clattering and banging.

"Out ya get," shouted an officer. "Stand over there. Don't move." Then, "Move! In there, quick march. Bags there, clothes there. Name?"

"Max Brandrett, sir," I said.

"One jacket, one trousers, one shirt, two socks, two boots. First timer, you wear a star. Get dressed. Follow me. Through there. Along there. Up the steps. Stop. In there."

I looked inside. It was crowded and austere: a small cell with three men; flaking whitewash; a stone floor and two wrought-iron bunk beds.

"Look after 'im," instructed the warder.

The door slammed shut behind me.

"What's yer name, son?"

"Max."

"You sleep in that bottom bunk."

When the bell rang, I followed them out onto the landing where the springy trampoline-style suicide nets stopped the 'jumpers' from killing themselves, and downstairs to the dining hall. One metal tray, one scoop of chips with a frazzled fishcake, and a hunk of bread. Then upstairs, wash face and clean teeth. Clanking keys. Lights out. Shouting. Banging. Yelling. Whistling. Screaming. Snoring. Cold.

"Just crap in the potty. It stinks the cell out, so make sure you shut the lid after. You'll get used to it."

Bell. Slop out bucket. Stench of shit. Freezing washdown. Clean teeth. Breakfast. Porridge. Rock-hard bread-roll. Margarine.

"Brandrett! Up to see the governor."

I stood before the governor and he advised me, "Work hard and stay out of trouble. What work have you done in the past?"

"I'm an artist, sir," I said. "A painter."

"An artist!" he exclaimed. Then, turning to the officer, he said, "Perhaps Mister Sweet, you can find him some paints and brushes?"

My cellmates were a kindly trio. Enrique was a stowaway who was serving time for trying to smuggle himself into Britain. Tom and Bernie were a pair of small-time racketeers who had been nicked for selling underweight sacks of coal and watered-down Esso Blue paraffin to the pensioners. Although I liked them, I had no wish to live with them.

"A single cell, Mister Sweet?" the governor queried with the screw, with an uplifted bushy eyebrow. "Why?"

I politely interjected, "Sir, I'd really like to spend my time here doing something useful, sir. I could paint, sir, but there's not enough room in the cell, sir."

My request was granted and after only a couple of nights of sharing, I had my own cell, plus oil paints and an easel. The screws and the governor were somewhat aghast when they saw my old Dutch shipping scene, and quickly I was painting pictures to order. Apart from the staff's pets and kids, I did a comical painting for

Mister Sweet in which the Great Train Robbers were escaping from a prison cell. He loved it so much that he promised to put twenty-five pounds into an envelope for when I was released. The cons also loved the pictures I did for them, often in honour of distant wives and girlfriends, and they rewarded me with sugar or biscuits or pats of margarine or ounces of Ringer's A1 Tobacco.

Each day we were let out into a small exercise yard, surrounded by a high fence. The screws would keep an eagle-eye on us as we walked round in circuits. For obvious reasons, we weren't allowed within ten feet of the perimeter fence, and a painted band of whitewash on the ground marked the exclusion zone. As most of us went round clockwise, a smaller group of prisoners, a dozen or so, walked anticlockwise in a smaller circle just inside ours.

Growls of "Fuckin' nonce!" and "Pervert!" and "Scum!" were literally spat into the faces of the others as they shuffled past on the inside track. Most of them would turn away to avoid the hatred and phlegm, but some would retaliate with threats.

I observed as a couple of old lags were soaking a pair of thick woollen socks under a tap. A screw noticed them, nodded and looked away. Later, I saw one of the lags repeatedly bashing the dampened sock across the metal bedstead in his cell.

"It hardens 'em up like concrete clubs," said one of the blokes. "Then they hold the geezer down - and wallop! They pummel his guts till 'is liver bursts."

Cons were expected to work, and I had a couple of jobs in the workshops, breaking up obsolete Bakelite radios and making rope fenders for Scarborough and Yarmouth fishing trawlers. But it was my pictures and the tobacco trade which earned me extra treats and privileges, plus respect and protection. I didn't smoke much and so I would 'lend' a spare quarter-of-an-ounce of snout to a fellow inmate, and a week later he would give me half-an-ounce in return. As trade grew, a rugged Irishman called McGinty volunteered his services as my 'collector'. Literally, he would go round the wing and collect my debts, although the cons were generally an honest lot and I was never aware of any bother.

And if a bloke was genuinely down on his luck and couldn't repay me, I'd tell McGinty to lay off him.

"You're a real sort, you are, Max," the senior inmates told me, smiling heartily. "You're a proper geezer. We'll miss ya."

I had obeyed the rules of prison survival, working hard, respecting the old lags and the screws, and had kept my nose clean. I'd been locked up for eight weeks, and my good behaviour meant that I was entitled to be released early, as long as the governor approved. On my last night I lay awake, listening to the sounds of haunted men. As morning glimpsed through the small window at the end of my cell, I eagerly awaited the order to 'slop out' and begin the day began as I always did, with a freezing washdown and a breakfast of porridge, rock-hard bread and margarine.

"I'll be seein' ya," McGinty choked. "Now you be sure and look after yourself, Max."

"Here, I want you to have this," I told him, handing him all my prisonly possessions: snout; biscuits; marge etc.

I was taken in to see the governor. He finished reading the file on his desk and closed it. "Well Brandrett," he said, "you're going home. And I hope you've learnt your lesson and closed this chapter of your life for good."

"Yes sir," I assured him.

"You are an exceptionally talented young man, Brandrett," he praised.

"Yes sir," I agreed.

"But I fear, Brandrett," he sighed, "that your talent could lead you into a life of crime. Does life imitate art, Brandrett, or does art imitate life? Hmmm?"

"Definitely one-or-the-other, sir," I smirked.

"Goodbye," he said. "Stay out of trouble, Brandrett, and one day you'll be famous."

Just before 8 A.M. I was marched away to the gatehouse where I was reunited with my pair of suitcases. I relinquished my itchy prison clothes and dressed up in my spruce collar-and-tie and snazzy suit.

"You look like a different man," smiled Mister Sweet. Then, handing me an envelope, "I've put in a bit extra, just to see you on your way."

The clock ticked eight and a guard opened the small walk-through door which was built into the corner of the main gate. A rectangle of fresh daylight filled the doorway, like a glorious blank canvas, and the air smelt clean.

Turning to Mister Sweet, I said, "If ever you want a picture…"

I stepped outside and the door banged shut behind me. Stretching my arms aloft and looking up to the heavens, I inhaled deeply and held the air in my lungs for as long they could take it. The prison was just a short way from the town centre. I strolled slowly in the misty morning, just to observe the various colours of life as they sped or ambled by. It was magical to hear the birds twitter, and human chatter, and buzzing traffic. Settling on a park bench with a flock of chirpy sparrows flitting in-and-out of the hedgerows, I took out my envelope and looked inside. When I had arrived at the prison, I owned twenty pounds. During my time inside, that twenty pounds had grown to almost seventy, thanks in part to Mister Sweet's generous donation.

The inns of Dorchester started to open their doors at midday, and I was the first customer to take advantage of the facilities at the Bull's Head. There was a private cubicle with soft toilet-paper, and a hot tap and scented soap.

"Yes sir, what can I get you?" asked the cheery landlord when I returned from the loo to the lounge bar.

"Rum and black?" I requested, slightly hesitantly.

"Of course. You can have whatever you like, sir," smiled the man. "Are you just passing through or..?"

"Dunno," I shrugged. "I'm at a bit of a loose end. I've just come out of nick."

"Aha! I didn't wanna say, but I thought maybe…" he admitted.

"That obvious, eh?" I grinned.

Between serving customers, Gerry the landlord kept coming back to where I was sitting on a high stool at the end of the bar, as I recounted tales of my life.

"So you actually rode on the elephants!" he gasped. "But you're an artist, are you?" After we'd been chatting for some time, he said, "Listen Max, don't be offended, but the bull's head on my pub-sign needs of a lick of paint or something. I don't suppose..?"

I went outside and gazed up at the squeaky sign. The poor old bull was worn out and neglected. His face had almost faded away and he looked quite sad and blind. And the picture on the other side was even tattier. With no plans in mind and nowhere special to be, I decided to titivate Gerry's cow.

"We've got plenty of empty guest rooms this time of year, so why don't you stay here, on the house?" he suggested. "You can get settled in, have some dinner, and start work in the morning, if you'd like."

My bedroom was warm and clean. As I crossed the creaky landing, my nostrils were treated to the sweet aroma of malty beer. The bathroom smelt of fresh pine, the piping hot water steamed-up the mirrors, and the towels were thick and fluffy. It was luxury! As I opened my suitcases and rummaged inside, I was amazed to discover my stolen soda syphon was still there. Presumably, I thought, the cops who had nicked me for stealing the clock and the chandelier thought it too trivial to bother with. It was worth a quid, so it was an unexpected bonus. The prison governor had also been kind enough to let me keep all my prison-issue paints and brushes, so that was another bonus.

"Can I ask you something, Max?" asked Gerry, as he served me up a big dinner and poured me a big glass of wine. "What did you actually get sent down for?"

"Nothing bad," I assured him. "I was in a hotel up the road, and a chandelier and a clock just fell into me lap. Coppers thought I was trying to nick it!"

"Don't look now," he warned me, "but that bloke you were just talking to, he owns *that* hotel! He's a regular in here."

"Oh," I sighed. "Are you gonna chuck me out, or can I finish me dinner first?"

"Shhhh," he winked. "Mum's the word."

After a social evening with the pub locals, and a night of blissful sleep, I arrived downstairs in the morning to a full English breakfast. Gerry had a handyman at the pub and he had already been up his ladder and taken down the weary sign. I worked on it in the warmth of the pub's garage, carefully rubbing down the picture on either side, before repainting all the areas of lifeless pigment. I carefully painted and blended in my new bits with the old, so that my work was subtle and unassuming. I also redid the lettering on the pub's name-sign in bold white characters. Then, after a coating of revitalizing varnish, the Bull's Head was alive once more.

A few days later, and with another fifty quid in the kitty, Gerry patted me on the shoulder and asked, "So where will you go next then, Max?"

"Wherever the fancy takes me," I smiled.

And the first place I went to was the train station, whereupon the booking clerk peered through his ticket window and gasped, "You! What the 'ell are you doin' 'ere!"

"This *is* a ticket office, ain't it?" I submitted. "I'll give you one guess."

I took a train and travelled west to Penzance on the extreme tip of Cornwall. The season was almost at an end, but one of the holiday villages was still offering short breaks for pensioners, and I got work as a kitchen porter, with chalet accommodation and grub included. I knew the routine of the camps as well as I knew every one of the comedian's weary jokes. When the pensioners had all gone, the camp needed sprucing up, so I decided to stay on to do a bit of painting and decorating. When I'd had enough, I meandered my way around to St Ives. The town had a reputation for its hippy types and, although I had never considered myself to be one of *them*, they were life's drifters, just like me. Dozens and dozens of them sprawled across the golden beaches, smoking dope, playing their guitars and bongos, before crashing out in cuddly heaps on the sand. When the sea and the skies turned black, and the freezing rain lashed across the boggy beaches, we huddled around campfires in the woods, or sought refuge in the local church. However, some of the 'free spirits' weren't quite so free when the constabulary arrived to round them up, and sent them off to the local magistrates' court. I hitched to Exeter, but within a few days I found myself sitting on a National Express coach to London.

It was a good feeling to be back on familiar turf, renting a flat in Shepherd's Bush and setting up my pictures amongst the familiar characters of Portobello Road. A few yards down from the Earl of Lonsdale was an alleyway with an archway over the top. Offering protection from the rain, it was a popular spot for street vendors, and it was an ideal site for exhibiting my pictures. I carted a good collection of paintings in bin-liners on the tube, then paid for my pitch and started setting up. A small trolley rattled past me over the cobbles. As I glanced up, I saw that it was being hauled by a young lady with a wild mane of long red hair. She stopped a few yards away and I was curious to see what goodies she had brought to sell. It was immediately apparent that she was well-organised and well-practised, and in a few minutes she had set up an impressive display of amulets and homemade jewellery, pre-mounted on natty presentation boards. Our eyes met and there was a twinkle.

"Hi!" she called out, breezing towards me with her radiant dress flowing around her ankles. "Where's your dog?"

"Bonnie's staying with someone else at the moment," I told her.

"Oh, right. I'm selling jewellery and stuff," she beamed, toying with a pair of giant, gypsy earrings which swung audaciously from her pink, delicate lobes. She approached and inquired, "So how old is this picture?"

"Has it got a date on it?" I asked her.

She peered below the blasting cannons and shattered hulls of sinking galleons, and frowned at the faded numbers, "eighteen-twenty-seven?"

"I guess that'll be when it was painted then," I shrugged.

"Wow!" she gasped. "It's amazing to think…"

Between customers and sales, we visited each other for a chinwag and a cigarette. As trade ebbed away after lunch, the dealers boxed-and-bagged their unsold bric-a-brac, and piled their antique tables-and-chairs onto the roof-racks of their sagging estate cars, and left.

"So Caroline, how d'ya fancy a bite to eat?" I suggested to my new buddy.

A guy who ran a large antique bazaar nearby let us store our stuff at the rear of his premises, and I escorted Caroline up to the Earl of Lonsdale for a nibble and a well-earned glass of vino. Our conversation was so chirpy and cheeky that we could have been old friends. She liked my stories and I liked her spirit.

"Where on earth do you get all those old pictures from?" she quizzed.

"Just some place I know," I teased.

"What? A shop or something?" she quizzed further, her earrings swinging wildly as she shook her puzzled head.

"Well not exactly," I said. "I'll let you into a little secret. I get 'em from my flat."

"Your flat!" she exclaimed, looking quite bewildered.

Her sweet-and-spicy scent filled my nostrils as I whispered into her ear, "Don't tell anyone, but I do 'em myself."

"*You* paint *them*!" she gasped. "What, all of them? Holy shit, Max!"

The following day, on the Sunday, she fancied a trip down to Club Row, and so did I. We buzzed down to the East End in her pretty Volkswagen Beetle and browsed cheerfully amongst all the dross in search of treasure. She was looking for undiscovered and under-priced trinkets, and I was looking for old frames and canvases. We scoured together, unearthing unusual objects, keen to learn more about each other's interests and fancies.

"Seven delightful old landscapes. That'll be forty quid to you, mate," one of the traders told me, as I was eyeing up some naff pictures which I wanted to buy.

I sighed deeply and was shaking my head in mock disbelief, when Caroline suddenly cut in, "Forty quid! For these old pot-boilers! You're taking the mickey, mate! Come on, Max…" As we made for the door, he called us back, and Caroline scowled, "Twenty quid, mate, take it or leave it."

"Phwoar!" the man chuckled, and sighed at me, "She drives an 'ard bargain, does your Mrs!"

Caroline's flat was just off Portobello Road, above a greasy spoon café. It was on the top floor, and a skylight bathed it with a warm and natural brightness. The rooms were a good size, high-ceilinged, and the fragrance of exotic incense wafted freely. Strewn around the place were dishes of beads and fancy stones, and coils of multicoloured twine and snippets of shiny wire, and all types of miniature tools. Vibrant fabric throws were draped across the furniture, and Indian and African wall-hangings graced every room. Plates and bowls in various stages of completion sat around a potter's wheel, along with paints and brushes. Due to its size and location, the apartment would normally have been quite a costly place in which to live. However, Caroline's father owned the property and only charged her a peppercorn rent.

As we shared a desire to create and sell pieces of art, we found ourselves spending more-and-more time with each other. Caroline was a beautiful, full-figured woman, fun-loving and passionate. She demonstrated an abiding interest in me and my life, and she was always eager to explore new things and new experiences. Although I had divulged a good deal to her, she wanted to learn more about the auction rooms and the methods by which I sold my work. I took her to Lots Road and Phillips. She stood by, observing as the 'experts' assessed my paintings, telling me who had painted each one, before giving me their estimates of suitable reserve prices. Then, on auction days, she loved to hang onto my arm and watch me raising bids on my own pictures. As a companion she was a real asset, looking every bit the glamorous wife of a potential buyer. However, I never allowed her to get too involved and she never placed a bid on any of my fakes.

We raced out of London and up the A10, with the sun tickling our skin and the wind whistling through our hair. I had money in my pocket and not a care in the world. I'd borrowed a smart MGB sports car to take Caroline away on a break, and thought that she might like to take a trip along memory lane with me.

"Here we are, North Elmham," I announced, as we approached the road-sign on the edge of the sleepy village. "That's the church. And a bit further on you'll see Watts Naval Training School across the fields on the right. It's a massive old Victorian building with a pair of turrets and hundreds of gabled windows. It's an impressive old place. It's elevated on a huge hump, so you can't miss it."

Caroline peered sideways across the flat landscape. I slowed down a bit, then a bit more, and a bit more, until finally I pulled over onto the grass verge. She looked at me and shrugged, and I looked at her and shrugged back. It was nowhere to be seen. Even as we drove up the long, straight driveway, I was desperate for my old school to appear out of thin air, as if by magic. The school's train station was still there, deserted and disused, and the little chapel where the bodies of ill-fated Barnardo's boys were laid to rest, and the stone bridge across the river. But no school!

"Nope," gurgled a couple of listless farmers who were chewing the fat, "the school be gone many a year now, demolished into the ground."

"We used to play *there*, right across the school fields, right over to *there*," I gestured extravagantly across the landscape. "East Front versus West Front. And there was a ship's mast, a hundred-foot tall, which the masters forced the boys to climb up. Where's that gone?"

The farmers shook their vacant heads. Then, just as we were leaving and I had given up all hope, one suddenly blurted out, "Could try America. Some say they took yer flagpole *there*."

We stopped in a pretty Norfolk village, at a traditional country inn. It offered big and comfortable beds, and big and tasty dishes. Nearby, en route, we'd passed an antique shop which I was keen to visit.

I told the dealer that I was 'trade' and he inquired, "What genre of antiquities are your bag?"

"Pretty much anything," I shrugged. "I get most of my stuff from London. I've got a couple of old paintings in the car, but I don't suppose you'd…"

"Au contraire," he insisted. "I would *love* to see them." And when I returned from the car with a shipping scene, he pretended to be quite downbeat about it, but I saw his eyes light up and he opined, "Hmmm, the artist is… It looks like… Albert something. Ah, yes, Albert Derby."

"One of the Norwich School?" I suggested.

"Of course, early eighteen-hundreds, an apprentice to John Crome," the man declared. "How much would you erm..?"

"Unfortunately I've already bagged that one," Caroline interjected. "It's for our library at home you see." Then nudging me, "Don't you remember, darling?"

"Of course," I uttered. And then to the disappointed chap, "Sorry."

As we were almost out of the door, he called out after us, "I could offer you five-hundred for it."

"Hmmm," mused Caroline, "perhaps it *is* a little dark for the library."

We left and went back to the hotel with five-hundred-and-fifty quid. In the bar, after supper, we got chatting to a cheerful American couple who were on vacation, and who just happened to love old porcelain and paintings.

"My-my! That is some pig!" gasped the wife when I showed them a primitive painting of a Potbellied Black, blessed with prize-winning genitalia. "Back in the States we have an artist called Grandma Moses. Have you heard of her?"

"Oh yes," I said. "But *this* painting probably predates her by fifty or a hundred years. It *is* signed by Abraham Haynes. Do you know of Abra..?"

"Abraham Haynes! Oh, honey, I just have to have it for our kitchen," she insisted to her husband.

The pig added another four hundred to our coffers, which wasn't bad for a fake painting by a made-up artist. The next day, we tootled along to Barsham in Suffolk. Luckily, the rectory where I had been a foster-child was still standing, and it looked as glorious as ever. I felt quite proud to point out to Caroline the tall trees which myself and my brother had climbed as children, and which Horatio Nelson may also have climbed almost two-hundred years before us. I was keen to show off my former residence and didn't hesitate to go up and ring the doorbell.

"It *is* an historic building," admitted the owner, "but it is also our private home."

"I'm terribly sorry," I apologised. "It's just that… Well, it's just that when I was an orphan, the Reverent Soden took me in, and looked after me, and I just thought…"

"Oh dear!" gasped the embarrassed man. "I'm so sorry. Of course, do come in."

The owner and his wife welcomed us with a cup of tea and a slice of malt-loaf. And as we toured the property, they were happy to let me impart my knowledge about the buildings and grounds.

"The priest's hole was in the corner of this bedroom," I told them. "Although I don't think they'd have got many priests in that little gap! There used to be lovely stables with a thatched roof and a reindeer weathervane, and an ancient flint-walled kitchen-garden. I can't believe they've been demolished! There was a peach tree, and I almost got into trouble for knocking Reverend Soden's prize peach off it with an airgun. He used to smoke this Erinmore pipe tobacco. I can smell it now. It was delicious."

"They loved *you*," giggled Caroline as we drove away, and the charming couple stood waving us a fond goodbye.

I was saddened to hear that the kind-hearted Reverend Soden was quite feeble and had gone into a nursing home.

On a lane near the village of Waterford in Hertfordshire, a series of high, pointy gables appeared above the treeline, and I rejoiced, "Thank god for that! This is still standing too!"

I had ignored a signpost which declared the vast mansion

'Private Property', and within a moment of parking the MG, a groundsman confronted me, and I told him, "I used to live here."

"Well Goldings ain't Barnardo's no more," he said. "Private flats now. But I suppose it'd be alright if you and the young lady wanna take a look around."

"What a beautiful house," Caroline delighted. "And these views down to the woods and the river… quite breathtaking!"

We were directed to find the janitor, and he advised us which areas of the estate were accessible to ex pupils. The lofty entrance hall, the size of a cricket pitch, still boasted its grandiose splendour: acres of light-oak panels; the gargantuan, stone fireplace with its ornate mirror above; the broad staircase and intricately carved balusters and bannisters; giant-sized oak doors and a viewing gallery aloft. The room echoed with the hubbub of rushing boys and ringing bells and bawling masters. And the smell of wood-polish and body-odour lingered from my past.

"That's where they used to roast the younger boys," I told Caroline, indicating the gaping hearth. "You remember Tom Brown's School Days?"

She gasped with horror and stared into the fireplace. Then, as she gripped my arm and kissed my shoulder, I was unable to keep a straight face. "You liar!" she giggled.

As Portobello Market was on the doorstep of Caroline's flat, it seemed sensible to move in with her. I had been spending more-and-more time with her anyway, and it meant that we could roll out of bed at eight o'clock on a Saturday morning and be set up and ready for work by nine. During the week, she would sit at her kitchen table, crafting her avant-garde jewellery, while I stood at my easel, drawing and painting. The flat was bright and airy, and we found each other amusing and stimulating. Often, we would go away on leisure trips, with a bit of business thrown in, jaunting around the country, stopping wherever the fancy took us, meeting interesting characters and getting a kick from every picture we sold. On occasion, we revisited antique shops and dealers of old, and they were all over-the-moon to see us and discover what treasures I'd brought up from London in the boot of the car.

I still loved the buzz of Portobello, with its miles of assorted antique dealers who came from all corners of the U.K. and beyond, along with colourful characters like Bill the showman and escapologist. Many traders would arrive the eve before market day and slump overnight in their rusty vans or flagging estate cars, crushed between mountains of bone china or horse brasses, their pockets stuffed with valuable gems, and with just a steering-wheel for a pillow. We would all visit each other's stalls, or meet up for a yarn in the Lonsdale or Star at close of play, and I felt privileged to be part of such a large and peculiar family. Business was okay, and Caroline did pretty well from her silver rings and bangles. Life was sweet, but I had itchy feet and a mind which was constantly wandering. Whatever I did, I wanted to do more. And whatever I had, it wasn't enough. It wasn't just about money, but about life - and living. I knew people who worked 10 hours a day for 50 quid a week, and had 2 weeks holiday in a caravan each year, and contented themselves with a pair of kids, and MFI and DIY. If it was okay with them, that was good. But that was never going to be the life for me.

I loved to copy the style of numerous painters, altering the angles and viewpoints of existing paintings, yet carefully capturing the essence of each artist so that my work looked as though it may have been an earlier prototype version of a more famous picture. I enjoyed sourcing old frames and mounting my pictures so that the overall effect looked totally authentic. Then there were the encounters with the auction houses, relying on my acting skills to persuade the experts that I was a run-of-the-mill antique dealer, competent enough to know when I'd happened across a valuable work but, at the same time, too likeable and too stupid to be a con man. And then there was the auction itself, the frantic toing-and-froing between rival bidders, sometimes spurred along with a little help from me. Finally, there was the payoff for my efforts, measured in thousands of pound notes. Every part of the game excited me and made me dizzy for more.

I painted a pleasing coastal scene near my home turf in Shoreham-by-Sea. It was loose and moody, atmospheric like any good Samuel Palmer. Caroline came with me and we watched it sell at one of the salerooms for £2,500. It was like playing Russian roulette, and I suppose I came to believe that the gun wasn't loaded.

"Ah, good afternoon, sir," greeted the familiar valuer at a gallery in upmarket New Bond Street. "And what does sir have for us today? More of your delightful John Ward paintings on chamfered oak board?"

The pair of 10x8 marine pictures which I had taken to him a few months before were outstanding in every detail, and had made me a profit of £3,500, and probably the same amount for them.

"Just one today," I beamed. "I bought a job lot of stuff, a few nice bits of porcelain and clocks, and *this*... As soon as I saw it, I thought of *you*."

"Most considerate," warbled the chap. Then, upon close inspection, he observed, "It appears to be a Samuel Palmer. If you'll just give me a moment, I would like to consult with my colleagues."

I waited, eavesdropping on the snooty comments of the Saturday critics who were bumping their way around the display of pictures on the walls. Mayfair galleries were small but pricy. I stood back from the counter as a couple of American collectors negotiated loudly with staff, and a nice-looking lady with a gentleman companion smiled at me, and a bearded young artist presented a large abstract work for consideration, and a pair of eagle-eyed chaps in beige raincoats came in through the front door and weaved their way inside. The valuer reappeared and nodded to the rain-coated gentlemen, and then at me. I had a bad feeling.

"Excuse me, sir," said the raincoats, "we'd like a word with you."

There was no point in trying to make a run for it.

I turned to the gallery buff and shrugged, "So you won't be taking the Samuel Palmer, then?"

I went quietly, without fuss, escorted through the recoiling clientele who looked on with raised eyebrows and curled lips. A panda car drew up and a couple of uniforms pushed me into the back. We pulled off, went round the corner, and pulled up. It must have been all of a minute's drive. Inside the police station, the detectives sat me down in a beige room.

With beery London accents, they put their case against me: "The gallery's 'ad a complaint from the chap who bought these…" They slapped some photos of the small 'John Ward' shipping scenes down on the desk. "He's paid seven grand for 'em, and apparently they're bloody fakes! Well, you wanna comment?"

"Seven grand!" I shrieked. "The geezer's been robbed! Should've bought 'em off *me*, and I'd have let him have 'em for half that price."

"Less off the fuckin' wisecracks!" they snapped. "So, where d'ya get the pictures from?"

"Out of a paint pot," I smirked.

"Yeah, well we'll see if you're so fuckin' clever when we've turned yer drum over, won't we?" they snarled.

"It's not my flat," I contested. "It's my girlfriend's, and she's had nothing to do with any of this. Honest, that's the truth."

"Honest!" they sneered. "You're just a fuckin' common crook!"

They chucked me in a cell and left me. Some hours later, they hauled me back to the interview room, armed with all the evidence they needed to paint a picture. They'd been to Caroline's pad and taken my paints, plus a pile of worn-out canvases and worm-holed frames in various stages of distress, and printed pages of fake-worthy paintings alongside my own sketched and painted versions, some finished and some still roughs.

"A right little a van Goch, ain't we!" they scoffed. "Well, what yer gotta say?"

I 'fessed up to everything. There seemed little point in doing anything else. I was kept in the cells overnight, and first thing in the morning, after a cup of weak tea and a slice of dry toast, I was stuffed into a cop car and taken away. We left the West End behind us and joined the Brighton Road, accelerating through the perilous ghetto of Brixton and speeding past the notorious Cat's Whiskers nightclub in Streatham. An hour later, I was standing in the dock at Croydon Magistrates' Court.

"You appear without representation," the stern-faced magistrate disapprovingly observed.

"I do, Your Worship," I confirmed. "But only because I accept my guilt and would like to apologise."

After a brief hearing, and taking into consideration other counts of fraud and deception, His Worship's expression softened as he summed up: "Mister Brandrett, you have admitted your guilt and co-operated with the police. And whilst your crimes weren't violent, they did have pernicious consequences to innocent members of society. In your case, I feel that a sentence of community service… would *not* be appropriate. I sentence you to six months imprisonment and a fine of five-hundred pounds. Take him down."

I sat in my stifling cubicle in the back of the police van, swaying about and jerking to-and-fro, stopping and starting as I peered out through the dark window at the world spinning by outside. Ordinary people, men and women, and happy families, breezed along the pavement, ambling into HMV or Woolworths, or coming out of a Wimpy Bar with a dripping burger. Wandsworth Prison was a dark and dingy Victorian institution. We were squashed, three to a cell, with a book, a bucket and a few sheets of abrasive bog paper. There were fifteen hundred of us crammed into five wings, and at the end of the landing was a working gallows. I didn't know how long I would be held there, but I just got along, making sure I didn't get on the wrong side of my cellmates, slopping out and sketching the screws.

"Brandrett, you're being moved," the governor announced. "You're leaving in thirty minutes. Goodbye."

After just ten days, my temporary buddies bid me farewell and I ended up in Ford Prison, halfway between Portsmouth and Brighton. It would have been ideally located for friends and family to come and visit me, had I let them know that I had been incarcerated (Caroline was the only exception and my only visitor). In contrast to the claustrophobia of Wandsworth, Ford was an 'open' prison which was bright and airy, formerly a World War Two airbase. The barrack blocks had been converted into single billets and I found it quite cosy. The prisoners were considered decent chaps, low category and low risk, many of them quite well-to-do, who'd happened to be caught with their hand in some till or another. A lot of the time we weren't kept under lock and key, but were allowed to roam around almost freely. I was given paints and canvases, and the kindly governor allowed me to hold art classes for the inmates. Although time dragged, I kept my nose clean and, after three months, I was granted early release for good behaviour.

"I never want to go inside, ever again," I gasped, squeezing Caroline almost to death on the morning she came to collect me. "Not ever."

As she drove me away to freedom, I held my chin up to the open window and felt the air wafting over my face and rushing into my lungs. It wasn't the same air as prison air. She pulled the Beetle over at a restaurant in Arundel, and I ate a juicy steak and drank tasty wine.

When we arrived back in Portobello, I lay with her on the sweetly scented bedsheets, and she sighed wearily, "You will stop it, won't you, Max?"

"Yeah, course I will," I smiled.

Life was okay, painting, working the market, the odd trip away, the country shows, the medieval fairs, the few quid in my pockets, the chats, the pals, the pubs, Caroline…

For a few months, I faked interest in painting my own pictures and resisted the craving to paint my beloved fakes until, one day, I told her, "I'm going to pop down to Brighton for bit."

"Great. How long were you thinking?" she asked.

"Just a few days," I shrugged. But as we parted with a kiss, I think we both had more than an inkling that it might be longer.

The front door of my sister's council house in Bellingham Crescent opened and my mum bellowed, "Eee! Where has thee been hiding theeself? Thou's lost weight, son!"

My sister's three young children hid behind the settee, as I lounged back in an armchair with a strong brew and a plate of chocolate biscuits. "Sorry I haven't been to see you, mum, but I've been a bit tied up."

"Are thee stayin'?" she inquired eagerly.

"Yeah, thought I might get a flat," I said.

Mum was like a live-in helper for my sister and her kids. There was a cheap bedsit for rent in Seven Dials, not too far away, and I moved in. It was a handy spot, but more importantly it had enough space and daylight for me to paint quite freely. A car dealer I knew had a red, open-top MGB Roadster for sale, and I bought it on the loose arrangement that I would pay him back whenever I had a few bob. I telephoned Zena and she was happy for me to take Bonnie off her hands for a while and give her a break from having two big hairy dogs barging around her house. The moment Bonnie saw me, she charged about, scampering up and down Zena's hallway with her tail wagging, whacking into the furniture and jumping up to lick my face.

"Linda's not in," Zena sighed wearily.

"Sorry to hear about Eric," I commiserated.

"It's what happens when you marry someone older," she shrugged. "But Linda hasn't taken it very well at all I'm afraid, what with..."

"I'm sorry," I sighed. "I never meant..."

Bonnie sat on the passenger seat of the MG, with the breeze flapping her fluffy ears as she lapped up the views of our old stomping ground. We passed within half-a-mile of Ford Prison, and when I spotted the turnoff, I gave her a pat and chuckled, "Daddy is *not* going back in there again."

CHAPTER 8: UP THE PROM AND DOWN THE HILL

Bonnie bounded up the concrete steps and crashed into my sister's sitting room. My mum greeted her with cuddles and chicken scraps. They were good pals and loved to spend time together, especially on odd occasions when I couldn't take Bonnie somewhere with me.

A guy with a Groucho Marx moustache and long hair waltzed up to the bar in Ye Olde King and Queen, a huge Georgian and Tudor style theme pub opposite Victoria Gardens in Brighton. I sipped my drink and as he turned towards me his jaw dropped. He looked, then looked again, then blurted, "F'in''ell! Maaaax! It's me, Dave!" After he'd bear-hugged me and we'd spent a couple of hours reminiscing, he roused, "Listen, I'm goin' down to Jenkins nightclub later, grab-a-granny night. Come along, it's a right laugh."

The evening had been set up primarily for people in their forties, and above, to meet up and have a dance. But it wasn't entirely full of decrepit geriatrics. There were a few mature stunners who took a shine to some of us younger chaps, and Dave was quite keen to show off his moves, on and off the dancefloor. It transpired that he had a wife and kids, whom he fed and clothed by making miniature, wire sculptures: penny farthing bicycles; aeroplanes; automobiles; birds and animals and the likes.

Dave and I would truck around together and tout our art in the local galleries, or spend time larking around on the seafront. "Hold that pose," we'd tell the pretty girls, "we're from the Argus and we wanna take yer picture."

"Where's your camera then?" they'd challenge.

"Well 'ow about a private interview instead?" we'd cheekily suggest.

At Dave's flat one evening, we walked in to find that his wife had company, in the shape of a titillating and busty model called Jane. After we'd settled down with a drink on the couch together, Jane frowned and wagged her finger playfully at me and said, "I definitely know you from somewhere. Hmmm. I know! The auditions for the Penthouse Pets!" And we coupled up for a short spell but, as always, I was really just too engrossed in painting.

A guy came up as I was browsing in a small and empty Brighton gallery and asked, "Are you buying?"

"Just looking," I replied.

"Oh," he grizzled, appearing rather narked, and walked away muttering expletives. Then, a couple of minutes later, he came back to me and growled, "Listen, if you ain't gonna buy nuffink, then you can ffff…" He stopped short as a tweedy, middle-aged gent entered.

Dashing eagerly up to the potential customer and smiling, he greeted him in an affectedly posh tone, "Good morning, sir. Is there anything in particular that sir is looking for this morning?" After a brief look around, the chap left, empty-handed.

As if I was his old mate, the guy turned to me, shaking his head and grumbled, "The fuckin' people what I 'ave in 'ere! Honestly, they drive yer round the fuckin' bend!" Then he tutted a lot, before sighing, "So what is it you're lookin' for?"

"I'm an artist," I answered.

"Yeah? What sorta stuff?" he asked.

"Shipping scenes," I said. "But anything on old canvases really."

We chatted for a bit and he dragged out an old canvas and challenged, "You paint me some nice boats on that, and if it's any cop, maybe you and me could 'elp one another out."

When I returned with a painting of Dutch flagships in a choppy harbour, he took one look and yelled, "Fuckin' 'ell! That's Hendrick bloody Vroom all over that is! Are you sure you done this?"

"It's *your* canvas," I shrugged. "Well, what d'ya reckon?"

"Put it there, son!" he chuckled, squeezing my hand with an almighty handshake.

Sid and I became good mates, and I would churn out pictures for him, and he would turn them around in his gallery in double-quick time. "If that picture had a signature on it," he would brag to his customers, "it'd be worth four grand. But for you, I'll do it for five 'undred." I didn't make a lot of money out of it, but I was still selling through other dealers, so I wasn't making a bad living.

Sitting in the front room with my mum, with my sister's kids silently amusing themselves behind the sofa, I suggested, somewhat concerned, "Why don't I take them out? I could take 'em down the pier. Do they ever get out of this place?"

The three little souls followed me outside and stood in a row, watching me open-mouthed as I pulled back the hood of the MG. I plonked the trio down on the narrow bench at the back, and Bonnie jumped into the passenger seat.

"All aboard!" I hooted, driving away and glancing backwards to see if I could detect a smile on the children's pallid faces.

On the beach, and on the pier, they toddled along behind me with candy floss and cowboy hats, and smoking sweet cigarettes.

"Do you wanna paddle in the sea..? Do you wanna watch Punch and Judy..? Do you wanna go on the fairground horses..?" My invitations were met with a sombre look and a shake of their cute, curly tresses.

I was about to suggest a chug along the seafront on the Volks miniature train, when a soft female voice purred, "Bonjour. You 'ave a very cute doggie."

"Her name's Bonnie," I said, looking up and seeing a chic and sexy young lady wearing a pretty foulard across her bouffant of dark silky hair. I was quick to add, "And my name's Max, if you're interested."

"I am Marie-Claude," she announced, smiling and gently caressing me with a handshake. "You 'ave beautiful children, too."

"The nippers ain't mine," I assured her, looking down at the three sticky-faced cherubs with toy cigarettes sticking out between their lips. Then, just to confirm, "The kids belong to my sister."

Marie-Claude smiled and twiddled her fingers at the little ones, and they seemed almost to smile back. We all wandered along the esplanade in the sunshine and had exotic sundaes at Marrocco's Italian ice-cream parlour.

"So, were you spying on me at the pier?" I chuckled.

"No, no, no, I was not spying on you," she rebuffed, "I was just observing your dog."

"Listen," I said, suddenly spotting the time, "how d'ya fancy going out later? We could meet at the clock-tower. How would five o'clock suit ya?"

Her face dropped and she shrugged, "The famille I am staying with, they aff their supper at five o'clock."

"No problem," I persevered, "how about half-past five?"

A cheeky smile came over her and she chirped, "Okay, at five-thirty, I will meet you at the clocks-tower."

I got back to my sister's and walked up the garden path with the kids dawdling along behind, and a bunch of flowers in hand. Opening the back door, I took off my shoes and noticed that the clock had already passed four. As Bonnie went bounding into the house, I called out, "We're back. We've had a lovely time. I've got some flowers for... Oh! Hello." Sitting in the lounge with my mum were Zena and Linda, staring silently into empty teacups. "Sorry, I didn't know that you... We got caught up... I wasn't expecting..." I babbled. "Anyway, it's great to see you both, really great." My mum took the children and Bonnie to the kitchen to wash their paws and faces.

"We thought we'd call round," Zena told me. "It's just that Linda hasn't been too well lately, and you are still married to her."

"Of course," I acknowledged.

However, it was obvious to see, despite a cloak of makeup, that Linda wasn't the Linda of old. She looked thin and white, and her eyes faintly flickered beneath a pair of black and hollow sockets. I didn't know whether to kiss my estranged wife, or whether it might kill her, or send her into a screaming fit of rage against me.

"She's been under the doctor for a while now," sighed Zena,

"and she's just not snapping out of it. I'm not saying that you're totally to blame, but… She just wants to know…"

"I just want to know," Linda whispered coldly, "if we can give it another go, or whether we're totally and utterly finished?" I hesitated, caught off-guard. She seemed to brighten a little, and smiled softly, "We *were* in love, weren't we, Max? We were good together, weren't we? You know we were. Couldn't we just give it another try? Please?"

Pausing to soften the blow, I declared, "We *were* in love, but… I haven't changed. I can't change. It's not your fault. I'm sorry. Truly I am."

There was a moment's silence, then Zena sighed, "I think we'd better go. We came on the train, so…"

"I can run you to the station if you like," I suggested. "I mean, we could still be friends, if that's what you wanted."

Linda stared into my eyes and nodded with a soft, mournful huff, then said, "Come on, Bonnie, we're going home now."

Bonnie and Linda squashed into the back of the MG and the four of us drove to Portslade station, the tang of salty sea air wafting across our lips. I left them at the front entrance. They didn't want me to hang around and give them hugs goodbye, so I didn't, except for Bonnie. The speed of their departure, however, did mean that I still had enough time to get back to my flat for a quick wash-and-brush-up.

Dressed to the nines in a swanky corduroy jacket and a pair of tight flares, I drove towards the clock-tower to meet my date. I did, however, hastily pull over at a phone box en route. There was a call which I had been putting off, and which I had promised to make that day.

"Hi!" I greeted into the mouthpiece. "It's Max."

"I know," Caroline's voice rattled in the earpiece. "How are you?"

"I'm fine," I raced. "I've only got one ten P, so…"

"I see. So when do you think you'll be coming back?" she asked.

"I'm not sure," I replied. "Things are a bit crazy here at the moment, but I'll give you a buzz next week."

"Okay. Love you," she kissed.

The phone beeped and died.

I made it to the clock-tower with minutes to spare. When Marie-Claude appeared through the haze of ordinary people, she looked dazzling. She looked fresher and prettier than I had remembered, with her flowing locks cascading around her slim, bronzed shoulders. As I drove her along the seafront, she threw her arms aloft in a gesture of wild abandon. We both knew that it could only be a brief affair, but that only served to heighten our desire and passion. Overlooking the moonlit waves from a hotel room, we tore off each other's clothes and cavorted from boudoir to balcony. Three weeks later she was gone. We had promised to write letters and meet up again one day, but she returned to the privileged lifestyle of a diplomat's daughter in France, and I returned to the business of faking pictures.

I sauntered into Jack Powell's antique shop in Portslade with a good collection of my rare paintings for him to choose from, only to be warned off. Jack told me that a couple of coppers called Pugglesham and Fitchman from the Fraud Squad had been sniffing around, and they were keen to see me nicked and banged up, by hook or by crook. It wasn't exactly what I'd wanted to hear, but it wasn't totally unexpected, and I wasn't going to let it put the kibosh on things. I still had a living to make.

As I did the rounds of my usual shops and galleries in Brighton, I kept getting the cold-shoulder, and hearing the same story: "I couldn't touch your paintings with a bargepole, Max. Pugglesham and Fitchman have been round - and they're onto you."

With one eye peeking over my shoulder, and a bag of pictures to sell, I was walking through The Lanes in Brighton when I caught a glimpse of a beige raincoat in the shadows. I quickened my pace and noticed that there was a second beige figure darting in and out of the shop doorways behind me. As I twisted and turned through the maze of narrow streets and alleyways, it was obvious that the shady pair was sticking steadfastly to my tail. I slowed down and halted abruptly, and wasn't at all surprised when they did likewise. As I lit a cigarette, they did their feckless best to melt into the colourful mix of Brightonians and tourists. When I continued, they continued. When I speeded up, they speeded up. I wondered if they could be the dynamic duo of Pugglesham and Fitchman? Whoever they were, they were coppers, and I needed to get rid of them.

I knew The Lanes very well, and I knew all the odd little shops and quirky dealers. Picking up the pace, I could see that my pursuers were breaking into a sweat to keep up. I trotted them around until I could think up a way of detaching them from my backside. Then I thought of a shop which offered the perfect solution. The owner was a pal of mine, and I was familiar with the layout of his place. It was a popular outlet for desperate men in beige raincoats, a place where the over-eighteens could procure naughty lingerie, erotic toys, dirty books and porno films. I glanced behind me and went inside, leaving my antagonizers lurking uncomfortably outside on the street.

"Hey Gerry," I blurted to the owner, "see them two, they're a pair of bloody perverts. They'll be in 'ere sniffin' yer knickers and interfering with yer blow-up Barbies! Alright if I pop out the back way?"

Gerry instantly got my drift, smiled and pulled out a pickaxe handle from under the counter. And as I was legging it, the cops came in, and Gerry ambushed them and threatened to call the law.

"We *are* the fuckin' law!" I heard them yelling, by which time I was halfway over the back wall.

The next day I moved flat. But over the next few weeks, even when I was taking my sister's kids out for a stroll, or visiting one of my brothers, or taking my mum out shopping, I was constantly looking over my shoulder. Whatever else, I didn't want my family to have any involvement in my unorthodox profession. The sheer embarrassment at the thought of being carted off in a squad car in front of my mum made my blood run cold. And the word was out amongst the local dealers that my paintings had become too hot to handle.

The squeal of screeching tyres amid the row of mundane shops in George Street was an unusual distraction for the sleepy folk of Hove. Just as I swivelled round to see what all the fuss was about, a pair of weighty coppers in uniform had their grubby mitts on my collar.

"Max Brandrett," the officers stated, "you're wanted at the station."

"Can't it wait?" I moaned. "I was just off to the pub for my lunch!"

A gaggle of passers-by giggled.

"Alright smart-arse," grunted the cops, "get in the car."

As we sped off, I hoped that nobody who knew me had witnessed the incident. They took me off to the huge main police station at Edward Street. It was right next to the courthouse, and I was worried that an appearance before the beak might be my next port of call.

"Name and address?" demanded the custody sergeant.

"Tell me what I'm supposed to have done," I objected.

"You're a wanted man, Brandrett," he smiled. "Our colleagues from Mayfair nick are coming down to see ya. They wanna word with *you*."

Two men in familiar beige raincoats were peeping out of a doorway, but they quickly shrank back out of sight.

"Oh, well that's alright then," I sighed, relieved that if I was going to be nicked by the Met, then it probably wouldn't make the pages of the Brighton Evening Argus. "Any chance of a chicken sandwich? I'm famished."

My police cell was quite comfortable, complete with a plastic-coated mattress and well-bleached toilet. I lay back, staring at the whitewashed ceiling and wondered what was about to happen and where I would end up. Visions of paintings and dealers and galleries flashed through my mind, as I tried to work out what allegations might be levelled at me, and what excuses I might offer in my defence. But there were so many pictures I had painted, and so much cash.

At teatime, I bashed on the cell door, and when the wicket clacked open and an eyeball appeared, I grumbled, "Silly question, but how much longer are you gonna keep me in 'ere?"

"They're on their way," a voice called back. "D'ya wanna a packet of crisps?"

By supper time, I was getting quite worn down by the police's lack of activity. I could hear the unlocking and locking of cell doors, and the heavy threats as my neighbours came and went, but there was never as much as a rattle of keys at *my* door.

"Oi! I'm getting sick of this!" I grizzled. "Oi!"

"Oh yeah," said a fresh-faced bobby who had been sent to investigate why there was a noise coming from the cell at the end of the corridor. "I'll try and find out what's happening." Sometime later he returned, opened the cell door and grinned, "Oh well, it seems like the Mayfair squad aren't coming to see you after all."

"What d'ya mean, not coming?" I demanded. "Why not?"

"None of your business," asserted the grouchy custody officer who discharged me. "There's yer keys, there's yer wallet. Sign 'ere and fuck off."

"Well how am I supposed to get home?" I questioned.

The grouch leaned down and scowled into my face, "We're watchin' you, Brandrett."

"A taxi'd be nice," I suggested.

"On yer bike," he grunted.

As I was released through the cop-shop gates at midnight, I took a long and grateful breath of fresh air.

I had been compelled to give the cops my proper address, or face the possibility of them turning up at my sister's, or at one of my brother's. Unemployment was high and my chances of making an honest living in Brighton were low. I had rent to meet and bills to pay, plus the constant threat of being pulled in by the police, followed by the prospect of another, but probably longer, prison sentence. It was obvious that I had to make a quick decision and get out of town before the long arm of the law grabbed me again.

"I'm popping back up to 'The Smoke' for bit," I told my mum.

"Tha's always on the move, you!" mum sighed. "Why can't tha just settle down?"

"I dunno," I shrugged. "I guess it's in me blood."

She stroked a wisp of straggly hair away from my face and stared intently into my eyes. Was it, I wondered, that when she looked at me, she could see my father?

"Ya take care, son," she whispered.

I hugged her and left.

Portobello Road was deathly quiet. It was a drizzly grey weekday, and the antique shops were closed, and the market stalls were absent, apart from the few at the bottom of the hill which sold fruit and veg. I pulled up my collar and wandered cautiously past the café and stared up at Caroline's flat, contemplating whether or not to ring the bell.

"I think she's gone, Max," said an old neighbour. "India I think, or Thailand, or some place on the hippy trail. Sorry mate."

For once, even Portobello Road seemed like a lonely place. I wandered down to Shepherd's Bush and got chatting to a friendly old couple in a pub, and they offered me an upstairs room to rent in their house. It was small and cheap, and it had a basin in the corner, which I thought would be quite handy as they were okay with me painting there. I plonked my suitcase down on the bed, took out my washbag, cleaned my teeth and rinsed my face, then went off to see if any of my old mates were out-and-about. I arrived back a few hours later to find the couple seething under a pile of soggy rubble in their sitting room. Looking up at the view of my bedroom through a gaping hole in the ceiling, they told me how they had been alarmed by heavy drips of water, quickly followed by a groaning noise and a deluge of lath-and-plaster. The only explanation was that I had left the tap running, and the only outcome was that I had managed to achieve the shortest room-rental in history.

I found myself a big bedsit in Hammersmith, near Charing Cross Hospital. A couple of days later, I was back in the hustle-and-bustle of Portobello Market, renewing a few old acquaintances and flogging a few pictures. Swarms of tourists jostled about, filling Portobello Road from side-to-side and up-and-down, as far as the eye could see. They fought to see the millions of treasures on display on the hundreds of stalls, scavenging and bickering like pigeons to try and get the tastiest morsels. Fresh faces beamed from behind the stalls which were once mine and Caroline's, but I was quite happy to exhibit my pictures on the railings, set back from the trampling masses. It was a shame that my beautiful Bonnie wasn't with me, and I did keep my eyes peeled in the vague hope that Sam (my old 'dad') or Bill (the escapologist) might appear. The customary clatter of foul-smelling litter trolleys, piled high with shattered rubbish and squashed vegetables, signalled the culmination of a fruitful day's trading. And afterwards, in the Earl of Lonsdale, the traders swapped boozy tales of tasty trades and dirty deals. The cut-and-thrust and the atmosphere of the market suited me well, and every time I returned to Portobello it felt as if I had returned home.

When I wasn't at the market, I spent my time painting, or digging out old 'potboilers' amongst the capital's jumble. The sniff of a rich oak or mahogany panel, a hundred or two hundred years old, was enough to send my pulse racing. And whenever I was lucky enough to unearth a piece of nature's special timber, shaped and planed and sanded by a master-craftsman, and expertly layered with resin and linen, but adorned with some atrocious, amateurish painting, it seemed only right to honour it with a worthy painting and give it a new lease of life.

It had been some time since I had hit the London auction houses, and I hoped that when I arrived with a crazed old equestrian scene and a mixed bag of trivial tat, the staff wouldn't recognise me. I was also more than a bit concerned that the Fraud Squad in London might have circulated my details to galleries and auctioneers. As I waited my turn at the reception desk, I decided that if anyone showed the slightest hint of suspicion about me, or the pictures, then I would have to bluff my way out of it, or run.

"Mornin' sir," I smiled at the snooty bod. "I picked up a few smudges on me travels and wondered if you could tell me if they was worth anything?"

As the chap peered and sighed, then peered and sighed some more, I held my breath and waited, watching for signs of a twitchy finger on an alarm button, or a surreptitiously raised eyebrow to signal for a colleague to call the law. And if he requested to take my painting away for further examination, I wondered whether it would be best to let it go and slink off, or refuse permission and make a hasty exit with my pictures, or just hold my nerve and wait until he returned? In the past, playing father and son with Sam, we just had the gift-of-the-gab, the brass-neck, the front to fool even the most diligent of experts.

"I would like a second opinion on this one," stated the man, singling out my equestrian scene, "if sir has no objection?"

"Is it a gooden then?" I asked. "It's just that..."

Before I could finish, he had walked off with the picture. I willed him not to disappear out of sight to summon the security guards. When he stopped nearby to consult with an older chap, I thought my palms might melt. The pair cogitated, swirling and stroking their fingers above my paintwork, and nodding and shaking their heads in quick succession.

Eventually they came back with the picture and announced to me, "*This*... in our opinion... more than likely... as far as we can tell... is a fay..." My heart stopped until they continued. "... famous painter of horses called John Best. He was a student of a very distinguished artist called George Stubbs. You may have heard of him?"

"I've heard of *him*," I nodded, "but not the other gentleman."

"Anyway, it could be quite valuable," they concluded.

And, luckily, they weren't incorrect about that.

I liked my roomy bedsit in Hammersmith. I had a lovely studio set-up, the house was comfortable, and the other tenants were a friendly and decent lot. I was drawing and painting, socialising and selling, and all-in-all I was more-than-happy with life. Then, one nippy market day at my pitch, I saw two windswept figures, arm-in-arm, walking towards me up Portobello Road. I instantly recognised the man with the Father Christmas beard, but wondered whether either of *them* would recognise *me*.

Just as they were about to pass by, and I was about to call out to them, the fancy young woman glanced up at me and smiled, "I know you, don't I?"

I pointed at the gentleman and recalled, "We once had a tiff over some old 'potboilers' which we both..."

"I remember, in Club Row," the lady grinned.

"You have a very good memory," I complimented.

She asked her companion if he remembered me.

"No, not really," mumbled the old chap. "I've met hundreds of young artists."

"I'm Jane," smiled the woman. "And this is Tom."

"Max," I said, shaking her hand.

"Did you do *this*?" Tom inquired sedately, staring at a seemingly ancient painting of Lord Nelson.

"That's right," I said. Then, gesturing at my assortment of exhibits, "I did all of 'em."

He squinted at each of my works in turn, rubbed his ruddy nose and murmured, "Hmmm, not bad. I wonder if we should have a chat sometime?"

I met them in the Earl of Lonsdale and we had a long conversation over big glasses of red wine and rum. Tom had been an art restorer, then an art forger for a number of years. Jane was many years his junior, as was I. They invited me up to their maisonette in north London and he proudly challenged me to examine his fakes, some completed and some still works-in-progress. As I looked at the tone of his colours and compared them with those in the prints which he was trying to recreate, I could discern slight differences, but I said nothing.

"You see how in this painting I've captured the technique of Samuel Palmer's romanticism?" he smiled. "I've studied the man and his methodology until I'm a master at it. It takes a lot of practice and a lot of time."

I agreed with him, and as the three of us sat in his living room and drank, a cigarette almost slipped from his sleepy fingers, only to be saved by Jane in the nick of time. As Tom snored in his chair, Jane and I smoked rollups and discussed our shared love of painting, and the songs of Bob Dylan and Tom Paxton.

A few days later, as I was in my room, finishing off a twenty-four by thirty-six inch Battle of Trafalgar oil painting by Clarkson Stanfield, a voice shrieked from downstairs, "Max! Phone!"

I went down and answered the call abruptly, "Hello."

A mellow voice replied, "Tom Keating here. Come up to my studio. I've had an idea."

At around mid-day, I rang on the doorbell and waited, and rang again, until eventually Tom emerged. He looked saggy, like a bloodhound, and he peered out at me, possibly wondering for a moment why I'd called.

"I'll make some coffee," he puffed, as we went inside. "Jane's not here. She's out looking for frames and labels and whatnot. She's awfully good at that, and mocking up bits of paperwork. Do take a look at my latest. It's there on the easel. It's an Alfred Vickers. Not finished of course."

Paintings were strewn around all over the place for anyone to see. There were obvious copies of Monet, Van Gogh, Renoir, Turner, Picasso... and a few lesser-known artists, plus some of his own portraits and nudes. As my eye was drawn to a re-concocted version of the Hay Wain, Tom returned and handed me a mug of muddy coffee.

Gazing admiringly at his own version of Constable's masterpiece, he noted, "See how I've expressed the clouds with broad, flowing brushstrokes, just as Constable would have done? And if you look at the way I've cleverly swung the scene round at an angle to change the perspective... This is what I'm working on at the moment. Are you familiar with Alfred Vickers' work?"

"Father or son?" I asked.

"Well I can do both," he said, leading me to his easel. "This is it. A nicely proportioned river landscape with fishermen. There's a lot of sky. Quite tricky, but I think I've captured it."

His flow was barely interrupted by Jane arriving home. Gone was her more bohemian look, and she was styled more like a businesswoman, with her hair up, and a plain blouse and a dark skirt. From the depths of her oversized handbag, she brought out a Victorian photograph album and a couple of ancient copies of Punch magazine. She laid them on the table and began stripping the sepia pictures from the album leaves and tearing the dividing sheets from the magazines.

"It seems like sacrilege," she sighed, "but the paper's old, so they're wonderful for doing paintings and sketches on. And I got these from my friendly printer..." She took out a few small labels with the names of various galleries printed in old-style type fonts. "The designs are copied from authentic old labels, but they'll need ageing of course."

"So Max, what delights did you bring?" asked Tom.

He gawped at my Battle of Trafalgar scene, shifting from side-to-side and rubbing his furry chin, before pronouncing, "Hmm, Clarkson Stanfield, not one of my favourites. But not bad, boy, not bad. Your cracking effect is pretty good, but I'll show you a better one - using bee glue. Maybe we could work out something between us, and see how it goes?"

"So which galleries do you normally sell through?" asked Jane.

"All over," I shrugged. "And auction houses."

Tom frowned, "Don't you find auction houses a bit snotty?"

"The snottier the better," I grinned.

We arranged to go together and take our two pictures to two separate, posh auctioneers in central London on the same day. As Tom drove us in his outdated and temperamental Hillman Minx to our first port of call, he seemed quite hot and shaky, and chain-smoked all the way. We decided that we would try and pass off his Vickers' river scene first. I had explained to him how Sam and I had successfully played the system as a pair of slightly gormless dealers who were supposedly father and son. However, I knew that the plan would only work as long as the staff didn't have a photographic memory of my old 'dad' and we didn't overplay the stupidity routine and arouse suspicion. I really didn't fancy another spell in nick, and I had no idea how Tom would have coped with the rations of rotten grub and slopping out a bucket of his own crap every morning!

"Just follow my lead," I told him, as he parked in a back street. "If I think they've got wind of us, I'll shake my head at you and we'll make our excuses and get out. Okay?"

Luckily, I had never seen the character at the reception desk before, and he greeted us most politely: "Good morning. And what is it that we'd like to sell today?"

As I handed over the small muddle of pictures, I spouted, "Oh, just some old smudges, sir. We picked up a job lot. Poor old bird passed away." Then to Tom, "Where was that big hass, dad?"

"Hmmm?" mumbled Tom, who seemed to be daydreaming and miles away.

I prompted, "The big hass, dad, where we picked up these paintin's. What was that place?"

"Erm, Suffolk I think, or was it Essex?" Tom pondered.

"Oh, Constable Country!" piped the estimator, raising a surprised eyebrow at us.

"That's right, sir," I quickly chipped in, before Tom could put his foot in it again. "But these ain't by Constable are they, sir?" I chuckled.

"No, no, no, hardly. But this one may possibly be by Alfred Vickers - Senior if I'm not mistaken," he advised. "Oh, and that's interesting, the verso has a sale sticker."

"Oh, is that good, sir?" I queried.

"It means that at some stage in its history, this painting has been sold by the gallery on the label," he imparted. Then, squinting, "The label is very badly faded, but it looks authentic. So would you like us to sell the picture for you?"

"Only if you can get a good price for it," grumbled Tom.

After the chap had satisfied Tom that his distinguished

organisation was up to the job, we went back to the car to fetch our next offering, my Clarkson Stanfield Battle of Trafalgar scene. It was well received by the auction house around the corner, and afterwards Tom was keen to cool down with a glass of vin rouge at a local wine bar.

"Ah! That's better," he gasped, taking a mighty glug of his medicine. "I really don't like all this yes-sir-no-sir-three-bags-full kind of kowtowing nonsense," he grumbled. "I certainly don't wanna sound like a bloody imbecile!"

"It's just an act," I shrugged. "And if brings in the cash, then who cares?"

He glowered at me, then drained his glass and called out across the bar, "Waitress! Two more glasses of Chateau Latour."

I was summoned to Tom's studio and asked whether I would like to try my hand at doing some touch-up work on his unfinished Hay Wain. It really wasn't the best piece of work and I don't think anyone would have believed that it could have been painted by Constable's gifted hand. It was sloppy and the detail was sadly lacking. However, I spent some time repainting the dodgy bits and, when I had finished, Tom actually muttered that it wasn't a bad job. I didn't know what his intentions were regarding the picture, whether he was really going to try and pass it off as a genuine article, but when I returned to the house one day it had gone.

"Come with me, boy, I'm gonna show you a secret," he announced, beckoning me to the kitchen with his smouldering dog-end. "This is how you age a picture. Watch and learn. See *this*, it's bee glue…" He unscrewed the lid of a broad jar and held it up to my face. "What d'ya reckon?"

"Bloody stinks!" I cursed, shrinking back from the dark-brown substance.

"Yeah, it does," he coughed. "But it's really 'ard. Fuckin' useless as it is. So what I do is…" He used a knife to scrape at it, and tipped the lumps and scratchings into a small saucepan until it was half full. "Give it a soft heat over a gentle flame for a few hours, and voila! More wine, boy? You're lookin' a bit empty."

We were in the studio all afternoon, retouching a few of Tom's unfinished works, when Jane came through and told us, "Your gloop's ready, and I've made us some supper."

I followed Tom as he toddled into the kitchen, then watched as he plunged a wooden spoon into the gently gurgling pan of mucilage. It ponged fiercely, like damp, mouldy leather.

"Beautiful," he sniffed, stirring the smooth, gummy paste round-and-round.

After our meal, we cleared the plates and bottles from the far-flung corners of the giant kitchen table, and laid out one of the larger Van de Velde (the Younger) oil paintings which I'd done.

"Go on, boy," Tom urged me, "slap it on."

I took the pot from the flickering stove and dipped in the soft, springy bristles of a varnishing brush. As I began slowly covering the ships and sea and sky with horrible slime, Tom was henpecking me to be bolder and splosh it all over. After a proper, stinky coating, I rinsed off the residue with warm water. Then later, as we carefully wafted the painting over Tom's faithful electric fire, the glue heated to a perfect temperature and began to sizzle and crackle out loud. Jane appeared with a Hoover, and we emptied a bagful of dust and fluff onto the surface and rubbed it in. To mask the awful, lingering smell, we sprinkled on talcum powder, before administering a final wash and dry. The result was amazing. The maze of tiny, dirt-encrusted fractures which were shattered across the picture could have led anyone to believe that the ravaged paintwork had been there for three centuries.

Tom held the painting up to the light and commented with a faint grin, "Get it back under glass and we've got ourselves a gooden there. Don't worry, I'll give you a fair price for it."

It was a few days later when Jane contacted the two auction houses about my Clarkson Stanfield and Tom's Alfred Vickers.

"Well, yours did okay," Tom sighed. "But mine must have had a bad turnout on the day, or a duff auctioneer or something."

Mine made £4,500 and his £1,750. I suspected that the

authenticity of his Vickers had been questioned, and Jane privately concurred. However, Tom did pay me a hundred quid for my work on the Hay Wain, although I never did find out where it went or how much he'd made.

"Can ya do pen-and-ink drawings, boy?" asked Tom.

I replied a few days later by delivering him a moonlit churchyard in the style of Samuel Palmer. He seemed to like it, and suggested that Jane could sell it and we would split the profits. Even though Tom was doing less-and-less, and I was doing more-and-more, it didn't bother me, as long as there was dosh in my pocket, grub in my belly, schmutter on my back, and a song in my heart.

We pottered off down the A24 with a stash of fresh paintings in the boot of Tom's quirky Hillman. He enjoyed our little jaunts into the countryside, and enjoyed them even more if they proved to be fruitful. The galleries in the sleepy rural towns were a far cry from the international auction houses of London, but the dealers were probably all-the-more-hungry as they had to swim in smaller ponds. And so, by presenting them with a mouth-watering delicacy, like a Samuel Palmer or a Cornelius Krieghoff, most of them just couldn't resist the temptation. Our usual modus operandi was to park up, take a picture each and set off for opposite ends of our chosen high street, then work our way along the galleries towards the middle. If one of us, or both of us, sold a painting for a tidy sum, then we would skedaddle to the next town before word had spread amongst the dealers. One minor masterpiece turning up on a small high street would be thought of as good fortune, but three or four would probably be considered as a miracle too farfetched to believe. And if the description of the sellers in each case happened to fit that of myself and Tom, then..!

As we arrived at the quaint little town of Arundel, I directed Tom towards the Castle at the top of the high street, but we ended up instead in a car park down towards the river at the bottom end. It didn't seem important, as most of the galleries were near the middle. Tom took out an oil painting of the French seaside in the style of Boudin, and I was going to try my luck with a winter coaching scene. We ambled towards our destination, stopping on the way to replenish our stocks of rolling tobacco and cigarette papers. As we puffed our way merrily up the street, we separated and I tagged along behind him at a safe distance. He stopped outside a likely-looking gallery and stared in through the window, before cutting me a glance and disappearing inside.

I looked at a couple of galleries down the street, chose one, and said to the owner, "Morning mate, I picked up a few pictures here-and-there, and I was wondering what you thought of this old beauty? It ain't signed, but… John Maggs, d'ya reckon?"

The dealer raised his wary eyebrows and examined it closely, before performing the usual rigmarole of umming and ahhing, and questioning the painting's authenticity. The glint in his eye told me that he didn't want to miss out, and when I took the picture and made for the door, he called me back and haggled with me until his offer was irresistible.

As I was leaving with a fat cheque in my hand, and a long shopping list in my head, I called back to him, "Cheers mate. See ya again sometime."

"Yes, yes," he snorted, "do come back if…"

I walked out of the door - and whack! I was knocked off my feet and found myself sprawled across the pavement with Tom on top of me. A man was running down the street towards us. Tom scrambled to his feet and ran, and I did likewise.

An angry voice yelled from up the street, "Oi! You bastard! Stop 'em!"

As we ran for our lives, I glanced back and saw that others were joining the chase.

"Quick! Get to the car!" I panted. Then, "Where's the fuckin' car? Tom! Where is it?"

"I dunno," he shrugged, coughing and gasping.

"Quick! Get in 'ere!" I snapped.

As we dived behind some bushes and ducked down, Tom leaned on me and wheezed, "Pills! I need me pills!"

"Shhh!" I whispered, "Just don't croak on me!"

I heard the wild posse go chasing by, pounding and puffing, cursing and swearing. We waited, not moving a muscle, until we were sure that the angry mob had withdrawn back up the street to their shops and galleries. However, we knew that the phone lines to the local cop-shop would be melting, and we were wanted men. When everything seemed calm, we broke cover and snuck around the streets in a desperate search for the elusive car park. But, even when we found it, I feared that somebody might just report seeing Father Christmas and an Edwardian gentleman fleeing town in an aged Hillman Minx! Driving off down the country lanes, with one eye constantly looking behind us, we finally came to rest and found sanctuary in a pleasant Surrey pub.

"Bloody idiot!" panted Tom, supping his wine. "He should never have taken it out of the frame! Idiot!"

Dealers would sometimes want to examine the raw painting without its shield of glass. Unfortunately, in this case, as the dealer was taking it out, a glob of wet paint smeared itself across the bottom corner of the glass, which wasn't the best look for a Boudin painting which was supposedly a hundred years old! Although Tom tried to argue with the guy that it had been recently restored, he was forced to abscond before the man beat him to a pulp.

"He was a big guy," insisted Tom.

"He looked old," I teased. "Definitely older than that picture."

When we got back to London, we didn't even risk trying to cash the cheques at the bank; we knew that they would have already been cancelled.

"But I bet they still sold our bloody pictures though," I told Tom.

Jane had made some good contacts in the art world and had been accepted in some quarters as a bona fide dealer. We'd make up a tale about where a fake picture had come from and how she had come to acquire it, and then she would fiddle a receipt or any paperwork to suit its imaginary provenance. Sometimes, in a second-hand shop or wherever, she would find an antique frame which still had a gallery's numbered sale-sticker on the back, but which was missing its original picture (it was obvious if it had been replaced at some time by an inferior modern work). Using her charm and nous, she would visit the said gallery and tell them that she was carrying out some innocent academic research, then persuade the staff to let her peruse their volumes of old sales records. Left alone to do her work, she would locate the entry which corresponded to the number on the sale-sticker in order to glean details about the original artist and the subject matter of the original picture. Then she would ask me to recreate the artist's original picture to fit her frame. Obviously, this was much more of a rigmarole than simply steaming off the sticker and using it on the back any old fake, but the overwhelming advantage was the fact that the picture and the frame looked totally authentic together, and could fool even the most rigorous research by an expert or busybody.

"You love it here, don't you?" Jane grinned, as we stood in the sunshine at my pitch on Portobello Road.

"Yeah, I do," I answered. And then to a curious punter who was eyeing up a primitive pig painting, "That's no ordinary pig, darlin', that's a two-hundred-year-old prize porker. Not only that, *that* picture used to be hangin' on the wall of Osborne House in the Isle of Wight. It was a great favourite of her majesty Queen Victoria. You can believe me, darlin', that's gospel that is."

"Wow! What type of pig is it?" asked the lady.

"It's a Gloucester Old Spot," I said. "And she called it Albert, on account of she loved him so much."

The lady gave me a tidy sum for the historic painting, slipped it into her bag and sauntered off as happy as Larry.

Jane chuckled, "You've really got the gift, haven't you, Max?"

"Just the way I was born," I shrugged.

Jane and I would hang out together. We had fun chats and I'm sure she enjoyed the company of a guy her own age. Our friendship didn't seem to bother Tom, who was getting more doddery and more tetchy; more angry about the dealers and the galleries and the world. And there were times when I would put a little spark into Jane's life, as well as providing her and Tom with a huge and steady supply of top-end fakes.

I mainly enjoyed doing lighter stuff, like Cash Coolidge's poker-playing dogs, and Louis Wain's crazy cats, and Samuel Palmer's woolly sheep, and Krieghoff's adventures of native life in Canada. But I wasn't averse to producing the heavier works, like the Turners, Constables, Rembrandts, Goyas, Gainsboroughs, Caravaggios… I'd turn out landscapes, seascapes, portraits, water-lilies, sunflowers or abstracts. To me, it was all art, and I was game.

"Best you stay away," Tom told me one day. "Jane can come and collect the pictures from you."

Reports had been circulating that somebody was investigating the authenticity of several Samuel Palmer pictures.

At my flat, Jane puffed on a cigarette, exhaled lustily and revealed, "Tom wants me to jet off to Tenerife with him."

"Are you going?" I asked.

"No," she sighed, with a wry smile, "opposite direction. I'm off to Canada. You know that I've…"

"Yeah, I understand," I said, and quipped, "You just can't resist Krieghoff!"

"If it was about painting Krieghoffs and Palmers, you know who I'd choose," she smiled. "But things could get rough around here, and the old man's up for a fight."

CHAPTER 9: FOREIGN AFFAIRS AND HOME TRUTHS

A guy walked down Portobello Road towards me and stopped to have a look at my pictures. "Love these old paintings, man," he grinned. "Are they real, or are they fakes?" He didn't look like undercover 'Old Bill'; he looked like a gypsy, and his hair was far too long, although he did have the height and gorilla-like build of a copper. I was quite wary, guessing that anyone, even a rozzer, could grow a bit of shaggy hair on top and wear cool clothes and string a few beads round their neck. He continued apologetically, "Sorry man, when I say fakes, I mean, are they like prints or photocopies or summat? They look really real, but ya never know these days." By this time he was chuckling, and I had a good feeling about him.

We went to the boozer when I'd finished for the day and got chatting. Bruno was a lot like me; he was a free-and-easy soul who liked to laugh a lot, who loved women, who played guitar and sang folk songs. That evening, I strayed down to Streatham and breezed into a buzzing pub where, through a fog of thick cigarette smoke and beer fumes, I watched him perform 'Streets of London' and a couple of songs by Wizz Jones, a great guitarist who I knew from the gigs in Cornwall, and 'Worried Man Blues' by Woody Guthrie.

In the cool evening air of Notting Hill Gate in late September, Bruno and I sat on the pavement and poured out a few of our favourite tunes, me joining in on guitar for my two showcase numbers, but otherwise just harmonising along with him. And as the army of fleeting feet began to wane, and the drizzle began to fall, I said to Bruno, "Come on, mate, let's hit the road."

"Bloody good idea," said Bruno. "How d'ya fancy Italy?"

"Do they have Orangina in Italy?" I asked.

Although I had only meant, "let's hit the road - and go to the caff for a bacon sarnie," a few days later we had passed through the port of Calais and found ourselves hurtling down the A1 autoroute in an articulated lorry. After gesticulating to a stubbly French lorry driver in the café on the ferry, he had kindly offered us a lift to somewhere, although it wasn't quite clear exactly where, and we didn't much care. As Bruno and I sat in his elevated cab, chatting and admiring the passing French landscapes, our chauffeur remained virtually mute and chain-smoked his way through a pack of Gauloises, before unexpectedly pulling up and dropping us off somewhere on a ring road outside Paris. However, for two young guys with large thumbs and guitars slung across their backs, it wasn't difficult to get lifts. There was a steady stream of lorries and vans, and even the odd, family car which stopped and squeezed us in, between pets, kids and elderly relatives.

I gazed in awe as we passed through the lush green, snow-peaked mountains of the Alps and arrived at the Mont Blanc Tunnel. As we drove through it, the thought that millions of tonnes of rock and ice were pressing down on us, right above our heads, sent a claustrophobic shiver down my spine. In ten minutes we shot out into blinding Italian sunshine and meandered our way towards Turin. Goat herds wandered aimlessly amongst warm, shallow-roofed chalets in the foreground, overshadowed by a background of freezing Alpine spikes. That night, lying on a straw-filled palliasse, I gazed up through the holey roof-trusses of an ancient barn and watched the drifting clouds give way to the brightest stars I'd ever seen. Come morning, I awoke to discover that Bruno had gone. I found him outside, lying unconscious on a hay bale and cuddling an empty Chianti flagon, with a swarm of fidgeting flies stuck to his face.

As I yelled at the angry insects and frightened them off, Bruno's swollen eyelids painfully parted, and he groaned blearily, "What's happening, man?"

"Pappataci, pappataci!" chortled the farmer, which I gleaned from my tiny Italian dictionary was their word for sand-flies.

His wife applied some lotion to the bites, shaking her head and frantically trying to explain to Bruno, who understood a bit of Italian, why it was a silly idea to sleep outdoors, even when it was too hot indoors. Over supper, the farmer invited us to stay on for as long as we liked, but by this time we were, understandably, itching to move on.

The next day we had been singing and playing in a bar, and as we sat devouring our wages of sausage pasta and carafes of wine, a stylish middle-aged gentleman approached us. By the squeeze and vigour of his handshake, he made it obvious that he had appreciated our impromptu performance. Although he only spoke in broken English, we conversed quite well and laughed a lot.

"Max e artista," explained Bruno, painting a pretend picture in the cigarette smoke which filled the air.

I dug in my bag and showed him a couple of sketches I'd made of Turin.

"Brilliante!" the man gasped, kissing his fingers. "Magnifico!"

Before we knew it, he had insisted on taking us to his beautiful home. His wife was attractive and English, and she interpreted as I recounted amusing tales of elephants and my youth. The afternoon drifted into the evening, until Bruno and I decided that it was time for us to find a bed for the night.

"No, no, no!" cried our new amico as we stood up to leave.

We were fed and watered and given luxurious king-size beds with goose-down pillows and mulberry silk sheets. In the morning, as we were about to leave, I spotted a monochrome photograph of two grass-stained footballers, grinning in baggy old-fashioned kits, obviously on opposing teams, but each with an arm slung around the other's shoulder.

"Ferenc Puskas?" I inquired, recognising the legend. Then, as I peered more closely, "And *you!*"

"Si, si, Puskas my friend. He Hungary, me Italy. He win, we lose," our host shrugged, but still with a beaming grin across his face.

It had been a great night, and as we left and I gave him the sketches of Turin, he hugged me and almost cried. He, too, was obviously a legend, although I didn't know his name.

Youth Hostels welcomed ex Barnardo's boys and we were never short of a bed for the night, even if the bunks were a bit short for Bruno's feet.

"Ay up, me duck," chirped a young female voice as we lay snoozing. "Alreet if we move in next door to ya?"

"Yeah, be our guests," I heard Bruno yawn.

I opened my eyes and stared down to see two bright-and-breezy backpackers unfurling their sleeping bags on the mattresses alongside us. They took their washbags and rushed out of the dorm, returning a few minutes later, fresh-faced and cool-breathed.

"I'm Angela," beamed the taller blonde one, before introducing the busty brunette, "and this is me mate Suzanna. We've come from Derby."

The next morning, we decided to move on to the port town of Genoa with the Derby duo and find a hostel together. Suzanna seemed to gravitate more towards me, and Angela seemed quite smitten with Bruno. However, neither Bruno nor myself had made any kind of serious advance towards either of them, although we'd chatted about the possibility.

During the heat of the day, when all the other travellers were off sightseeing, and our dorm was empty, Suzanna lay on her tummy on the top bunk and watched me drawing on my sketch pad. As she raised her chin, her curvaceous breasts flitted into view under her flowing top, and her peachy bum wiggled provocatively in the air.

"Bugger!" I cursed, and started furiously rubbing out all the pencil lines from my paper.

"What is it?" she gasped, quite concerned by my outburst.

"Ah, just this bloody sketch," I grumbled. "I can't get it right."

She looked worried and I sighed, "It's a portrait of Nell Gwynne. I promised to do it for a famous London restaurant, but I'm just not getting her shape right. It's so bloody difficult when you ain't got a model."

After a moment, she ventured, slightly nervously, "I don't s'pose I could 'elp could I? I'm no model, but…"

"Yeah, actually you look just like her," I smiled. "Hop down and stand over there for us, would ya?" She took my instructions and posed perfectly, and then I directed, "Could ya just loosen yer top around yer shoulders for us? That's it, pull it down a bit lower. Yeah, if ya could slip it down so that…"

"Would it be easier if I just took me top off?" she grinned.

"If ya wouldn't mind," I shrugged. "And if it's no bovver, maybe you could take off yer bra? That's it, hold yer boobs up a bit. It's alright, no-one'll recognise ya. It's just so I can define the proper shape of the female form, that's all." I doodled a bit, and did noughts-and-crosses, enjoying the view, before declaring a while later, "That's it, all done."

"Can I see it?" she urged, eager and excited.

"Oh, sorry," I sighed, "it's only the preliminary sketch, and us artists always say it's really bad luck for a sitter to see an unfinished picture. It's a tradition."

Despite the obvious obstacles which our bunk beds presented, and the fact that we were living in a communal dormitory, Suzanna and I enjoyed a couple of weeks of hot passion, as did Angela and Bruno.

And when they were leaving the hostel to hitch back to Blighty, Suzanna hugged me tightly and giggled, "Ooh, I'm so excited! I can't wait to move down London and see me picture in Nell Gwynne's restaurant! You'll call me, won't ya, Max?"

"The second we get back from India," I assured her.

Bruno shot a stunned glance at me. We kissed the girls and said "arrivederci" on the doorstep, and waved at them as they disappeared across the cobbled piazza.

"India!" chuckled Bruno, as we strolled out for fried eggs and espresso.

"Well, I 'ad to tell 'er summit, didn't I?" I smiled.

I found some sheets of old hardboard dumped on the side of the strada. I cut them into rectangles, painted a load of colourful, miniature caricatures, and flogged them to the tourists.

As a punter reeled off a pile of 500 Lire notes into my sweaty palm, I counted, "Thirteen thousand... fourteen thousand... fifteen thousand. Molte grazie, mate."

"Fifteen grand a picture," praised Bruno. "Can't be bad."

"So how much is that then?" I asked.

"About a fiver. Or is it a tenner?" shrugged Bruno.

"It's like bloody Monopoly money!" I laughed.

Bruno made a few bob performing in bars, we mingled with the locals at the galleries and gelaterias, and busked around the streets. But when the biting rain hit Genoa, I was ready to get back to the comfort of my cosy flat in Cricklewood. I'd got the place through a contact in Portobello, and the Irish couple who owned it were happy to let me go back when I returned from my travels. Bruno's landlord wasn't quite so accommodating and so he dossed down on my couch. He showed me how to do some simple sculpting and how to play better guitar, then shot off to Cornwall to do some gigs and poetry readings. He stayed at 'The Cottage', a venue I knew well, and a favourite haunt of songsters like Ralph McTell, Pete Stanley, Wizz Jones, Martin Carthy, Noel Murphy, and John the Fish. I carried on as usual, drawing and painting, selling my work at Portobello, and conning the highfalutin mugs at the auction houses and galleries.

"D'ya know, I've been thinking," Bruno mused, on the night he returned, "I reckon we *should* go to India."

I knew it was a long flight but, unlike Bruno, I wasn't much of an international traveller.

"I'll sit by the gangway," I told him, as we boarded the plane, wringing my clammy mitts and listening to my pounding heartbeat.

"Why? Where ya gonna run to?" he tittered. "Don't worry, just relax, get pissed, have a smoke and turn the headphones up full blast."

Some hours later, I hobbled stiffly into the airport terminal at Delhi. We navigated our way out through the sweating masses to the exit and onto the concourse outside. It was sweltering and seething and smelly. A deranged army of antiquated black-and-yellow taxis fought for position, cutting each other up and blasting their horns. As we sat in the back of one, bumping and rattling through the dusty potholes on the main road to the city, our grinning driver told us through his set of gleaming gnashers that he would take us to the best hotel, and also chauffeur us around for the duration of our stay. "I vill come back and collect you for guided tour at two P-M," he beamed. And as the swanky concierge moved him on, we ran round the corner and found a cheap hostel.

Mothers with flocks of children sat on the dirty verges where they lived, desperately holding out their malnourished fingers and pleading for pennies. Some of the kids had truncated limbs and many were sick. Sacred cows wandered, shitting on the pavements, and peasants washed themselves and their clothes in the river, as others crapped and pissed in it. Men and women grunted and spat thick phlegm all over the pavement, and some just squatted wherever they happened to be and did their toilet. The fiery stench of smoke and curry soaked into my muggy clothes and skin, and the air was hot to the touch. I got a dose of Delhi Belly and lay writhing on a lumpy bed, sweating and freezing, puking and pooing, until eventually I was resurrected.

We visited the manic train station and discovered a giant and confusing queue in the booking hall, and a system which required a dozen or more railway officials to issue one ticket. On the platform, we could see that the carriages to Mumbai (Bombay) were packed tightly with humans who were standing, sitting and crouching inside. Outside the carriages, they were hanging off the ledges, doors and roof. It would have taken us twenty-four hours by rail, but instead it took us just two by plane.

Mumbai (Bombay) was sweltering and seething. However, like Brighton, at least it did have a cooling sea breeze. Otherwise, it was pretty much the same as Delhi, dilapidated and desperate. We were propositioned by packs of hefty 'ladies' who swaggered along the promenade, coyly shielding their faces and trying to touch us up. And in the steamy backstreet markets, females peered out at us from behind the bars of their gloomy cages. There were rows-and-rows of them, some of them children, some of them withered women. Certainly there was nothing of interest for me there, and I departed feeling somewhat deflated and a couple of stone lighter.

Bruno's parents lived near Petersfield in Hampshire, and when I went down to visit him, I was quite impressed. His dad was a seed merchant and vegetable wholesaler. From what I could see, judging by the cars and the big detached house, it must have been a pretty lucrative enterprise. However, the business end wasn't so pretty, and Bruno and I helped out by sorting thousands of loose potatoes into sacks. We had never argued and never got on each other's nerves. We weren't moaners or fighters. But we were a formidable duo: Maximillian and Bruno. There were a few gigs in the area, and we played and sang together, and painted, sculpted and socialised. Bruno was doing a bit of recording, but wanted to do more. He went off to see some guys he knew who had just set up their own studio, and I headed back to London.

It had been quite some time since I had seen Tom Keating and Jane Kelly. When I saw them again, they were standing in the dock in court number 1 of the Old Bailey. I looked down from the public gallery and Jane's eye caught mine. She had been publicly brought back to the U.K. in handcuffs and wasn't her old self. Tom was haggard and wheezing, but was seemingly happy to have his day in court. He'd hired the best barrister in the business, Jeremy Hutchinson QC, who'd previously defended the likes of Christine Keeler, George Blake and one of the Great Train Robbers. Tom didn't seem the slightest bit daunted by the event. He had pleaded innocent and sat casually drawing sketches, presumably in a gesture of two fingers to the judge, the prosecution briefs and the establishment. Jane had pleaded guilty.

She looked less relaxed, although I guess she was hoping they'd be more lenient with her because of her confession. At the end of the day's business, there was a bit of a bun fight outside the court; photographers and journalists jostled to stick their cameras and microphones up Tom and Jane's noses. I stood back out of the line-of-fire. I didn't think I had anything to worry about because neither Tom nor Jane had any reason to shop me, and they didn't have any solid evidence anyway; it would have been their word against mine as to who had painted what. However, I was always aware that a hand could feel my collar at any moment.

I visited Jane at her hotel, and she flew back to Canada with a slap on the wrist from the judge. Tom went to hospital; the judge had taken pity on him and had let him off on the grounds of ill health. Although he wasn't supposed to survive, he did somehow manage to toddle away from death's door.

Shepherd's Bush had more than its fair-share of car dealers and scrap merchants, some of them could have been the model for Arthur Daley, and some for Harold Steptoe. When I saw a gleaming mint-condition MG on a lot one day, I couldn't resist it. It was the GT fastback model with a tan leather interior and light walnut dashboard, and its bodywork was emblazoned with startling sunburst-yellow paintwork. She was quite individual and striking. The guy selling it was an Irish scrap dealer, tough as old boots and as rough as nails. However, he had a soft spot for horses and horse racing, and his favourite racehorse of all time was the legendary Arkle which, in the mid-sixties, had won nearly all its races, including the Cheltenham Gold Cup three years in a row, two Hennessy Gold Cups, the King George V1 Chase, the Irish Grand National, and many, many more. I produced an action painting of the beautiful bay, ridden by Pat Taaffe, as it led over a fence in the 1966 Gold Cup, and the motor was mine. It was a stunning-looking car; a real eye-catcher.

"Couldn't give me a lift could you, old boy?" Tom asked me. "I've not really been driving since…" Then, smirking like the cat who'd got the cream, "It's just they're keen that I should do my own T-V show you see. I'll be explaining how the great painters created their work. It'll be an education for you."

At the television studio, I sat in the background as Tom was dressed and titivated until he assumed the very image of respectability and sobriety. There was a lot of fuss over him, and a production lady requested, "I know that you take on the actual spirit of the artist while you're painting, so could we see some of that please?"

He went out to do his piece, and as the cameras rolled and he started to splash some paints around, he went into a sort of trance, and started making faint grunting and groaning noises. I thought it was all odd, and afterwards I told him that he looked as if he was about to have an orgasm. "So when you're telling the audience that you know what an artist is thinking… Well how do you know that?" I challenged. "You don't really know why an artist has used this brush or that brush, or why they've used this colour or that colour, or what's going on in their head, do you?"

"It's all about a higher plane of consciousness," he replied.

"A higher level of bullshit!" I said.

It wasn't the first philosophical discussion we'd ever had, but it was one of the last.

I was doing some legit paintings for a couple of galleries whose clientele liked classic reproductions on modern canvases, of stuff like Botticelli's Birth of Venus, Monet's Poppies in a Field, Vermeer's Girl With a Pearl Earring, Turner's Fighting Temeraire, the Mona Lisa, the Hay Wain and all the others. However, it was a bit tedious and I wasn't exactly living what I would've called the high life, so I did occasionally slip back into my bad old ways and hit the auction houses with some of my Louis Wains and Cash Coolidges etc.

The scrap dealer who sold me the MG had mentioned at the time that he'd like me to do some more racing pictures for him, and so I thought I'd drop in on him and see what was doing. Pulling up in his yard, there was a lot of activity, cars and vans and people milling around all over the place. As I got out of the car, a large and partially mummified figure shuffled stiffly towards me, its arms held aloft at chest-height by steel rods which were attached to the wrists at one end and to a waist-belt at the other.

"Y'alright, Maxie?" emanated a familiar but muffled Irish voice through a slit in the head-bandage. "Is the car goin' alright?"

"Yeah, fine," I answered. "What's with the..?"

"Ah, I got blasted with a sawn-off shotgun at point-blank range," he grumbled, his eyes rolling around behind their peep-holes. "They say I'm lucky to be alive."

"Bloody 'ell!" I gasped. "Who was it? Why d' they do it?"

"Ah, you make plenty of enemies in this business," he dribbled. Then groaning and flinching, "Sorry Max, I think I'd better go and have a wee lie down for a minute."

As he tottered off towards his Portakabin, and I was about to get back in the car, a woman suddenly grabbed my arm. I swung round and was confronted by the sight of a couple of coppers lurking nearby.

"You're a bit late," the woman complained brusquely. "Anyway, you'd better come with me."

"Another time perhaps," I told her, shrinking back towards my motor, with my keys at the ready.

"We're shooting in five minutes!" she exclaimed huffily.

"Shooting!" I spluttered.

"Yes," she said. "And you've got to have your costume and make-up done." Then, glancing quickly at her clipboard, she demanded sternly, "You *are* an actor, aren't you?"

After the confusion had been cleared up, and the real actor had arrived, the lady invited me to stay and watch them filming a reconstruction of the shotgun shooting for their true-life crime show on the telly. I did see the programme, and reckoned that I could have done a better job than the actor who turned up to play the part of the crook. It was obviously a case of attempted murder, maybe connected to drugs, or money, although I never did find out.

Although I wasn't a great one for watching TV, I did enjoy the

Antiques Roadshow and had to chuckle when I saw a bloke whip out one of my primitive pig paintings and ask the expert if it was real. "It certainly looks like it," said the specialist, "but one can't be too sure." I can, I thought.

The next time somebody felt my collar, it was, unfortunately for me, the real thing. Pugglesham and Fitchman had been on my case for a long time and had evidence that I'd 'Obtained money under false pretences'. They were actually quite pleasant guys and, although we were on different sides of the fence, we got on pretty well. I was straight with them, and them with me, and they saw to it that I was granted bail, pending trial. I hired a high-profile barrister from Brighton to defend me. Keith was known for being a bit iffy and a bit slippery, although he came across as a charming and respectable English gentleman. He was just the type of chap I needed to fight my corner. His fees were exorbitant, although he was happy to accept a dodgy picture in lieu of cash, which suited me perfectly.

"Max, you've got nothing to worry about," purred Keith, his persuasive tone as smooth as the cool Chardonnay which was lubricating his vocal cords. "Relax, we'll have you out in time for lunch. Just relax."

We were in the posh lounge bar of the White Hart Hotel, directly across the road from Lewes Crown Court. The clock was ticking and I sank another glass for a bit of Dutch Courage, before I had to face the music.

"Well, we had better get going. Don't want to keep the judge waiting," advocated my advocate.

"Here barman, can you keep that on ice for us?" I requested, chuckling as I handed him our half-full bottle. "We'll be back to finish that in a bit."

"That's the spirit," smiled Keith, slapping me manfully on the back.

As I stood enclosed within the tiny confines of the dock, I glanced across at Keith. He looked 'the business' in his wig and gown, shuffling a thick wad of papers about and discreetly issuing orders to his minions. I just wanted it to be over with, and to pay my fine, and to finish my wine, and to visit my mum, and for her to never find out about it. It didn't seem too much to ask. The charges were read out, alleging that I had profited by deceiving a gallery owner into believing that my work was something which it wasn't, which was obviously true, and I was asked how I would plead.

"Guilty, Your Honour," I stated, staring innocently into the eyes of the avuncular gentleman.

Keith earnestly assured him that I was truly sorry, and that I had never intentionally gone out to pull the wool over anyone's eyes, and that I was suffering from a heart condition which needed ongoing medical treatment. Nevertheless, the old bugger-of-a-judge still said he was going to send me down. "Mister Brandrett," he sighed, "I do not see you as a malicious criminal, but why-oh-why do you continue to use your God-given talent in this way?"

"I just can't help myself, Your Honour," I told him. "I dunno what it is, but I just see the work of a great artist, and suddenly I'm standing there with a paintbrush in me hand, and a beautiful old canvas on me easel, and I get the shakes, and I just can't help myself, and I find myself havin' to copy it. It's like an addiction, Your Honour."

"Very well," he sighed. "I sentence you to a term of six months imprisonment. Take him down."

I glanced over at Keith and he shrugged, and I knew that *I*, at least, would never see that bottle of Chardonnay again.

Winchester prison was totally unremarkable; just hundreds of blokes locked in squalid cells and vowing that when their sentences were served, they'd never return. I managed to soft-soap the prison governor and pull off what was becoming an all-too-frequent arrangement whereby I was allowed to have my own private cell and access to art equipment.

"Just as long as you're not thinking of painting one of your fakes during your stay, Brandrett," the governor warned me, with a headmasterly wag of his seasoned finger.

"Of course not, sir," I assured him. "As if!"

I was in my 'studio' one rainy afternoon when the governor and a screw breezed in on an impromptu tour, just as I was finishing off on an old horseracing scene. The pair gawped over my shoulder as I coolly added some final touches.

"Excellent Brandrett, really excellent," praised the governor. "Not a George Stubbs copy I hope?"

"Definitely not, sir," I assured him. "It's more of an Alfred Munnings, sir. In the style of Alfred Munnings, sir. Obviously not a copy, sir. It's on a new canvas and it'll be signed in my own fair hand, sir. Oh yes, it's all above board, sir."

But not everything was above board. A girlfriend and I had devised a system whereby she would go to libraries and razor out the blank flyleaves from old books and magazines, and smuggle them into me, rolled up inside the arm of her coat. She'd go through the prison x-ray machine and past the sniffer dogs and, as we held hands across the desk, I would slide them out and slip them up the sleeve of my own jacket. It worked a treat, every time. And we would smuggle out my finished pictures in the same way, but in reverse. The antique sheets of paper were ideal for doing pen-and-ink drawings, and I did mainly Samuel Palmer's. They were like an insurance policy for me; a policy which would mature on completion of my term in the nick.

"I've painted one or two pictures for the warders, sir," I told the governor. "Portraits of loved-ones, wives, children, pets... Is there anything I could do for you, sir?"

"You could paint the mallard for me if you like," he suggested.

"Oh, well that's different. A beloved pet is it, sir?" I queried.

"No Brandrett," he sighed, "it's a train."

He hung the speeding blue locomotive in pride of place on his office wall. As he was wishing me farewell on my final morning, he told me once again how much he loved it, and warned me once again to stay out of trouble.

"Don't worry, sir," I said, "from now on I definitely won't be havin' any dealings with the law. You have my solemn word on that."

He smiled and I was led out of his office and out through the prison gates to freedom. The taste of liberty was as wonderful as ever, and I shut my eyes and felt the sun's warm rays on my face, and inhaled deeply.

"Max, I 'ope you don't mind us dropping by, but we'd like a word," a copper's sarcastic tone announced.

It was 8 o'clock in the morning, and when I opened my eyes, Pugglesham and Fitchman were poised with their handcuffs. I went quietly and they whisked me away for questioning about a number of suspected fakes which were under investigation.

"Not guilty," I insisted indignantly again-and-again as they interviewed me. "It definitely weren't me."

They turned off the tapes, and Pugglesham said, "Sorry about doorsteppin' you at the prison, Max, but we've been told to improve our clear-up rate."

"Oh well, it doesn't matter," sighed Fitchman. "Now Keatin's brown bread, we'll just put these down to 'im, like all the others."

"D'ya wanna lift anywhere, Max?" offered Pugglesham. "I'll get one of the plods to drop you off if ya like."

I got back onto the rollercoaster of life, riding up front and ready to face whatever thrills-and-spills came my way. I carried on selling a few pictures here-and-there, and dropped in regularly on my mum with bits of cash and gifts. She was living in a basement flat, and when I dropped in one day, my sister and her kids were there. We suddenly heard a disturbance outside; the din of a crazy man yelling, his voice rising louder as he hobbled slowly down the front steps. We all knew the voice. It was my sister's one-legged ex-partner, and the father of her children. My titchy mum pushed us out of the way, grabbed a large leg-of-mutton which was lying on the kitchen table and charged down the hallway to the front door.

"Ya take one more step and I'll crown thee, ya bastard!" she shrieked, swiping her bloody shank at the giant oaf and cracking him hard across his solitary shin. He toppled and fell like a giant sack of spuds, then shuffled, cowering, on his backside up the steps, with my mum shouting after him, "Come back and thee'll get it across ya thick skull! Now thee leave 'er alone - or else!" She returned to her boiling kettle and smiled, "Sit down, Max, and we'll 'ave us a nice brew."

"I reckon he was hopping mad that you hit him, mum," I grinned.

"If I'd crowned him proper, son, you'd be eatin' murder weapon for yer tea!" she quipped.

Outside Al Duomo, *the* restaurant to be seen at in Brighton, there was a fantastic and oddball car for sale. I didn't really know what it was, but it looked like a cross between a classic old British sports car and a gangster's getaway car. It was a low, open-top two-seater, long-nosed, with old style mudguards and big round headlamps, and sleek bodylines which gleamed in a tasty cream colour. It had no doors, and getting aboard entailed stepping up onto the running boards and clambering through the windows to squeeze into its leather-and-walnut cockpit. Getting out also required a measure of elasticity. It was curious and fanciful, daring and flamboyant. It was called a Madison Roadster, and I knew that it was the car for me. It belonged to Antonio, the restaurant's art-collecting owner, and he was prepared to part with it for the princely sum of three paintings. But also, as part of the deal, he agreed that I could have free meals for life.

A few weeks later, I rolled up outside the restaurant, accompanied by a glamorous and supple young lady. Fifty hopeful diners who were queuing outside watched in awe as we elegantly limboed out through the Madison's windows. I took my companion's diamond-glistening hand and, looking like film stars, we casually sashayed past the general public to the front of the line.

"Yeah?" grunted the doorman.

"I'm Max Brandrett, the artist," I announced.

"Yeah?" grunted the doorman.

"I have a special arrangement, free meals for life," I announced. "Ask Antonio."

"Antonio's dead," grunted the doorman. "So you can fuck off to the back of the queue!"

It was a crying shame; Antonio had died suddenly on holiday in Spain. He was a nice guy, and fairly young, and it totally buggered-up his promise of "Free meals for life."

Over the years, I'd always wanted to know about my dad. Unsurprisingly, the few words which my mum had uttered about him usually contained the phrase "useless bastard" and I could understand that. I had a hazy childhood memory, or a dream, that he was standing beneath a flickering lamppost by our house, his cigarette smoke gently wafting in the breeze as he gazed in through my bedroom window. But when I looked back, he had gone. I thought that he had been looking for me, or perhaps waiting for me. My mum had given him the 'Spanish Archer' (El Bow) for his intolerable behaviour towards her, but I wondered if, maybe, he had wanted to get back with her? Because he wasn't the other half of the equation in co-creating my brothers and my sister, I couldn't expect them to help me find out about the man, or his fate. But, however curious I was, it was crucial that I didn't upset my wonderful mum. Yet, more than ever, I wanted to find my dad, to meet him and talk to him. All I knew was that his name was Joe Brandrett, and apparently, he was a horseracing tipster, and probably a bit of a hustler. The Salvation Army offered a service to help inquisitive souls like myself to find lost relatives. And find him they *did*.

"You're the spit of 'im!" beamed my older cousin Jimmy when I met him in Manchester. "A chip off the old block!" We sat in a backstreet café and drank stewed tea and ate sweet Eccles cakes, as he told me all about my dad: "He dressed dead smart. Wore a flash coat with a velvet collar, just like your'n. And 'e spoke nice. Always at the gee-gees, sellin' his tips, at Aintree, Cheltenham, all of 'em. He was a great tipster and 'e knew all the top jockeys, Gordon Richards, Greville Starkey, Lester Piggot, and that crazy tipster Prince Monolulu."

"I gotta horse!" I chuckled, mimicking the famous Abyssinian tribal chief.

"Top man your dad," sighed Jimmy. "Classy, a real gent."

Jimmy took me to the house where my dad had been living. Apparently, he had lodged with the landlady for several years, although Jimmy didn't know if they were connected romantically. But he had died of a heart attack, and I was sad that I would never be able to meet him or show him my paintings. I gave Jimmy a couple of horseracing pictures and he was gobsmacked.

"This is Joe's boy," Jimmy proudly announced to the cloth-capped regulars who were shoving ha'pennies and toppling skittles as they swilled their mucky pints. "Here, get that down yer throat," my cousin beamed, handing me a glass of the same.

"Was my dad a bit of fighter?" I asked him, reluctant to taste the bitter ale.

"There were times 'e struggled to make a crust," shrugged Jimmy. "Always duckin' and divin', but 'e was never a quitter."

I ventured, "What I meant, Jimmy, was whether he was handy with his fists? You know, if he got the hump with someone, or got drunk, would he thump 'em?"

"Joe! No, no, no! Not Joe!" he rebutted soundly. "He 'ardly touched a drop and 'e always used that silver tongue of 'is to get 'im outta scrapes. He might've got into a scuffle with a drunken punter or two, but he'd never lash out, not ever, not Joe." Then, raising his glass, he toasted, "To yer dad," then necked it in one, and slurped, "Your round, our kid."

I felt as if a guilty weight had been lifted from my shoulders. My dad might well have been a bit of a scoundrel, a waster, a philanderer, a Jack-the-Lad, a silver-tongued spiv, an absent father, but he wasn't a drunk or a wife beater. And he was a well-respected man who was liked and who had talents, and who made his own way in the world as best he could with the hand he was dealt.

Driving across from Lancashire to Yorkshire, I went off in search of Guisborough, the hometown of my mother, and a place where she had told me we still had relatives. It seemed like such a remote place, stuck way up at the top end of the North York Moors, where the only visible signs of life were heather and sheep. It was easy to understand why my mum had chosen to move to the hustle-and-bustle of Brighton. However, I found that the tiny town of Guisborough itself was quite quaint and picturesque, and as I drove through it to find my uncle's pub, I spotted a couple of promising-looking galleries. My Uncle Bob was the landlord of the Red Lion, across the road from the towering ruins of the medieval priory.

"Ee, come in, lad," he greeted, looking down at me from behind the bar. "I expect thee'll be gaggin' for a decent pint of ale."

"Actually, I drink wine," I told him, trying to ignore his surprising lankiness.

"Wine!" he shrieked. Then, to the collection of bushy-eared farmers at the bar, "Ya can tell he's not a bloody Yorkshireman!"

"Ee, get off with ya, ya daft bugger!" I grumbled. "I'm as Yorkshire as ye and thee!"

The next day I thought I would chance my arm and, adopting the guise of a gormless southern antique dealer, I managed to get the wily Yorkshire gallery owners to pay a champion price for a couple of ambiguous shipping scenes and a Louis Wain.

My uncle, too, was a wily old devil, and I asked him how he had come to buy a public house from the proceeds of my grandfather's will, when my mum had received nout.

"She'll get 'ers presently," he replied, quickly dismissing the subject.

I presumed that the family had once been quite well-heeled, having owned the local smithy and a couple of shops which supplied boots and shoes to families throughout the entire area. Anyway, I thought, at least I was taking back a bit of 'brass' from Guisborough for my mum.

CHAPTER 10:
CHAMPIONS AND CHOPPERS

"Would you consider donating a painting?" I was asked by Toby, a Brighton businessman and patron of the Variety Club of Great Britain. "It's for sick and underprivileged kiddie…"

"I'll do it. You can 'ave that one if you like," I told him, indicating the oil painting which he happened to be holding up in his outstretched arms.

"Blimey Max!" he gasped. "I was only looking at it, I didn't mean..!"

Arriving at the gala dinner and auction at Brighton's Metropole Hotel, I wandered through the glitzy foyer and spotted a flock of penguin-suited gents and chic ladies fluttering eagerly around my picture of the majestic, classic-winning racehorse Dancing Brave. Among the smiling faces, I instantly recognized Vera Lynn, Dora Bryan and Jimmy Hill.

"Max!" rang out a cheery voice above the chit-chat and giggles. I turned to see Toby breezing towards me with a large, bearded character. "I want you to meet our chairman, Mike Mendoza."

"Thanks a million for your donation to our auction," beamed Mike, shaking me earnestly by the hand.

"Let's hope it makes a million," I quipped.

"Well, whatever it makes, we're truly grateful," he said, before darting off to greet another wave of celebrity guests.

"And of course," said Toby, batting away a party balloon, "you get to go and have dinner with the winning bidder. And what with phone bids, that could be anywhere."

"Like where?" I asked.

"Anywhere," grinned Toby.

I was shown into the sparkling ballroom. Thirty or forty large circular tables, each accommodating parties of ten glittering guests, were laid with immaculately pressed white tablecloths, rows of crystal glasses and precision ranks of silver-plated cutlery. As I was ushered to mine, a bloke I had crossed paths with before, a sculptor, stared up at me and sneered, "I don't think you're meant to be sitting here, old chap."

"Funny, my name's on the card for this seat. But I guess reading's not one of your strong points, is it, *old chap*?" I grinned, sending his companions into titters of laughter.

"Hey Max! Max! Over 'ere!" I heard a friendly voice from the past shouting from a nearby table.

Harry Fowler M.B.E. was a cheeky chappie from South London who had acted in scores of films over the years, and who had a face which most people knew, even if they couldn't always put a name to it. He was enthusiastically beckoning me over and shuffling his party around to make a space for me at his table. Even before I'd settled, he was boasting to his pals that I was the world's greatest artist, but the world's worst driver.

"Me and Max met in Mallorca a few years back," he explained to his gang. "We 'ad a brilliant bloody 'oliday! Your mate still around is 'e, Max?"

"No," I sighed, "I haven't seen Sam Cohen for donkey's years - unfortunately. I never did find out what happened to 'im."

"Bloody good bloke," chuckled Harry.

"Yeah, he was the best," I said.

"D'ya remember, at first I fought 'e was your bleedin' dad!" roared Harry.

"Yeah, I remember," I smiled.

And as Harry recounted some tales to his fellow diners, I remembered my Mallorcan holiday with Sam. It was one of many great times we'd had together, always laughing and larking about. Even at the airport, and on the plane, we played out our silly father-and-son routine, with me asking him in a soppy voice as the stewardess was pouring us our drinks, "Daaaad, how much is a patater werf in English money, daaaad?" The poor girl's hands were trembling so much that she spilt the wine all over us. Our holiday came courtesy of Bonhams' affluent clientele, and we arrived with flash suits and bulging wallets. It was boiling hot and we stayed in five-star luxury and splashed out on the finest food and drink, and spent most of our time lounging on the beach and swimming, or cruising around the island in hired convertibles and speedboats.

"So we'd spent the 'ole night in this bar, pissed as farts," Harry was recounting, "and Max and Sam say they wanna go for a drive on the beach in these two open-top jeeps what they've 'ired. So it's the middle of the night, I look out me bedroom winda and see 'em racing each other rand and rand, and then whoosh, they drive flat-out, straight into the fuckin' sea! There's an almighty great splash and then nuffin. Then suddenly, I see these two emerge like a pair o' wet kippers and leg it up the beach! It was a right laugh!"

After a sumptuous supper, the audience applauded the man with the cheeky grin who stepped out onto the stage. "Good evening, my lords, ladies and gentleman," his voice echoed through the P.A. system. "Welcome to this Variety Club charity gala night in sunny Brighton, even though it's dark and it's raining. I'll be your M-C and auctioneer this evening, and if you don't like it, you know what you can do! For those of you who've been asleep for the past fifty years, my name is Norman Vaughan." To which there was rapturous applause. Then, much later, after music and entertainment and a number of auction lots had gone under the hammer: "Now we come to the grand finale of our wonderful auction, a fine horseracing painting which has been very kindly donated by the brilliant local artist, Mister Max Brandrett. Where are you, Max?" A spotlight searched the table where I should have been sitting. "Is he hiding? They always say artists are very shady, and a bit sketchy. Boom-boom!"

"He's over here," yelled my old mate Chris Ellison, whose table I had joined for a drink.

Not hearing him, Norman continued, "Anyway, what am I bid for this wonderful, original painting by Max Brandrett? One thousand pounds from the lady at the front…" And after a frenzy of activity: "…I've got a bid of five-thousand-three-hundred pounds from our mystery phone bidder in sunny California, where I've been told it really *is* sunny. Any more bids in the room?"

There was silence, and Chris nudged me and grinned, "Looks like you'll be havin' dinner in L-A then, mate."

"Any more bids?" prompted Norman. He scanned the hall, then suddenly there was a bit of a commotion at the back of the room, and he asked, "Is that another bid, sir? Six-thousand pounds? Wonderful! Sold!"

"You can forget California, Max," grumbled Chris, "that geezer lives in Hove. Hangleton Road if my memory serves me correctly."

At the end of the night, Chris's raffle ticket came up and he won the star prize: a big colour telly.

"Ain't yer gonna put yer ticket back in the pot?" I asked him.

"Am I f'!" he exclaimed. And I helped him carry it out at the end of the evening and load it into the boot of his mate's Rolls Royce.

"Sorry you missed out on L-A, Max. But thank you," said Toby.

"You're welcome," I said. "Just let me know if you want any more paintings."

That night I lay on the bed and listened to the spiteful rain lashing across the rotten windows of my bedsit. The lightbulb flickered and I wondered how many coins might be hiding in the cash box of the electric meter. As I nibbled on a stone-cold chicken leg, a floating party balloon kept tapping annoyingly on the ceiling, agitated by the hissing breeze. I stared at the pale ceiling and thought about the posh nosh which I might have got to eat in L.A., and the free, sun-drenched vacation which I had missed out on. "Six thousand pounds," I slowly repeated to myself. "Six thousand bloody pounds!" I roared. Then I burst out laughing until the velvet seams of my tailored trousers almost split open. I was a kid from a basement in Buckingham Road, with no shoes and just Weetabix-and-water for my tea, and my life was great.

I had obviously inherited my dad's passion for the turf, and my horseracing pictures were always in demand, although there was, as always, a limit to how much I could earn by painting Max Brandrett one-off originals. On occasions, I had turned out pictures for commercial studios and knew that there was a healthy trade in selling limited-edition prints. I splashed out on a few hundred reproductions of my paintings and hired an enterprising couple to hoof them around the country's racecourses in their van. On race days, they would set up my market stall and keep it stocked-up, whilst I did most of the selling. Somewhere amongst the purveyors of caps, canes, hats, hipflasks, wellies, wallets, pots, pans, pottery, jumpers, jackets, jewellery, antiques, wet fish and raw meat, you'd find me buttering up the punters and persuading them that their living rooms needed a Max Brandrett racing picture hanging on the wall. Mainly I would sell numbered prints, signed by myself, although I would always offer a few originals to the toffs and yuppies with deeper pockets.

I used to have a trade stand at all the main meetings, including the Grand National. The crowds at Aintree were especially lively in comparison to Epsom or Ascot, Newmarket or Cheltenham, and there were always a few Scallies about who wanted to blag or bully the traders into giving them a knockdown deal, or who just brazenly tried to stuff things like framed paintings up their jumpers and leg it.

It was a busy day, and business was good, when a local fella came up and chirped, "Oi mate, I want that piccy of Red Rum. And I mean the real paintin', not one o' them bloody copies."

"That's two-thousand quid to you, sir," I informed him.

"No way!" he choked. "Listen, I bet yer love a bitta meat don't yer? How d'ya fancy free chicken-breasts, jumbo-sized bangers, juicy beefsteak, pork-chops, liver-an'-bacon? Have whatever yer want, mate, free for a year. Eh, wadda yer say, mate? I can see ya dribblin' already!"

"That is a mouth-watering offer, sir, but I'm afraid I'm a vegetarian," I told him. "But if you've got two grand…"

The butcher went away disgruntled, and a grey man in a dead-black suit wafted up and pointed his bony finger at an oil painting of Bob Champion winning the Grand National on Aldaniti. "Would you consider an offer on that painting?" he inquired.

"Depends what the offer is," I replied.

"How would you like a free funeral?" he smirked enticingly, before enthusing, "I'm talking the full works, a beautiful Rolls Royce hearse, a chauffeur-driven limousine, half a dozen pallbearers, and an oak coffin with handles of your own choice."

I grinned, "Although that's the second best offer I've had today, I don't feel I'm quite ready for the off yet, sir."

"Well what if," he persisted, obviously put out at being talked back to, "I throw in a free burial plot as well?"

"Too many worms," I objected.

"Oh, well you can have a cremation if you prefer," he beamed, hopefully.

"Now if you could do me a flaming pyre up the Ganges, complete with…" I began to suggest, but he went blustering off into the crowd before I could finish.

"Rhyme 'n' Reason, a Grand National hero," I told a couple who were examining one of my numbered prints of the 1988 winner as he jumped Becher's Brook. "Are you fans?"

"No," scowled the man. "You nicked it!" He delved into a leather camera bag, drew out a photograph and held it up in my face. "There! Your painting is a copy of my photographic image. I own the copyright and I want my commission."

"My paintin's not a copy," I calmly replied. "Look, my 'edge is bushier than yours."

"If you don't pay me something, I'll have the Clerk of the Course throw you off," he angrily threatened.

"John Parrett?" I queried. "He 'appens to be a pal o' mine, and I'll have you turfed out if ya threaten me again. Now sling yer 'ook!"

A chap rolled up with a black box hanging from a shoulder strap. "Are you Max Brandrett?" he asked politely.

"You're not the Fraud Squad are ya?" I joked. He looked a bit taken-aback, and I confessed, "I'm only kidding."

He chuckled and pulled out a microphone and told me, "I'm recording some radio interviews and I wondered if I could talk to you?" Then, after he had listened with mouth agog for a few minutes, he asked, "Would you consider doing a proper interview in our radio tent?"

I followed him trackside to the makeshift studio and carefully stepped over the spaghetti of wires, as a tribe of engineers fiddled with their knobs. A glamorous blonde lady with a beaming smile looked up from behind her microphone and welcomed me with a beautiful Irish lilt, "Hello, I'm Gloria Hunniford." We chatted 'off air' for a few minutes, and then she interviewed me. It was broadcast live over the airwaves and through the loudspeakers to the heaving crowds across the Aintree course: "So you're a Barnardo's Boy with no formal art training, yet you can paint all these wonderful pictures..! You're so immaculately dressed that I thought you were a trainer or an owner..! And so the Elephants became your best friends..! But your art forgeries did land you in a bit of trouble, didn't they..? These days of course, you do a lot for the Variety Club, don't you..? I could carry on listening to you all day, but sadly we've run out of time. A huge thank you to my fabulous guest, Mister Max Brandrett. And I hope that my next guest is having a nice relaxing day out, having won this race in the past, that's the legendary jockey, Mister Bob Champion C-B-E."

"Loved your interview, Max," said Bob, when he saw me in the bar after he'd done Gloria's show.

"Thanks. I loved yours too," I said. "We've got a lot in common, you and me. We're both Sussex boys, and I gather that you were brought up in Guisborough, which is where my mum's from?"

"Blimey! What a small world," he grinned. Then later, when he asked me to show him some of my work, he raved, "Fantastic pictures, Max! If you like, I'll sign some of those Aldaniti prints for you."

The road north from Liverpool took me to the seaside town

of Southport. As I explored the place, I found that some of the older buildings and public gardens, and even some of the tattier parts, reminded me of Brighton. There were quite a few antique shops and art galleries around the area, and some were interested in buying my pictures to sell on, and some wanted to display them on a sale-or-return basis for a share of the profits. Judy had a shop, and she bought and sold a variety of bits-and-bobs, like Capodimonte ornaments, glassware, pieces of jewellery and Persian knick-knacks, and she kindly agreed to stick a couple of my prints up on her chintzy walls. To say that she was she was well-connected, well-preserved, and well-endowed, would be to do her a disservice. She was delightful and beautiful, with a good sense-of-humour and a big heart. And, after a couple of extended dinner dates, she suggested that I might like to move in with her. Her flat was large and luxurious. From the lounge, you could go out through a set of French Windows, down some steps onto a glorious patio and garden which had ornamental statues and overflowing pots of sweetly scented flowers. She was a social butterfly and the queen of Southport's aristocracy, and she kindly introduced me to a few prospective buyers who wanted to splash-their-cash on art. We hit it off well and she liked the fact that I was a bit quirky and could be outrageous, different from her normal coterie.

"I say, Max, how long was it you were in prison for?" a sneering guest asked loudly across the nattering dinner table at one of Judy's lavish soirees.

"Depends on which time you're talking about, Roger," I reposted.

"Ah, yes! Of course, you've been in jail several times, haven't you, Max?" he prodded.

"Let's put it this way, Roger, I've gobbled more porridge than you've gobbled women," I sniggered.

The assembled company stopped and tittered, and gazed into their suppers. Roger sat glaring at me with gritted teeth.

"More Champagne anyone?" Judy smiled.

"I've got a blow-up sex doll," I said. "Her name's Mandy."
"Really?" somebody remarked.
"What fun," remarked another.
"Have you got one, Rodge?" I queried.
"Certainly not!" he snapped.
"Oh, shame," I said. "I reckon with your personality you'd get on well together."

He wanted to hit me, but thought better of it, then left early, complaining of a headache.

"You are so naughty," giggled Judy as we lay in bed, gently blowing jets of cigarette smoke up into the glistening chandelier.

I *was* naughty, and I knew it, and after six months I knew that it was time to move on and take my naughtiness elsewhere.

The Variety Club held dos up and down the country, and I was often invited to attend. In return for a rattling good night out, I donated pictures for their fundraising auctions. There was a big bash being held at the Chester Grosvenor, a large, luxury hotel in the historic city centre, and it was suggested that I stay the night and make the most of the place. It was a huge old building, built in Victorian times, but with the façade of a Tudor mansion, and my room was comfortable and the food was excellent. Come the evening, I trotted off to the banqueting hall on the first floor and was shown to the top table, and introduced to my fellow revellers.

"Oh! You're the artist!" whooped a stunning lady wearing a sparkling diamond tiara.

"We saw your painting in the foyer," said her husband Gerald, a suave and handsome chap with a glowing smile and a gentle tone. "It's quite wonderful," he purred, raising his noble chin and slowly exhaling a fine rivulet of cigarette smoke.

"I second that," grinned an older gentleman called Peter, his Scouse accent mellowed by a lubrication of good living. "Welcome to our circle," he beamed, raising his Champagne flute.

They were a friendly bunch and, although we were like chalk and caviar, we got along like a house on fire, even though I didn't actually have a house, or anywhere else to live. My picture attracted lots of bids and pats on the back, and sold to a celebrity for four grand, although, at the suggestion and insistence of the charity, they took just three thousand for themselves and handed me one back.

The next morning, when he was leaving, Gerald came to say his goodbyes. We shook hands solidly and with a real sense of connection and friendship. "I would love you to do a painting for me one day, Max," he said. "One of my horses maybe?"

"It'd be a pleasure," I assured him.

"Great," he grinned, "I've got a quite a lot. Take care of yourself."

"And *you*," I returned.

"Oh, by the way," he suddenly continued, "if you want to stay on here, be my guest. And do stay as long as you like. I own the place."

I marched up to the reception later and told them, "I've decided to stay on here for another few days."

"Of course, Mister Brandrett, the Duke of Westminster did tell us that you might," smiled the receptionist.

One of my other tablemates, Peter, took me along to watch his beloved Tranmere Rovers. He was the chairman of the club, and we sat in the warmth and comfort of his private box as his 'Superwhites' slithered and slogged for ninety minutes and ended up the superbrown victors.

"My company does Christmas hampers and kiddies' gift boxes," Peter told me. "With Yuletide around the corner, just go along to the warehouse and help yourself, mate."

"Thanks Peter. There *is* somebody very special who'd love one," I said.

After a week at the Grosvenor, the concierge approached me and nervously coughed, "We just wondered, sir, will you be checking out soon?"

"Hmmm," I mused for a few moments, "I don't think I will. I think I'll stay on for a while longer. And if you wouldn't mind finding me a larger room, the one I'm in is starting to feel awfully cramped."

I drove up from Chester to Birkenhead to make the most of Peter's generous offer of some Christmas goodies, but arrived to a massive shock.

"What can I do you for, mate?" asked one of the security guards, as I rolled up at the gatehouse in the Madison.

The sheer scale of the company's operations was quite staggering. The megalopolitan site was filled with acres and acres of warehouses and offices. I explained my business, whereupon the guard made a brief phone call, opened the barrier and said, "They are expecting ya."

I drove as the gateman instructed, turning along this road and that road, until I found the right building. I was met upon my arrival at the production plant and treated to a full guided tour. Hamper baskets and boxes rolled along streams of conveyor belts, and scores of busy hands packed them with all manner of festive treats.

"Where's yer van, mate?" inquired the lad who wheeled my chosen gift packages out into the yard on his pallet truck. When I pointed out my long-nosed two-seater, he giggled, "You're havin' a laff ain't ya!" Despite the Madison's short, stubby boot having virtually no space, it did have a chrome luggage rack on the lid, and we managed to lug my giant hamper basket onto it and lash it down with some elastic straps and string. The back end of the car slumped a bit, and the lad looked bemusedly at the train-shaped box which half-filled his trolley and asked, "So where are you gonna put this 'n then?"

We wedged the cardboard locomotive into the passenger seat, with it sticking up as tall as a man, and I managed to struggle through the four-hour drive to Brighton with a crooked neck and a funnel squashed up against my ear. But there was nothing which could dampen my spirits as I contemplated the happiness which I was going to deliver to a special person. It was a struggle to lift the box out when I arrived, but I raised it up and held it out in front of me as I waddled blindly through the front door and into the lounge. Setting it carefully down on the carpet next to the flashing Christmas tree, I called out, "Martina! You can come in now, I'm ready!" My darling little daughter padded in and gazed wide-eyed at the brightly coloured engine, which was thrice her size. She giggled and pointed at it with her tiny fingers. I opened up the lid to reveal a mountain of multicoloured sweets and treats. She laughed and began to dance about. Then, before I knew it, it was time for me to leave.

"Ee, Max! Where did thee get all this scran!" gasped my mum when I took her monster hamper round. She opened up the lid of the basket and shrieked, "Thou 'asn't been thievin' has thou! I'll knock yer block off!"

"Course I 'aven't, mum," I assured her.

She stared in amazement into the basket, and slowly trawled through the tins of meats and biscuits, and jars of jams and chutneys, and bottles of beers and wines, and bags of sweets and snacks.

"Ee, you're a good lad, Max," she beamed, and planted a warm kiss on my cheek. "Reckon we'll have a right grand Christmas!"

The Halcyon Gallery in Birmingham sold originals and prints. They asked me if I could supply them with paintings, and I moved into some nearby digs and set up a studio. The city was quite lively, and I spent my time painting and checking out the local music scene and social scene.

"Bloody nice car, mate," said a chirpy Brummie in a scrapyard, his fingers bristling with offensive tattoos and belligerent metal rings.

"It's a Madison Roadster," I told him. "I'm after some spotlights."

"Then you've come to the right place," he grinned.

As I followed him across the busy scrapyard, the chains on his scuffed-leather jacket and cut-off faded denim clanked with every step of his sturdy biker-boots. Metal studs were patterned into the outline of a skull-and-crossbones which was painted crudely on his back, accompanied by the words 'Saddle Tramps MC Birmingham'.

He dug out a nice pair of lamps and offered to fit them for me, after we'd had a brew. And as we got nattering, he asked me hopefully, "I don't suppose ya can paint motorcycle petrol-tanks can yer?"

I took the tank back to my place and spent a couple of days over it, designing it according to his individual demands. He wanted the image of a worm's body, with a fiery dragon's face, eating its way out of an apple. I made it colourful, with a 3D effect, and gave it a lustrous coat of varnish to seal it and finish it off.

"Hey Spider! Come and look at this!" the guy bawled when I delivered it. Spider was a lanky lad who had just pulled up and cut the roaring engine of his Harley chopper. "Come and see what Max 'as done!"

Spider loved it and asked me to do a painting on his petrol tank too; predictably, a hairy-legged tarantula with an ugly mug. But he was a really nice guy, as were all the guys in their chapter, and I was asked if I could do tank designs for a few of them. They paid me a hundred quid each and it was happy days.

"Hey, why don't ya move into our place?" suggested Spider, when he called in to see me at my digs. "It's better than this bloody dive. Ya can set up yer studio and do all yer paintin' an' that, rent free. And don't worry, nobody'll bother yer."

He took me in his car, a souped-up Escort with wide wheels and customised exhaust pipes which rattled the lids off dustbins, to show me where he lived. And before I'd even snapped on my seatbelt (he didn't bother with such tosh), my head was rammed back into the headrest as we shot from to 0 to 80 MPH in the blink of a squinting eye. I was holding on for grim death as he shot down the narrow backstreets, blasting his horn at anything and grinning and giggling like a maniac. He glanced into his rear-view mirror as a siren suddenly blasted out behind us. His right boot kicked the throttle to the floor and thrust us like a rocket onto the ring road, which I think he saw as his own personal racetrack. He flashed his headlights and skimmed past cars at over a ton, as petrified drivers swerved to avoid being obliterated by us. Without any attempt at slowing down, we screeched into Spaghetti Junction, almost tipping over, then suddenly veered across the normal run of traffic and skewed off down a slip-road and through an underpass. The exhaust noise was deafening, but the flashing blue lights persisted on our tail. We doubled back and did another couple of laps around Spaghetti Junction. Spider gritted his teeth and seemed to push up into a higher gear, expertly executing seamless acts of coordinated acceleration, braking and steering, until the cops had disappeared and we were free. He glanced across at me and lit up a fag and laughed.

I shared my new room with an easel and paints, and a gymful of bodybuilding equipment. The house was often full of Hell's Angels and their girls, and beer and drugs and heavy metal music. However, during the daytime, it was mostly quiet as my housemates were either at work, asleep, or humping. They were a sociable lot and they respected me, and seemed fascinated with my life and my art. And so there were never any problems, except late one evening when Spider knocked on my bedroom door. "Okay if I come in, Max?" he asked. And then continued, "Thing is, there's summat going down tonight, summat big, and I don't want yer to get involved. There's nothin' 'appenin' in the 'ouse, but you need to stay out the way. Just shut yer door and don't come out, just in case. Okay?"

"Okay," I agreed.

"Here, ya can do a bit of weightliftin', build up them muscles o' yours," he laughed. "Anyway, I'll be seein' yer."

"Yeah, I'll..." I began, but he was gone.

I knew that there were weapons in the house, shotguns, blades, wrenches, metal bars and an axe or two, and as I listened, I could hear the ominous clicks-and-clanks and mumblings which suggested that trouble was afoot. Then there was the slamming of the front door, followed by the roar of all the motorcycles firing up and driving away in a procession up the road, until they faded away into the distance, and it all went quiet. I smoked a few fags and painted. And as the evening wore on, I got bored and weary, and the weights on the other side of the room started to call out to me. First, I tried one of the single dumbbells, raising it up to my chin and watching my bicep bulge. Then I picked up two dumbbells, and raised them to my chin, one after the other, and then in unison. And then I tried it with bigger dumbbells, admiring the coursing veins in my forearms. And then I grabbed one of the long bars with weights on each end, and pumped it up above my head. And then I increased those weights so that it was a real effort to lift the bar and extend my arms up fully. I struggled, but I did it. I lay flat-out on the sturdy, narrow weightlifting bench and manoeuvred the heavy bar so that it was lying across my chest. And then I grabbed the bar firmly with both hands, and pushed for all I was worth, grunting as I managed triumphantly to raise it until it was right up in the air. And then my arms collapsed and it fell down, with the bar stuck across my throat - and I couldn't move!

"What the bloody 'ell 'ave yer done!" Spider roared with laughter, when he returned later that night, bloodstained and torn, and released me.

The next day, there were questions and house-searches by the cops, and arrests and news-reports of running street-battles between rival gangs of bikers, but none of my housemates mentioned it, and everyone seemed as laid-back and chirpy as ever. When the police asked me to account for my whereabouts, I explained how I had been "underweight" all evening. They accused me of being a smartarse and terminated their questioning.

Some of the lads mentioned a children's hospice in Selly Oak, and I agreed to donate a painting and a few prints for an upcoming fundraiser. The nursing staff loved my picture of Lester Piggott riding out to win the 1983 Derby on Teenoso, and although the original and prints were signed by *me*, they didn't bear the all-important signature of the legend himself. I put in a request for Lester to sign them, but the fee was a bit steep and I declined. However, when the hospice received the pictures, they did bear the jockey's signature, and although I had decided to move on, I felt heartened that the proceeds from the sale would help to fund the care of sick children and their families.

I got fitted for a new velvet-collared dinner jacket and trousers, and attended a Variety Club ball up in Liverpool. On my table, I was surrounded by a mafia of butchers, whose wives were like mutton dressed as overblown lamb. The night drew on, and the grand auction was held. The great-and-the-good loved nothing more than to display their generosity to their fellow members, but it was all in good humour, and all in a good cause. A set of five of my framed horseracing prints appeared on the big screen, and the bidding began at a thousand pounds.

"Five grand," boomed a familiar, gravelly voice at the front, and that was that, the pictures were sold.

"Max, would you like to meet him?" one of the organisers asked me. "He's gone backstage to the private bar, but I'm sure he'd love to meet you."

The room was dimly lit and filled with the smoke of a dozen-or-more bawdy blokes who were sitting around a large table, with one bloke at the head.

"This is Max Brandrett," said the go-between.

"Who?" snapped the shadowy figure, leaning back almost horizontally on his chair.

"The artist," said the go-between. "He painted the pictures you bought."

"Fark orf!" he snarled. "I 'ate em! Cant!"

"Sorry, I thought you liked them," said the go-between.

"Yeah, yeah, yeah," growled the grouch. Then piercing me with a steely gaze, "Sidown and 'ave a drink." He suddenly spilt forwards, and his giant forearms slammed down on the table like blacksmith's hammers on an anvil. "Come on, sidown, sidown," he beckoned, chuckling as he shoved the man next to him out of the way so that I could sit in his place. He slopped a glass of liquid out from a giant jug into a half-pint mug and shoved it in front of me. "Cheers!" he roared, downing his own glassful in one glug. "What d'ya say yer name was?"

"Max Brandrett," I told him.

"Who?" he demanded, his head swaying towards me so that he could take a closer look.

"I'm the cant who painted the pictures," I told him, staring him right back in the eye.

He roared with laughter and, bashing his glass into mine, spilling pungent gin all over the tablecloth, grinned, "You're alright, Max, you're alright!" Then, after a long pause, as his entourage looked on, waiting in anticipation for his next word, he giggled, "I love them pictures, Max! I love 'em! Have a drink!" Then he stood upright to attention, without a sway or stumble, giving me a clear view of his comical stripy school blazer and knee-length grey shorts, and plonked a schoolboy cap on his head, and grinned, "Right, Max, I'm off for a piss."

His cronies roared with laughter and yelled out, "Go on, Ollie!"

Oliver Reed marched from the table, watched anxiously by the waitresses, and into the corner of the room, where he unzipped his flies, flopped out his hefty cock and pissed all over the flock wallpaper. His people guffawed and whistled and shouted until he had performed his function. He sat down and somebody cried out to get him another jug of gin.

"You know, Max," he continued to me, lucidly and quietly, looking out across the table, "I dunno what 'alf o' these fuckers do. They're not like me and you. You're an artist, Max, a creator of art, a gentleman and a scholar."

And when we were having lunch together the next day, when he was sober, he submitted politely, "Here, this is for you, old chap," and handed me a folded cheque. "It's for the pictures."

"But you've already paid for them," I protested.

"If you prefer, we could settle it with a boxing match," he courteously suggested. "But I think I would beat you. What do you think?"

"Thank you, I'll take the cheque," I conceded.

Ollie was great company, and laughed like a drain when I told him how I could make an elephant go to the toilet, and how I'd painted art forgeries right under the noses of the screws in clink, and how I'd busked my two songs and sold pictures on Portobello Road with Bonnie the dog. We spent two days hanging out at the hotel, under the watchful eye of his oppos.

"Tomorrow, we're going to Guernsey," he suddenly told me. "Just you and me, in my helicopter. Don't look so scared, I'm not going to try and fly the bloody thing myself! You can meet my lovely hounds." Then, clicking his fingers loudly in the air, he cried, "Bring us six beers - each!"

I slipped away before I found myself whirring up into the clouds. The cheque was made out by him personally, for the amount of five hundred pounds. And I was in two minds whether it would be worth more as a collector's item.

A racehorse called Warning had been a leading two-year-old back in the nineteen-eighties, and had won all its races under the expert guidance of his jockey Pat Eddery. A year later, the colt was raced against older horses in the Queen Elizabeth II Stakes. He won by five lengths, and I felt prompted to paint a picture of the closing scene, which I entitled 'Striding to Victory'. Although the prints sold well, I knew that with the inclusion of the jockey's signature they would be even more appealing to racing fans. Eddery had won thousands of races across the globe and was considered by many to be the best jockey in the world. However, not all of the top riders were keen to endorse commercial products, but begrudgingly did so if they thought they could make a load of money for nothing. That wasn't the case with Pat.

"I just wondered, sir, if we could come to an arrangement where you'd sign some prints?" I requested upon being introduced to the great man, along with Terry his booking agent.

"How many prints are we talking?" Pat asked, in his quiet Irish tone.

"If I said eight-hundred-and-fifty, what would you say?" I ventured gingerly.

"I hope you've got a sharp pencil," he grinned.

He sat and signed all 850 copies of 'Striding to Victory' in exchange for the original painting. And from then on, we struck up a friendship.

He'd phone me up and say things like, "Max, if you want those Dancing Brave's monikered, I'm just helicoptering it over to Kempton. I could meet you there," or, "Fancy a game of tennis, Max?" We were both great tennis fans, watching and playing.

My own love of the game stemmed from setting up a makeshift tennis court with my brother at Barnardo's. We had tied a piece of string between two posts for a net, and used rolled-up newspapers as rackets. Because we were keen, and considered to be well-behaved, we were selected to serve as ball-boys at Wimbledon. Although it had been an absolute thrill to see wonderful players like Doris Hart, Drobny, 'Little Mo' and Lew Hoad, and drink lashings of Robinsons Lemon Barley Water, and eat punnets of fresh strawberries, I did manage to actually stop play one day. I threw a ball to an English player called Roger Becker, bouncing it once on the grass as was the prescribed method, but it inexplicably rose up and hit him in the gob. He was losing his match at the time and, in a foul mood, he yelled at me, "You stupid boy!" and told the umpire that he wouldn't continue playing until I had been removed. Luckily, the umpire took my side, and the player eventually agreed to resume. At the end of the tournament, us Barnardo's Boys were allowed to play on the hallowed turf, and I played a few games on No. 2 court.

Pat had a tennis court in the gardens of his beautiful farmhouse in Bucks, and jokingly I'd call across the net to him, "If I keep lobbin' 'em, Pat, you're never even gonna see 'em - never mind reach 'em!"

One night we were out for dinner in Newmarket with a restaurant full of jockeys, which might seem a bit odd, but even jockeys had to eat. It was a good-humoured affair and, at times, downright rowdy. And as we were eating and drinking, they were asking me questions, like, "So Max, did you ever ride on the elephants?"

"Yeah, I did. Leila was a sweetheart," I recounted. "She'd lift me up on her knee, and I'd climb aboard, and she'd just trot along, nose-to-tail with all the others, and then I'd stand up and jump across their backs, from one elephant to the other."

"And we thought a jockey needed good balance!" somebody shrieked.

Then someone asked me about the camels. "A bit bad-tempered," I said. "And if they were pissed off, they used to spit at yer. But I did ride 'em sometimes."

"God! What was that like?" they asked.

"Bumpy," I replied.

Pat and I spoke the next day, and he thanked me for a great night out. That's the kind of lovely gentleman Pat Eddery was.

I was invited as a special guest to a Variety Club dinner at the Metropole Hotel in Brighton. As the guests were arriving, I swanked up in the Madison, went to climb out, tripped and fell flat on my face. As a doorman rushed to my aid, I'm sure I could hear titters. Among my tablemates was Brian Hall, the actor who played Terry-the-chef in Fawlty Towers. He was a funny bloke, and as they were serving up the salmon, he chuckled to me, "You'd think I'd know all about food, wouldn't ya? According to Sybil Fawlty I'd been, 'a chef in Dorchester, but not actually in *the* Dorchester.'"

"I served three months in Dorchester," I told him.

"Bloody 'ell, Max! What d'ya do?" he asked.

"I was in this hotel at five in the mornin' and a chandelier fell on top o' me," I told him. "Well I didn't know they'd want it back, did I!"

We had a great laugh and became great mates, probably because we were both cheeky and down-to-earth Brighton boys. Just before the auction was about to begin, a spotlight glared in my eyes and it was announced that the charity was going to accord me their premier award, a Silver Heart, for my donation of pictures which had raised in excess of eighty-thousand pounds for underprivileged kids. I went up and received it with overwhelming pride, and gratitude that I had been able to make a difference to some children's lives.

CHAPTER 11: HARD KNOCKS AND HAPPY ENDINGS

I moved into a simple upstairs bedsit in Shepherd's Bush and stuck my award on the mantelpiece. The place was within striking distance of Portobello, and I was happy to be back painting and drawing, and selling at some of my old haunts. The only slight downer was the stroppy landlord, who lived on the premises and who seemed to be permanently scowling at me.

One afternoon, there was an overenthusiastic, almost manic, knocking of knuckles on my bedroom door. "Okay, okay, I'm comin'," I sighed, rubbing the paint off my hands. "Keep yer 'air on!"

"Police, for you," the landlord snapped, like a prickly terrier, his lip curling up the side of his face.

"Oh? Well what do they want?" I asked, working out how I might escape through the window before they could get to me.

"I've no idea what they friggin' want!" he growled. "You'd better get dan there and find out, hadn't ya?"

He walked behind me down the stairs, and watched me until I was within spitting distance of the two coppers who were lurking on the doormat. And even then, he stood in the hallway with his ears twitching.

"Are you Max Brandrett?" asked the officers.

"Listen, if it's about the T-V licence, gents, I'm just a tenant. That bloke *there* is the householder," I told them.

"It's not about that, sir," they replied, quite deadpan. "Perhaps if we could come inside and explain?"

"That might be best," I said. "The walls 'ave ears in this place."

The landlord snarled a little and scurried off in a huff. The constables plodded upstairs with me, and I welcomed them into my humble abode. They stood, looking solemn, with their helmets tucked under their arms, and I tried to recall what paintings I'd sold recently, or whether I was about to be set up for something.

"I was just doin' a picture for the Variety Club," I told them, by way of explaining the Albert Derby shipping scene on my easel, before they asked.

"You might wanna sit down, sir," said one.

The other one softly nodded at me, his eyes filled with pity. "It's about your mum," he said. "I'm afraid we've got some bad news…"

When I got down to Brighton, my mum had already been collected. I went to visit to her at the Bungard funeral parlour in Hove. It broke my heart as I wondered whether she had called out for me in the darkness, "Where are thee, Max? Where are thee, son?"

I moved into a room with a microwave and a bed, in Goldstone Road, just around the corner from the undertakers. I wasn't bothered about the place or the people; it was just somewhere to sleep.

"Nice place you got here, Max," cracked a facetious voice, just as I was chucking some mouldy scraps into the dustbin at the front of the house.

"Mister Pugglesham! Mister Fitchman!" I exclaimed, startled as I looked up and saw the two raincoats. "How the 'ell d'ya know I was here?"

At the cop shop, Fitchman said, "Let's just say, Max, you're never far off the police radar."

"You can say that again," I sneered. "You even found me in London!"

"Yeah, well we were very sorry to hear about your mum, Max," consoled Pugglesham.

"Ta," said I, taking a sip of their insipid dishwater. "But I'm sure you ain't invited me here for pissy tea and sympathy."

"Just to let you know, we haven't started the tapes yet, Max," indicated Fitchman.

"Thing is, Max, we've been contacted by our colleagues at the West Midlands Fraud Squad," said Pugglesham. "It's regarding the forgery of a jockey's signature on a painting and some of your prints. The pictures were sold at a charity auction at a hospice in Selly Oak, Birmingham."

"You know what we're talking about, don't you, Max?" pressed Fitchman.

"The jockey's wife *has* identified the signatures as fakes," said Pugglesham.

"And not very good fakes," added Fitchman.

"I was in a hurry and the hospice needed the pictures!" I protested.

"We totally get why you did it, Max," said Pugglesham. "And if in the taped interview you wanted to explain about helping dying kids and all that, and say how sorry you are, then maybe..?"

In court, I pleaded guilty and we went for the sympathy vote. I was advised that I could expect prison, depending upon the judge's mood on the day. And although the judge obviously wasn't suffering from searing indigestion, I think his breakfast sausages might have been a bit underdone that morning, and he gave me a seven grand fine.

"Max! What the bloody hell you been up to!" shrieked a friendly voice. "They found you unconscious in your bedsit and had to call an ambulance!"

As my eyes adjusted to the glowing hospital lights, my old mate Bobby appeared. Bobby and I used to play tennis at various local clubs, although I had been barred from most of them for putting off my opponents by chattering too much. Another guy called Micky was with him. "I've got colitis," I groaned, flinching at the stabbing pains in my stomach. "It's not the first time. I just remember everything shootin' outta both ends! Wouldn't bloody stop! Then I woke up in this place. Think I've been 'ere about a week, ain't I?"

When Bobby and Micky took me home two weeks later, I was still weak and could barely walk, despite being on heavy painkillers.

As we went indoors, Micky was ahead of me. "I've got some bad news," he sighed, pushing open my broken bedroom door. "Looks like you've had a break-in."

As we glanced around at the mess, Bobby asked, "Anything missing?"

"The microwave," I said, "and me Variety Club award."

"Listen," said Micky, "my cousin runs a rental agency. You can't live here, mate."

"All I can afford now," I said, picking my wallet out of the debris and finding it empty.

"Don't you worry about that," said Bobby, "we'll get you sorted."

Better than their word, they got me a beautiful ground-floor flat, just yards from the seafront and near the King Alfred Leisure Centre.

"There you go, old mate," grinned Bobby, as he handed me the keys.

And Micky said, "Trixie, my Mrs, is gonna bring you some shopping over."

"Now if there's anything you want," offered Bobby.

"What about the rent and the deposit?" I questioned.

"Now you're signing on the old rock'n'roll," laughed Bobby, "it's all taken care of, courtesy of the government."

"Blimey!" I chuckled. "That's a first!"

Slipping something into my hand, Micky said, "And there's a bitta bunce from me an' Bob, just to tide you over."

As I walked from the hallway into the lounge, then back to the bedroom, then along to the bathroom, and then to the kitchen, and flicked through the pile of 10 twenty-pound notes which they'd given me, I thought I must be dreaming. And when Trixie arrived, she brought bags of shopping with her; everything I could want. They all popped in to see me, and kept an eye on me, and did as much for me as any person could possibly do for another.

Micky and Bobby were a pair of shrewd antique dealers who had built up reputable businesses by buying and selling pretty much anything which could earn them a bob or two. When I was better, we sat in Micky's handsome garden, lounging next to the swimming pool where his precious fish splashed around amongst the lush pond weeds, and he asked, "So, Max, have you got much on at the moment?"

"It's just that we picked up this lovely old frame and canvas," basked Bobby. "It's magnifico, Max! A work of art!"

Then Micky sighed bitterly and carped, "Except for the shit that's painted on it!"

"It is horrible, Max," grieved Bobby. "Truly horrible!"

At their lockup, they made me shut my eyes, before shouting, "Ta-da!" and asking, "Well, what d'ya reckon, Max?"

"Shit!" I gasped, as I opened my peepholes. "When ya said *big*, you weren't joking! And when ya said *horrible*, you weren't joking!"

The canvas was seven foot wide by four foot tall, and had some distorted abortions of lurid green hills and chocolate-coloured trees splattered all over it.

"Don't worry, Max, we'll get it all cleaned up for you," encouraged Micky.

"And we've got a big place for you, where you can work your magic," rallied Bobby.

"Yeah, I can see it now," I said. Then visualising a scene on the canvas: "We'll have some massive, warring galleons, with huge cannons, and great blasts of gunpowder a foot across, and a …"

"Hang on, Max, hang on," Bobby interrupted. "The thing is, we've got this client, an American art dealer, and what he wants is something quite specific."

"Go on?" I prompted.

"He wants a religious picture," said Micky.

"What, a crucifixion?" I grinned. "Done plenty o' them in me time. What style? Caravaggio? Rubens? Raphael? Rembrandt? Michelangelo? Titian? Grunewald? Botticelli? I could even do you a Lowry, a Picasso or an Andy bleedin' Warhol if ya like! Anythin' ya want."

"No-no, not the crucifixion," said Micky. "Something more like this…" And he handed me a photocopy.

I looked at the historical painting which they'd photocopied from a book, and pondered, "A pair o' Jewish rabbis in a synagogue?"

"That's right," confirmed Bobby, "rabbis studying the 'oly scriptures, or something like it."

"I could do ya *three* rabbis if ya like," I offered.

"Three's good," smiled Micky.

"But the picture's gotta look old," stipulated Bobby. "You know, totally authentic."

"You can have whatever century ya like," I chuckled.

"How much?" asked Micky.

"Well it's a bloody huge job," I sighed. "Look, somebody's after me for seven big ones, so..?"

"Seven grand it is then," they agreed, and we shook hands on it.

It really was a huge job. They supplied me with cash to buy paints and materials, and Trixie dropped off fresh fish, meat, dairy and veg to the flat every few days, and they made sure that I was happy and healthy. The canvas was already stripped and rubbed down, and I toiled for sixteen, eighteen, twenty-hours-a-day, seven-days-a-week, for over two months, until the pictured was drawn and painted, baked and crackled with a wrinkled web of thousands of tiny cracks, all ingrained with grime and dust, then washed-and-dried and framed in all its glory.

"Well?" I asked Micky and Bobby.

They stared at the giant painting, then at each other, and were rendered speechless.

At a superb cordon bleu restaurant, we chinked Champagne flutes, and Micky said, "I've spoken to our client, and he's flying in from Boston next week to see it in the flesh. And Max, you'll be playing the painting's owner, right?"

"How's your Yiddish?" joked Bobby.

"I won't have to dress up, will I?" I sniggered.

"Well, it's funny you should say that, Max," answered Micky.

They thought that it would add to the authenticity of our yarn if I appeared dressed all in black, in a tall, wide-brimmed Hoiche hat and long coat. But, more than that, they said that Trixie could get hold of some ringlets and beard-hair which she could stick on my chops with glue. My reply was two words, each of them with just one syllable.

"Okay," battled Micky, "how about a kippah?"

"I feel like I'm being stitched up like a bleedin' kipper!" I protested.

When the dealer arrived, I greeted him wearing a black suit and tie, with a small Star-of-David pinned to my lapel. As Micky and Bobby ushered him into our private function room at the Grand Hotel, they told him, "This is Maximillian Brandrett, the owner of the painting. He inherited it from his grandfather."

I bowed my head and shook the dealer's hand and greeted, "Shalom." He smiled and replied, and so I said again, "Shalom." I was relieved that he, too, was clean-shaven and dressed in a normal suit, although he did have a kippah (skullcap) on his head.

The painting was under wraps, on a big easel in the centre of the room where the light and space were at their best. The window-blinds were open and, at our request, the room had been cleared of desks and chairs and lecture boards and coffeemakers.

"Coffee, gentlemen?" inquired the manager, suddenly entering with the briefest of knocks, and carrying a tray of jugs and cups and biscuits in his hands. He was a friend of ours and he had been briefed to keep shtum about me being an artist.

"Not for me," panted the American, mopping his brow and moving anxiously towards his goal. "If you wouldn't mind, I'm very keen to see it."

He stood back as Micky and Bobby slid the sheet away. It was a glorious moment, framed in gold. I glanced at Bobby, biting my lip, and waited.

"Holy cow, Max!" cried the manager, suddenly looking up. "That's some picture! How did you..?"

"How did he come by it?" Micky quickly interjected. "He's just about to tell the gentleman that. So if you wouldn't mind?" Then, under his breath, "Piss off!"

"Remarkable!" gasped the art dealer, peering intently at every molecule of paint and into every minute fissure. "Remarkable!" After an eternity, he swung to me and asked, "Do you know what year it was painted?"

"Eighteen-eighty-nine, sir," I replied. "The year my grandfather was born."

"And tell me, how did you acquire it?" he probed.

I instantly thought of the innumerable times I'd pulled off the silly father-and-son act with dear old Sammy Cohen. I cleared my throat and recounted, in a low and solemn tone, "The picture belonged to my dear old grandfather, back in Germany. As you know, the Nazis confiscated and destroyed a lot of paintings, and this one, depicting the rabbis in the synagogue with the holy scriptures, would have meant an instant death-sentence for the owner. So, my dear grandfather, Jacob, dismantled the frame and the stretchers, and carefully folded the canvas, and got false papers, and led his family out through Switzerland and France, hiding in the forest with the French resistance for seven months, until he managed to bribe a farmer to drive them to the coast, and then he paid for a little fishing boat to take them across the channel to safety. He kept the painting hidden in a coalhole for several years in London, scared that the British authorities might take it off him. And before he died, he made me promise that I'd sell it, to help support my own family. And now, alav ha-shalom, I offer it to you."

The man looked at me, misty-eyed, and hugged me, and whispered, "Alav ha-shalom."

In a way, I was sad to see the picture go. But it sold for a fortune. And Micky and Bobby did give me a tidy bonus for my labours, and for my theatrical performance.

"That dealer's already got a client for it," said Bobby, as the specialist airfreight firm were packing up the picture in a custom-built plywood case.

"Don't feel guilty, Max," smirked Micky, "he'll be making double what we did!"

I used to have literally hundreds of ladies from all over the country who wanted me to show them my tricks. It was all perfectly above board, arranged by a company which offered seaside breaks to pensioners. These trips included rudimentary art classes at one of the local hotels. Dressed to the nines, I would put on a good show and try to keep the old ladies entertained. The function rooms would fill up with a hundred-and-fifty senior citizens, many of them widows, either alone or in pairs, or in small groups, and I would show them how to paint skies and trees and seas and vases and fruit and dogs and faces, and anything they asked for. It was a pleasant way to spend an afternoon or two, and the fees were quite generous, especially considering that I was being paid for what came naturally to me.

It was just another gloomy Thursday when I stubbed out my cigarette and made my entrance into the roomful of expectant grannies. "Hello, I'm Max, and I will be your teacher this afternoon, so I trust you're all going to be on your best behaviour?" They grinned and giggled. I continued, "There will be tea, coffee and biscuits served later, or a free glass of sherry for those of you who fancy a tipple..." And from there, I went off into my usual demonstration.

Afterwards, an eager cluster gathered around me and asked, "Please, do tell us, Max, what subject matters satisfy you the most?"

"Female Nudes," I said. "And elephants - and nude elephants."

As the ladies tittered and hiccupped, I noticed amongst the time-ravaged faces, a fresh face. "This is my daughter Debbie," announced the glamorous mum, ushering the young brunette in my direction. "We were interested to hear that you like elephants. Or was it a joke?"

"I *do* love elephants," I said. "I used to have twelve of 'em."

"Now we know you're joking," sniggered mum.

"Leila, Mary, Camella, Suzy, Dayla, Dana, Rhani, Seeta, May, Mabel, Janie and Sally," I reeled off. "They were my twelve elephants at Chipperfield's Circus. I travelled all over the country with my girls."

"Wow!" gasped the daughter, her face suddenly beaming. "I'm in the circus, on the flying trapeze."

Debbie was on holiday with her mum, and had only dropped by to pick up her up after I'd finished my talk. There was an instant connection between us; like a secret language which circus people shared. She and her mother had to leave the next day, but she asked for my address, and then wrote to me. The next thing I knew, she came to visit me, and again, until we were spending more-and-more time together. And then, before we knew it, we were in a beautiful relationship. Debbie was adventurous, a free spirit, born to soar through life and scale new heights. She toured the towns and cities of Britain, and Europe, and the world, becoming ever more famous and evermore popular, until finally the call of the circus won, and she had to fly away from me forever.

An audience of local ladies began attending my artistic sessions, and each week I would amuse and entertain them with tales from my life, and chords from my guitar. It got to the point whereby, after a couple of small sherries, the old dears would call out their requests: "Max, do you know 'The White Cliffs of Dover'?" or "Max, could you please play 'Pack up Your Troubles'?" or "Max, would you just sing 'Hang Out the Washing on the Siegfried Line'?" or 'It's a Long Way to Tipperary' or any of the songs which brought back memories of the people and places they'd loved and lost. And they would chirp along, half-pissed, with their eyes slowly closing, singing mostly out of tune, mostly out of time, and in a clash of keys. It was a joy to entertain them, but also a relief to see their eyes open when the show was over. On one unfortunate occasion, a lady's eyes didn't reopen and, when gently shaken, her arms flopped to her sides, and her head slumped to her groin, and she had sadly passed on to 'The Garden of Earthly Delights', as the artist Hieronymus Bosch called it in his famous painting.

As well as passing on tips to my budding artists, such as how to paint skies with Brolac house emulsion in order to cut down on otherwise lengthy drying times, they would bring me their pictures for appraisal. I would patiently talk them through their compositions, offering constructive criticism and suggestions, and encouraging them in their chosen hobby. However, competition began to brew between the ladies and they all wanted to be 'teacher's pet'. At first, one of them gave me a home-baked sponge, and then the next week a lady arrived with a Dundee cake, then a lady brought me a barrel of shortbreads, then a box of liqueur chocolates appeared, then a fresh carnation for my buttonhole, then a rose, followed by a red rose, and the next week a silk hankie for my top pocket, then a box of hankies, then a silk tie, and a silk shirt, and expensive fragrances, and a tiepin, and jewelled cufflinks, and a Meissen antique figurine worth hundreds… "Stop, stop, stop, ladies, please! No more!" I told them. "I cannot accept your gifts, it's against the rules. And apart from that, my neighbours smell me coming and think I've turned peculiar!"

Violet was a fairly typical, little old lady, and I was quite happy to give her private lessons at her house in Eastbourne. She insisted that she would pay me fifty pounds per lesson, which was well above the going rate, and I made it clear that we would be painting for the full two hours. The avenue where she lived was wide and pleasant with lots of large detached houses. Spotting her house number on the tall, brick pillars at the front, I drove in and swept around the circular driveway, and parked outside the front entrance. It was a period property, probably a hundred years old, and its three storeys loomed high above me. I pressed the off-white china button marked 'Press' and waited. After a minute or so, I pressed it again, and waited. Then again, a minute later. There were no lights on inside, and no signs of life, and I was about give up when I heard Violet's strained voice calling out, "Alright, I'm coming." Then, "Max, is that you?"

"Yes Violet, it's Max," I called back, as a dim, obscure whiff of light appeared at the transom window above the door, followed by the clank of unlocking bolts.

The door slowly opened, but only about a foot, and Violet peered out at me with a broad smile and greeted, "Come in, Max, come in." As she stepped back and I stepped in, I went to push the door open a little more, but it was jammed. "It's a bit tight I'm afraid," she grinned.

"Lucky I'm not fat," I joked, and squeezed in sideways through the gap, and pushed the door shut behind me. Shuffling on tiptoes, bit-by-bit, I managed to turn myself around into the hallway.

"Follow me," beamed Violet.

Instead of a broad and airy passageway opening out before me, I found myself sandwiched in a narrow alley between walls of newspapers which were stacked up on either side, and which reached from the floor to the ceiling. Breathing in, I was just about able to sidle along and follow her towards the interior.

"It gets a bit tricky here," she called out, as she climbed up and over an armchair which was blocking the way. "Don't worry, the kitchen isn't too far now."

Squeezing from the claustrophobic tunnel into the kitchen was a bit like popping a cork out of a Champagne bottle. As I spurted in, gasping for air, I was hit by a blast of extreme heat and the over-riding smell of burnt toast.

"Would you like a cup of tea?" Violet casually inquired.

"So hot!" I panted. "Why don't you open the windows? Or the back door?"

"Ooh, far too many nasty men around," she frowned. "Now, I thought we could do it here," she smiled, showing off the small part of her kitchen table which wasn't covered in bottles and jars, and upon which she had set up an adjustable easel.

There was just about enough space to wriggle around the place between the piles of boxes and bin bags.

"Do you live alone?" I asked her. "Or is there somebody else here?"

"I'm quite alone," she replied. "And that is one reason why I invited you here. When I die, I want you to have the place, Max. There's no-one else I want to have it, only *you*."

I thanked her most sincerely, but declined her generous offer and sweltered through our art lesson until I had fulfilled my obligation. However, over the following weeks, others in the group also expressed a desire to bequeath me their houses, and those I also turned down.

The local council liked the fact that some of their senior citizens were being given the chance to get out of their homes and learn to paint and have a bit of a singsong. They suggested that if I wished to take out small groups of ladies on painting trips, then they would allow me the use of a community minibus. On a warm and glorious day, I chose nine of my fitter students and set off with a nurse to the local beauty spot at Devil's Dyke. My 'girls' babbled excitedly all the way, as I drove them up into the rolling green hills and parked at the Devil's Dyke pub. There were spectacular views of the South Downs and the colourful hang-gliding enthusiasts who ran off into thin air and swirled around against a backdrop of blue skies and puffy white clouds. The scene was totally idyllic.

"Now then, girls, if you set up your easels along here," I instructed, as we toddled along to a suitable spot, not too close to the blustery edge, "you'll get a perfect view of everything. Now, while you're doing that, I'll go and fetch the rest of the stuff from the bus."

I nipped into the pub to get the ladies a bottle of Bristol Cream, and got chatting to the barman for a few minutes, and browsed around at some of the pictures on the walls, then collected some bits-and-bobs from the van. Wandering back to our vantage point, I was puzzled to see that only four of my ladies were busily working away on their paintings. And next to them, five easels stood deserted.

"Where are the others?" I asked. "Ethel? Doris? June? Mabel? Clementine? Where did they go?" I was met with frowns and shrugs. "Well *you* must know," I said to the nurse.

"To the loo I think," the attendant nonchalantly replied.

"No, I would've seen 'em," I disputed. "I'll go and see if I can find 'em."

"Do you think I've used too much green in my sky?" one of them asked me.

"Later, Muriel, later," I told her, dashing off. "Now where the bloody 'ell..!" Then, to some people in the car park, and the barman, and some dog walkers, "You haven't seen five old ladies have ya? No? Okay, thank you." I went back to the four ladies who hadn't escaped, and fretted. "I can't 'ave lost 'em! What the hell am I gonna tell the people at the council!"

A chap in a deerstalker hat wandered up and inquired, "Excuse me, are you looking for five old ladies?"

"Yes, yes," I replied eagerly.

"I saw a farmer helping them onto the back of a tractor-and-trailer," he informed me.

"A farmer!" I gasped. "Where?"

"Just down the lane there," he said, pointing with his stick. "They drove off *that* way. But they'll be long gone by now I expect."

"Max, do you think I've used too much green…?"

"Later, Muriel, later," I snapped.

I ran over to the minibus and roared off down the lane in hot pursuit, although I wasn't sure in which direction they'd escaped. Heading away from Brighton and towards the open countryside, I did eventually track them down. They were sitting in a village pub - sozzled!

Deciding that it was time to spend some time in the company of females who were under the age of eighty, I placed a carefully worded advert in the Lonely-Hearts column of the Brighton Friday Ad. It read: 'Artist, a walking contradiction, partly truth, partly fiction, wishes to meet young lady for candlelit dinners. Guaranteed happiness. Free potted plant to all applicants'. The pot-plants, dozens of them, had been gifted to me by a well-wisher, and I had no idea what to do with them, except give them away on dates. I received a flood of replies to my advert and, as I sifted through them, I hoped that I would be able to pick out the roses from the thorns. However, as I began meeting up with some of the ladies, it was apparent that they could be quite economical with the truth.

"Okay," I instructed Peter, my friendly cabby, "call me as usual on my mobile phone in half an hour," as he dropped me off outside Brighton station.

With a copy of the Friday Ad. tucked under my arm, and potplant in hand, I waited at the ticket barrier by Platform 7, praying for a corker, and not a porker. And when I spotted a woman with a soggy Friday Ad. squashed under her sweaty armpit, my heart sank. She looked across and smiled at me through a cake of bright makeup, and as a violent wind blew up the concourse, her flouncy, floral dress billowed like a mainsail.

"I thought we'd go to the pub across the road," I said, hoping that I could bring our meeting to a premature end.

And as she sat slurping a pint of brown ale, I kept glancing at my watch, whilst trying to maintain an interest in her unpausing diatribe about all the wicked men she'd met on blind dates. Despite trying to use telepathic powers to make my phone ring, it didn't.

"Can we eat?" asked my date. "I don't eat a lot, although a lot of men presume I do. But I don't."

She was finishing up her caramel tart, topped with double cream, and some leftover bread and butter, before there was a trill in my pocket. "What!" I gasped incredulously into the brick phone. "The basement! Flooded! I'll be right there."

Other ladies who replied to my ad. were much more my type, or at least on the surface they were. Jennifer was an attractive lady, slim and classy, a little older than me, who approached middle age with an air of confidence and excitement. Keen to explore her own adventurous side, and my artistic prowess, she suggested that I should paint her - in the nude.

She came to my place and emerged from the bathroom in a luxurious silk dressing gown, asking, "So Max, where do you want me?"

"You choose," I said, wiping my brushes.

She looked thoughtfully around my sitting-room/studio and strode across to the sofa. I looked up and she whipped open her gown, like a common flasher on the heath, and let it slide shamelessly down onto the floor. Gently pushing up her gorgeous breasts, she gazed seductively into my eyes. "Well?" she smiled.

"Very well, thank you," I grinned.

She sat herself on the arm of the chair, crossed her legs and slowly raised her ankle until her toes were pointing directly at me. "I loved The Graduate," she purred, pouting brazenly, like Mrs Robinson in the film.

When I had finished painting, I declared, "All done, apart from a bit of touching up."

"And when would you like to do that?" she grinned, sliding a cigarette between her lips and lighting up.

"When would you like me to do it?" I asked.

"Not now," she snapped, fretfully stubbing out the cigarette. "I have to go."

"I could bring it over to your house when it's done," I proposed.

"Not my house," she rebuffed. "There's a hotel I know. You can bring it there."

At the requested hour, I walked up to the hotel reception desk with the two-foot painting carefully concealed under a wrapping of brown paper. It really was reminiscent of a scene from the romantic 1960's comedy film, with me inquiring which room 'Mrs Johnson' was checked into, and the clerk raising a disapproving eyebrow for a moment before deeming to tell me. Jennifer was waiting for me upstairs, lying on the four-poster bed in a flimsy nightie. I unwrapped her portrait and displayed it on the wide, Georgian mantelpiece.

It was the first time she had seen it, and she put her hand to her mouth and gasped, "Oh, my, god! That's amazing!" and got up to make a closer inspection. "Max, you're wonderful!" she screamed, and started kissing me all over.

When I came to, the light of the moon flickered softly between the fluttering curtains, and Jennifer's warm breath whispered across the pillow, "Hello sleepyhead," and her lips caressed my ear. "I've left your present on the mantel." I glanced across and saw a fancy envelope with my name handwritten on it in swirling script.

She stroked my hair and implored, "You *will* stay the whole night, won't you? The court isn't in session until the afternoon, so I…"

"Court!" I blurted.

"Oh," she sighed, somewhat sheepishly, "didn't I mention that I'm a magistrate? It doesn't make any difference does it, *you* being a… and *me* being a..? I thought you might find it a bit of a turn on," she giggled.

"Listen, no offence, but I think I'd better be going," I said. "I've gotta feed me cat."

"You haven't got a cat!" she laughed, and rolled on top of me and stared kissing me.

Throughout our night of passion, frolicking and humping, my eyes were drawn to the mantelpiece, and the envelope which contained six hundred pounds by way of payment for my services. I realised that, in her eyes, I was probably no more than a common gigolo, although I had no real cause for complaint.

The Royal Air Force Club in Piccadilly was a posh old institution, housed in three huge converted mansions on the edge of Mayfair. Along the miles of tall, arched hallways and landings, and up and down its five storeys of imposing staircases, the club had numerous function rooms, dining rooms, sitting rooms, a pub and squash courts, plus dozens of bedrooms for the use of members and invited guests. I checked in, courtesy of the Lord's Taverners charity, and looked out from my bedroom window across the tourists ambling along the tree-lined pathways in Green Park, and the swarms of workers buzzing about their business. Below me, the busy traffic bibbed and filled the air with a treacly haze of familiar grey fumes.

Had I been on the other side of the building, it would have been possible to almost touch the capital's upmarket galleries and auction houses. The thought had crossed my mind that I should have brought a couple of 'Albert Derbys' with me and chanced my arm. However, I had become too recognisable, and most of London's art purveyors had barred me. And besides, the art business had become wise to even the most talented of forgers, due mainly to its use of high-tech scanners and chemical analytics. Unfortunately, peddling fakes had become increasingly passé. For an old lag like me, the rewards were somewhat outweighed by the prospect of years and years in jail.

My purpose for visiting London was to attend a celebrity bash; a charity boxing evening organised by the Lord's Taverners, with the retired legend Henry Cooper as the special guest. I sat at a table ringside with Taverner's bigwig Tim Rice, and the Swedish ambassador. Tim was a lovely guy. He was over-the-moon when my donated horseracing picture made eight grand in the auction, and he was keen that I should do a painting or two for him. The Swedish ambassador asked me if I could paint something for his embassy, but when I suggested a snowy, winter scene, he leaned back on his chair and roared, "No, no, no! Not vinter! I see too much snow in Sveden already!"

I decided that I wanted to go back and live in London. I suppose I was still just a little boy, with ants in me pants. Packing up a few rare bits-and-bobs and furniture which I had somehow accumulated, I went back to Holland Road in Hove, where my mum had once lived, and booked my life's possessions into a storage depot, just until I got settled in London again.

The smoking carriage on the London-bound train was empty that day, and as I put my trusty bag of hand-picked clothes and paintbrushes on the rack above my seat, I tapped my jacket pockets expectantly, but heard nothing. As the train chugged through Preston Park and into the rolling hills of Sussex, I contemplated the grim prospect of sitting for an hour with no means of lighting the cigarette which jiggled tantalisingly between my lips.

"The next stop is Burgess Hill," reverberated the rattly announcement over the tannoy.

The wheels began to screech, and the carriage lunged backwards and forwards as it braked, and I made the decision that I would hop off and buy a box of Swan Vestas from the newspaper kiosk. I took my bag with me, just in case, and stepped carefully down onto the tarmac. I looked up and down the platform, but there was no kiosk. It was just a tiny station, with one line heading north and one line heading south. As I trundled up the staircase towards the exit and the ticket office, the guard's piercing whistle heralded the departure of my train. But it didn't matter, as time wasn't pressing on me. Refreshed by lungfuls of delicious tobacco smoke, I wandered outside and stopped to admire the station frontage, old and quaint, with arched windows and a pair of matched gables, like a toytown model. And as I wandered up the street, I found myself staring into an estate agent's window. Then I was sitting inside, discussing details of properties to let. And then, before I knew it, and by whatever quirk of fate, I became a resident of Burgess Hill.

It was a sleepy little town, with small shops, takeaways, estate agents, a few pubs, and the train station, handy for getting down to the coast and up to London. The lady at the lettings agency was most accommodating, and she let me have a week's free rent for taking on a mid-terraced house in Mill Road. And as long as I handed over four hundred quid for the deposit, she wasn't too bothered about references or any of the usual formalities, so I planned to move in pretty much straightaway. Mill Road itself was a long and unremarkable street of unremarkable houses and bungalows. My new home was located at the bottom end, close to the town centre. The property was in a bit of a state and needed a lick of paint and some TLC, and while I was tarting it up, the previous tenant called round and took an offer on the furniture, cooker and fridge, which was a good result. With two bedrooms upstairs and two reception rooms downstairs, it was beyond my needs, but well within my budget. I decided to set up my studio in the much larger front bedroom, which was lovely and light and airy, and go to sleep in the quieter back bedroom. However, before I could move in properly, I booked a room for the week at the Railway Tavern, a handy little hotel just around the corner.

As I sat in the bar, idling my way through a glass of fruity white, an attractive young brunette who was ordering a big wine and a packet of salt-and-vinegar crisps happened to smile in my direction. She jiggled over and forthrightly asked, "D'ya mind if I sit with you?" I stood up and pulled out a chair for her. She sat down and took a satisfying sip of her drink and gratefully nibbled her crisps, and grinned, "Ooh, I needed that! I haven't seen your face in here before... Max? What a nice name. I'm Carol. I love your jacket. You don't see many guys round here wearing a buttonhole. You do look very classy... You're an artist!" We chatted for bit and she asked, "Listen, not being funny, Max, but could I take your mobile number?"

I had no idea what it was about, but a couple of days later, sitting in the same spot, she told me, "I've got a proposition for you. I'd like to rent a room in this house of yours, as a treatment room. You can see my certificates if you like. Here..." As I was perusing her fancy scrolls, one from an Institution of Reflexologists and another from the Universal Aromatherapists, she explained that my house would make the perfect location for her surgery. "It's to help people who need pain relief, with sports injuries and the likes," she said. "I use essential oils and gentle manipulation techniques. I've got a compact massage table, so I'd only need a small room."

Two removals men arrived and humped her treatment couch down the hallway and into the back room, next to the kitchen. We agreed that, if necessary, a patient could briefly use the front room as a waiting area, and she would perform her business activities strictly between the hours of 11 A.M. and 5 P.M. This meant that I could paint upstairs during the day and have social get-togethers or whatever downstairs in the evenings, although I obviously had freedom of the house at any time. And for such a minor inconvenience, she offered to pay me fifty quid a week. It was a win-win situation.

Sweeping a bold brush across a big blank canvas as I created a dark and dramatic sky, I was vaguely distracted by fleeting glimpses of a balding head as it periodically bobbed by on the street beneath my window. I paused and peeked out from behind the curtain. A tall man with a large leather briefcase loped past on the opposite side, then reappeared a minute later, and loped past again, until finally he darted across towards my front door. The doorbell rang and Carol was quick to let him in. Curious, I stood motionless on the landing and listened. "Did you bring everything I told you to?" Carol demanded. There was a mumble, and then nothing except the sound of her sharp footsteps clicking along the hallway, then the snap of her surgery door as it closed shut. I shrugged and returned to my seascape.

"So what sort of equipment and stuff do you use for your treatments?" I asked Carol, as I stirred a tea bag around and around in her mug.

"Oh, just essential oils," she shrugged. "And these…" she smiled, holding up her healing hands.

She was a good tenant: she paid on time; came in at eleven and left at five; bought her own coffee and squirty cream; filled the fridge with jelly pots and chocolate spread; always washed the kitchen floor and cleaned the toilet; and generally spread a sweet aroma around the house. And she was a hard worker, treating an unhealthy stream of patients who visited her practice every day, sometimes including Sundays by special request.

"Hi, I'm Max," I told the pretty blonde who I found sitting on my lounge-room sofa and staring into a mobile phone. "Are you waiting for Carol?"

"Carol? Oh yeah," she muttered, stubbing her fag out in my ashtray. "I'm Charmaine. She's booked me to do a job wiv 'er. I'm early. She's just finishin' one off."

My canvas was filling up with warships and choppy seas, and so accustomed had I become to the frequent chime of the doorbell, that I'd hardly heard it ring. Glancing through the window, I saw a couple of neighbours looking over and making gestures at my house. Downstairs, the front door opened and I heard Carol snap, "You're late! Now get in! Get down there!"

I took no notice and resumed my work, concentrating intently on the hundreds of fine brushstrokes which would create the criss-crossed rigging of one of my fighting galleons. I was suddenly startled by a firm knuckle rapping on my studio door. My hand slipped, and I went to the door and sighed, "Yes? What?" A sour-faced little man with a briefcase raised his trilby hat and was about to speak, when I advised him tersely, "Charmaine and Carol are downstairs, mate. They'll see to you down there. Now if you don't mind!"

"Mister Brandrett? I'm from Burgess Hill Town Council. I've called to assess your rateable value," he declared. "I've already been downstairs, thank you. And she gave me this…" He held up what looked like a Chinese takeaway menu from an establishment called 'Fantasia'.

Hovering red-faced in the background, Carol sighed, "Sorry Max."

The agitated official demanded of me, "Well, what have you got to say for yourself?"

I pointed at the menu and asked, "D'ya fancy the 'Creamy Blowjob' or a 'Jelly Surprise'?"

There was nothing the council could do, apart from re-evaluate me and increase my Council Tax. Under the circumstances, and relieved that I wasn't going to evict her, Carol was more than happy to a rent increase. And I didn't mind if she wanted another couple of masseurs to come in and use my bedroom at the back of the house when I wasn't using it, as long as they put a cover on top of my bed. It was better that everything was out in the open, or at least most of the time it was. The topless girls in their maid outfits and PVC miniskirts were okay, but occasionally I'd find a disorientated Civil Servant wandering along my landing with nothing on but scores of multi-coloured clothes pegs clipped to his nuts and nipples. As time went on, the sight of scantily clad ladies and pervy pilots or flagellated farmers flitting around the place was something I hardly even noticed.

The doorbell rang and, knowing that nobody else was about, I went to answer it. The pleasant lady on the doorstep smiled and handed me a huge bouquet of mixed blooms. The card read: 'To my darling Carol. You are the most divine. Please marry me.

With all my love, for eternity, Charles'. And flowers arrived every Wednesday at 10 A.M., but the inscriptions became increasingly morbid: 'I cannot live without you... I will die if I cannot be with you... Please, please, please marry me or...' The flowers stopped one day, and Carol never saw the chap or heard from him again. It was a strange business.

"Oh god, Max!" sighed Carol, as she popped into the kitchen for a quick nibble of crisps. "My punter's only gone and brought a bloody doggie costume with him! What am I supposed to do with him?"

"Put him on a lead, call him Lassie, and take him for a walk?" I smiled.

"I'll give it a go," she said.

Then I suggested, "You can feed him out of a bowl on the floor, tell him he's been a naughty dog, and stick him under the bed for half an hour. He'll love it."

And after the customer had been dragged around the house on all fours, and force-fed a dish of jelly and cream on the kitchen lino, I heard blissful, puppy-dog whimpers coming from Carol's treatment room.

For another client, who was frightfully posh and was after the common touch, I suggested that Carol should dress up like Mrs Mop, give him a tickle with a feather duster, clout him with a broom-handle and give him a rub him down with a soapy cloth. Apparently, he loved it and brought various cleaning utensils with him whenever he visited. Others paid to come and hoover and polish, and the house always looked spick-and-span.

Although the locals seemed generally quite accepting of Burgess Hill's one-and-only house of ill repute, the landlord of the Hog's Head did appeal to me, "Please tell your girls to stop comin' in 'ere and propositioning my customers. I've got all these wives givin' me right earache!"

But, of course, they weren't *my* girls, they were businesswomen who were simply supplying a service and earning a crust. And their business did bring extra cash into the town. I'm sure that nervous punters would have ventured into a bar for a large measure of Dutch Courage before visiting the Headmistress's office, or into a café for their last supper before confessing their sins to the strict nuns, or into the high street chemist for some girly makeup, or the newsagents for chocolates, or the local pet shop or hardware store to buy their bits-and-pieces. And the taxi drivers knew only too well what kind of therapy the city gents who arrived at the station were after, and would make sure that they took them for a joyride on the scenic route to my house in Mill Road.

Most townsfolk, I'm sure, just had a titter and turned a blind eye. And as Fantasia's clients had no wish to be seen, they didn't linger on the street, but scuttled discreetly in and out of the front door as fast as their shaved or massaged or slapped legs could carry them. However, my faux friends at the Conservative Club proved to be more conservative than most people, and blanked me. It was obvious that publicly they had a deep-seated loathing of massage parlours, although I'm sure privately they weren't averse to a pretty girl giving their dodgy hip or dicky groin a good seeing to.

"Hello mate," chirped a cheeky chappie, as I sat in the Con. Club one day. I looked up, somewhat surprised, and through a set of rotten gums this bloke grinned, "You're 'Max the Forger' ain't ya?"

"That's what the polite people call me," I answered.

"Well I'm Ian the bank robber," he beamed brightly, but toothlessly. "Mind if I join ya? I've robbed all the banks in Burgess Hill I 'ave, but not just Burgess Hill. Between you-and-me, I've done 'em all over the place. But it's handsome to meet a kindred spirit. Cheers Max!"

And so Ian and I became mates; I suppose we were seen as the bad old boys of Burgess Hill, although I think he was really more of a dreamer than a bank robber.

"Here mate," I said to him, as we sat drinking at what had become our regular table, "I've got something for you," and handed him a Co-op bag, rolled and folded into a small present.

As he unfurled it and peered inside, he whooped, "Oh Max! Cheers mate! He stuck his face into the bag and rustled about for a moment or two, then suddenly popped out with a mouthful of yellow dentures.

"They need a bit of a polish," I told him. "But they're good quality. Victorian if I ain't mistaken. I got 'em from a car boot."

His new teeth didn't really fit too well, and after a week or two they were giving him mouth ulcers, so I suggested, "Listen, I've been up at the old folk's home doin' me art classes, and most of them old dears wear false gnashers. And at night, they plop 'em in a glass of Steradent by the side of the bed. Well, a man of your talents…"

A few days later, Ian appeared with a set of gleaming new dentures, although he did say that he'd had to sneak around for a while and try a few pairs before finding some which were a comfortable fit. Unfortunately, Ian's shiny new look faded after a while, and then I heard that he'd died. Out of the blue, a letter came from a solicitor to notify me that I'd been left something in his will. I was requested to meet the legal eagle at my dead chum's house, and I arrived with a dash of expectation. After all, I thought, what if some of Ian's bank-robbing tales weren't as tall as they sounded, and he'd left me a map of where he'd buried his millions?

"*This…*" said the lawyer, who was standing in Ian's decrepit kitchen, "is what he bequeathed to you." And he pointed at an obsolete Hotpoint refrigerator.

"A bloody fridge!" I groaned.

"And its contents," stipulated the chap, showing me the wording on the will. "He was most specific about it."

I took a deep breath and opened the fridge door, hoping that the icebox would be crammed with cool banknotes. A set of false teeth stared back at me, laughing. And it cost me thirty quid to dispose of the worthless appliance!

"The thing is, Max, we've got a new Chief Super, and he's a bit of a bible-basher," one of my friendly neighbourhood cops told me. "He's gonna be clamping down I'm afraid, and I thought I should let you know. Sorry."

Discretion being the better part of valour, and not wishing to spend any more time at Her Majesty's pleasure, the massage parlour promptly ceased trading and I moved to a flat in the town centre. And as it turned out, I had stopped off for a box of matches in Burgess Hill in 1999 and never left.

An email arrived out of the blue from a guy called Jon in Canada. I replied and we later spoke on the phone. Jon was an art collector and he had bought several paintings by the Dutch artist Cornelius Krieghoff, although he and his art dealer had suspicions that they weren't genuine. Krieghoff had lived in Quebec in the mid eighteen-hundreds and had painted everyday scenes of hunters and fishermen and rustic life, all set against the mountains and rivers of Canada's wild outback.

"We were wondering," Jon asked me on the phone, "if you don't mind telling me, whether you ever painted any Krieghoffs?"

"Plenty," I chuckled. "Over the years, maybe twenty or thirty, maybe more. I'm not really sure." Jon emailed me some images of the pictures he'd bought, and called me back. "Yep, I did all of *them*," I confessed. "I did those when I worked with Tom Keating, and they were sold to a restauranteur in Brighton."

"Ah, okay, that figures," Jon sighed, sounding relieved. "It's just that Tom Keating told the press after his aborted trial that he'd forged a lot of Krieghoffs."

"And a lot of other bloody stuff which he didn't do!" I interjected.

"Right," Jon chuckled. "It's just that we've seen Keating's work and, well, we weren't convinced that he was up to it. And we'd seen some of your work, and let's just say they were on a different level. So I'm really happy, Max, that I own some genuine Brandrett Krieghoffs."

And he commissioned me to do another painting for him, on an old canvas, and cracked and aged, in the style of Cornelius Krieghoff, but autographed with my own signature.

My mum passed away on May 11th, 1991. Some months before that fateful day, I paid her a visit. She was 78 and living in a warden-assisted flat in Portland Road, Hove.

"Don't stand there leek wet week!" she grinned when I arrived at her door. She hugged me and kissed me and stroked a wisp of hair aside from my cheek. "I'll put kettle on. Sit ya down. Where tha bin? Are thee in good fettle, son?"

"Very good, mum," I assured her. "I've been painting racehorses."

"What colour?" she asked.

"Well, there was a brown one called Dancing Brave, and a grey one called Desert Orchid, and another one which was sky-blue pink," I joshed.

"Ee, well better paintin' 'em than backin' 'em," she advised.

We sat with strong tea, served in china cups with saucers and a sugar bowl and shiny teaspoons. She set out a plate of assorted biscuits, arranged in a neat circle. Her hand shook slightly as her once deft and pretty fingers scrunched around her cup. She sipped, then looked up at me and smiled with a hidden sadness.

"What's up?" I asked.

"Nowt," she shrugged.

"You are happy here, aren't ya?" I probed.

"What's not to like?" she smiled.

"Something's bothering you," I pressed. "What is it? Ya can tell *me*, mum."

There was a long pause. Then she frowned, and asked me bluntly, "D'ya hate me, son?"

"No!" I shrieked. "Never!"

"I would've kept ya with me. If ya dad'd stuck around it woulda been different," she sighed. "But I had four of ya to look after, and I couldn't do it, son, not on me own. But I did try."

"I know ya did, mum," I said, trying to reassure her.

"Ee, but 'e were such a fast alley-cat!" she smirked. "Me friend Margaret warned me against 'im. But would I listen? Would I 'eck!" She got up and took a small photo from the drawer and handed it to me. "Tha's me and Marge. Max Miller was on at Hippodrome. Ee, we laffed like drains! Then Compton pub afterwards." She glazed over as the memories came flooding back: she was *there*, in the bar, with the fire burning and the piano plonking away; the country was free of war and everybody was happy. "He walked in, and I knew. Tall, very tall. Long, beautiful, shiny 'air, just like yours. And a suit like yours. Very sharp. With a carnation, and a red silk 'ankie. He were like a film star. Then 'e come over and chatted: 'Evening, ladies. Could I buy you ladies a drink? What's your name? What stunning cheekbones you have.' I thought I'd died and gone to 'eaven! And 'e 'ad the gif of the gab alright: 'Do you know Prince Monolulu? I was on Brighton Racecourse with him today. He's an African prince. He's a good friend of mine. How would you like to go dancing? I could take you to Sherry's if you like?' The Victor Silvester band were playin'. Me and ya dad danced all night. He hugged me so tight. And he smelt beautiful. And I loved it. And your dad loved it, too. Everywhere we went, 'eads turned to see who 'e was. He always made me feel special. He were very kind, and generous, and sensitive - when 'e was around!"

"I saw him, mum," I confessed, somewhat hesitantly, "on the prom."

"You remember?" she glinted. "You were only three."

"He had a camel-hair overcoat," I recounted. "And an orange cravat. And he gave me an ice cream cone."

"That's the last thing 'e did give us, the useless bastard!" she hissed.

I paused before prying, "But you don't hate him, do you mum?"

She stared into space, her thoughts and memories churning around inside, then smiled warmly at me, "How could I hate him, Max, when you're so much like him? You're my special one."

And I knew that whatever else I'd been, I was always my mum's special one.

OTHER BOOKS BY GADFLY PRESS

By Michael Sheridan:

The Murder of Sophie:
How I Hunted and Haunted the West Cork Killer

By Steve Wraith:

The Krays' Final Years:
My Time with London's Most Iconic Gangsters

By Natalie Welsh:

Escape from Venezuela's Deadliest Prison

By Shaun Attwood:

English Shaun Trilogy
Party Time
Hard Time
Prison Time

War on Drugs Series
Pablo Escobar: Beyond Narcos
American Made: Who Killed Barry Seal?
Pablo Escobar or George HW Bush
The Cali Cartel: Beyond Narcos

*Clinton Bush and CIA Conspiracies:
From the Boys on the Tracks to Jeffrey Epstein
Who Killed Epstein? Prince Andrew or Bill Clinton*

*Un-Making a Murderer:
The Framing of Steven Avery and Brendan Dassey
The Mafia Philosopher: Two Tonys
Life Lessons*

Pablo Escobar's Story (4-book series)

By Michael Sheridan:

The Murder of Sophie: How I Hunted and Haunted the West Cork Killer

Just before Christmas, 1996, a beautiful French woman – the wife of a movie mogul – was brutally murdered outside of her holiday home in a remote region of West Cork, Ireland. The crime was reported by a local journalist, Ian Bailey, who was at the forefront of the case until he became the prime murder suspect. Arrested twice, he was released without charge.

This was the start of a saga lasting decades with twists and turns and a battle for justice in two countries, which culminated in the 2019 conviction of Bailey – in his absence – by the French Criminal court in Paris. But it was up to the Irish courts to decide whether he would be extradited to serve a 25-year prison sentence.

With the unrivalled co-operation of major investigation sources and the backing of the victim's family, the author unravels the shocking facts of a unique murder case.

By Steve Wraith:

The Krays' Final Years: My Time with London's Most Iconic Gangsters

Britain's most notorious twins – Ron and Reg Kray – ascended the underworld to become the most feared and legendary gangsters in London. Their escalating mayhem culminated in murder, for which they received life sentences in 1969.

While incarcerated, they received letters from a schoolboy from Tyneside, Steve Wraith, who was mesmerised by their story. Eventually, Steve visited them in prison and a friendship formed. The Twins hired Steve as an unofficial advisor, which brought him into contact with other members of their crime family. At Ron's funeral, Steve was Charlie Kray's right-hand man.

Steve documents Ron's time in Broadmoor – a high-security psychiatric hospital – where he was battling insanity and heavily medicated. Steve details visiting Reg, who served almost 30 years in a variety of prisons, where the gangster was treated with the utmost respect by the staff and the inmates.

By Natalie Welsh:

Escape from Venezuela's Deadliest Prison

After getting arrested at a Venezuelan airport with a suitcase of cocaine, Natalie was clueless about the danger she was facing. Sentenced to 10 years, she arrived at a prison with armed men on the roof, whom she mistakenly believed were the guards, only to find out they were homicidal gang members. Immediately, she was plunged into a world of unimaginable horror and escalating violence, where murder, rape and all-out gang warfare were carried out with the complicity of corrupt guards. Male prisoners often entered the females' housing area, bringing gunfire with them and leaving corpses behind. After 4.5 years, Natalie risked everything to escape and flee through Colombia, with the help of a guard who had fallen deeply in love with her.

By Shaun Attwood:

Pablo Escobar: Beyond Narcos

War on Drugs Series Book 1

The mind-blowing true story of Pablo Escobar and the Medellín Cartel beyond their portrayal on Netflix.

Colombian drug lord Pablo Escobar was a devoted family man and a psychopathic killer; a terrible enemy, yet a wonderful friend. While donating millions to the poor, he bombed and tortured his enemies – some had their eyeballs removed with hot spoons. Through ruthless cunning and America's insatiable appetite for cocaine, he became a multi-billionaire, who lived in a $100-million house with its own zoo.

Pablo Escobar: Beyond Narcos demolishes the standard good versus evil telling of his story. The authorities were not hunting Pablo down to stop his cocaine business. They were taking over it.

American Made: Who Killed Barry Seal? Pablo Escobar or George HW Bush

War on Drugs Series Book 2

Set in a world where crime and government coexist, *American Made* is the jaw-dropping true story of CIA pilot Barry Seal that the Hollywood movie starring Tom Cruise is afraid to tell.

Barry Seal flew cocaine and weapons worth billions of dollars into and out of America in the 1980s. After he became a government informant, Pablo Escobar's Medellin Cartel offered a million for him alive and half a million dead. But his real trouble began after he threatened to expose the dirty dealings of George HW Bush.

American Made rips the roof off Bush and Clinton's complicity in cocaine trafficking in Mena, Arkansas.

"A conspiracy of the grandest magnitude." Congressman Bill Alexander on the Mena affair.

The Cali Cartel: Beyond Narcos

War on Drugs Series Book 3

An electrifying account of the Cali Cartel beyond its portrayal on Netflix.

From the ashes of Pablo Escobar's empire rose an even bigger and more malevolent cartel. A new breed of sophisticated mobsters became the kings of cocaine. Their leader was Gilberto Rodríguez Orejuela – known as the Chess Player due to his foresight and calculated cunning.

Gilberto and his terrifying brother, Miguel, ran a multi-billion-dollar drug empire like a corporation. They employed a politically astute brand of thuggery and spent $10 million to put a president in power. Although the godfathers from Cali preferred bribery over violence, their many loyal torturers and hit men were never idle.

Clinton Bush and CIA Conspiracies: From the Boys on the Tracks to Jeffrey Epstein

War on Drugs Series Book 4

In the 1980s, George HW Bush imported cocaine to finance an illegal war in Nicaragua. Governor Bill Clinton's Arkansas state police provided security for the drug drops. For assisting the CIA, the Clinton Crime Family was awarded the White House. The #clintonbodycount continues to this day, with the deceased including Jeffrey Epstein.

This book features harrowing true stories that reveal the insanity of the drug war. A mother receives the worst news about her son.

A journalist gets a tip that endangers his life. An unemployed man becomes California's biggest crack dealer. A DEA agent in Mexico is sacrificed for going after the big players.

The lives of Linda Ives, Gary Webb, Freeway Rick Ross and Kiki Camarena are shattered by brutal experiences. Not all of them will survive.

Pablo Escobar's Story (4-book series)

"Finally, the definitive book about Escobar, original and up-to-date" – UNILAD

"The most comprehensive account ever written" – True Geordie

Pablo Escobar was a mama's boy who cherished his family and sang in the shower, yet he bombed a passenger plane and formed a death squad that used genital electrocution.

Most Escobar biographies only provide a few pieces of the puzzle, but this action-packed 1000-page book reveals everything about the king of cocaine.

Mostly translated from Spanish, Part 1 contains stories untold in the English-speaking world, including:

The tragic death of his youngest brother Fernando.
The fate of his pregnant mistress.
The shocking details of his affair with a TV celebrity.
The presidential candidate who encouraged him to eliminate their rivals.

The Mafia Philosopher

"A fast-paced true-crime memoir with all of the action of Goodfellas" – UNILAD

"Sopranos v Sons of Anarchy with an Alaskan-snow backdrop" – True Geordie Podcast

Breaking bones, burying bodies and planting bombs became second nature to Two Tonys while working for the Bonanno Crime Family, whose exploits inspired The Godfather.

After a dispute with an outlaw motorcycle club, Two Tonys left a trail of corpses from Arizona to Alaska. On the run, he was pursued by bikers and a neo-Nazi gang blood-thirsty for revenge, while a homicide detective launched a nationwide manhunt.

As the mist from his smoking gun fades, readers are left with an unexpected portrait of a stoic philosopher with a wealth of charm, a glorious turn of phrase and a fanatical devotion to his daughter.

Party Time

An action-packed roller-coaster account of a life spiralling out of control, featuring wild women, gangsters and a mountain of drugs.

Shaun Attwood arrived in Phoenix, Arizona, a penniless business graduate from a small industrial town in England. Within a decade, he became a stock-market millionaire. But he was leading a double life.

After taking his first Ecstasy pill at a rave in Manchester as a shy student, Shaun became intoxicated by the party lifestyle that would change his fortune. Years later, in the Arizona desert, he became submerged in a criminal underworld, throwing parties for thousands of ravers and running an Ecstasy ring in competition with the Mafia mass murderer Sammy 'The Bull' Gravano.

As greed and excess tore through his life, Shaun had

eye-watering encounters with Mafia hit men and crystal-meth addicts, enjoyed extravagant debauchery with superstar DJs and glitter girls, and ingested enough drugs to kill a herd of elephants. This is his story.

Hard Time

"Makes the Shawshank Redemption look like a holiday camp" – NOTW

After a SWAT team smashed down stock-market millionaire Shaun Attwood's door, he found himself inside of Arizona's deadliest jail and locked into a brutal struggle for survival.

Shaun's hope of living the American Dream turned into a nightmare of violence and chaos, when he had a run-in with Sammy the Bull Gravano, an Italian Mafia mass murderer.

In jail, Shaun was forced to endure cockroaches crawling in his ears at night, dead rats in the food and the sound of skulls getting cracked against toilets. He meticulously documented the conditions and smuggled out his message.

Join Shaun on a harrowing voyage into the darkest recesses of human existence.

Hard Time provides a revealing glimpse into the tragedy, brutality, dark comedy and eccentricity of prison life.

Featured worldwide on Nat Geo Channel's Locked-Up/Banged-Up Abroad Raving Arizona.

Prison Time

Sentenced to 9½ years in Arizona's state prison for distributing Ecstasy, Shaun finds himself living among gang members, sexual predators and drug-crazed psychopaths. After being attacked by a Californian biker in for stabbing a girlfriend, Shaun writes about the prisoners who befriend, protect and inspire him. They include T-Bone, a massive African American ex-Marine who risks his life saving vulnerable inmates from rape, and Two Tonys, an old-school Mafia murderer who left the corpses of his rivals from Arizona to Alaska. They teach Shaun how to turn incarceration to his advantage, and to learn from his mistakes.

Shaun is no stranger to love and lust in the heterosexual world, but the tables are turned on him inside. Sexual advances come at him from all directions, some cleverly disguised, others more sinister – making Shaun question his sexual identity.

Resigned to living alongside violent, mentally-ill and drug-addicted inmates, Shaun immerses himself in psychology and philosophy to try to make sense of his past behaviour, and begins applying what he learns as he adapts to prison life. Encouraged by Two Tonys to explore fiction as well, Shaun reads over 1000 books which, with support from a brilliant psychotherapist, Dr Owen, speed along his personal development. As his ability to deflect daily threats improves, Shaun begins to look forward to his release with optimism and a new love waiting for him. Yet the words of Aristotle from one of Shaun's books will prove prophetic: "We cannot learn without pain."

Un-Making a Murderer: The Framing of Steven Avery and Brendan Dassey

Innocent people do go to jail. Sometimes mistakes are made. But even more terrifying is when the authorities conspire to frame them. That's what happened to Steven Avery and Brendan Dassey, who were convicted of murder and are serving life sentences.

Un-Making a Murderer is an explosive book which uncovers the illegal, devious and covert tactics used by Wisconsin officials, including:

– Concealing Other Suspects

– Paying Expert Witnesses to Lie

– Planting Evidence

– Jury Tampering

The art of framing innocent people has been in practice for centuries and will continue until the perpetrators are held accountable. Turning conventional assumptions and beliefs in the justice system upside down, *Un-Making a Murderer* takes you on that journey.

HARD TIME BY SHAUN ATTWOOD

CHAPTER 1

Sleep deprived and scanning for danger, I enter a dark cell on the second floor of the maximum-security Madison Street jail in Phoenix, Arizona, where guards and gang members are murdering prisoners. Behind me, the metal door slams heavily. Light slants into the cell through oblong gaps in the door, illuminating a prisoner cocooned in a white sheet, snoring lightly on the top bunk about two thirds of the way up the back wall. Relieved there is no immediate threat, I place my mattress on the grimy floor. Desperate to rest, I notice movement on the cement-block walls. *Am I hallucinating?* I blink several times. The walls appear to ripple. Stepping closer, I see the walls are alive with insects. I flinch. So many are swarming, I wonder if they're a colony of ants on the move. To get a better look, I put my eyes right up to them. They are mostly the size of almonds and have antennae. American cockroaches. I've seen them in the holding cells downstairs in smaller numbers, but nothing like this. A chill spread over my body. I back away.

Something alive falls from the ceiling and bounces off the base of my neck. I jump. With my night vision improving, I spot cockroaches weaving in and out of the base of the fluorescent strip light. Every so often one drops onto the concrete and resumes crawling. Examining the bottom bunk, I realise why my cellmate is sleeping at a higher elevation: cockroaches are pouring from gaps in the decrepit wall at the level of my bunk. The area is thick with them. Placing my mattress on the bottom bunk scatters them. I walk towards the toilet, crunching a few under my shower sandals. I urinate and grab the toilet roll. A cockroach darts from the centre of the roll onto my hand, tickling my fingers. My arm jerks as if it has a mind of its own, losing the cockroach and the toilet roll. Using a towel, I wipe the bulk of them off the bottom bunk, stopping only to shake the odd one off my hand. I unroll my mattress. They begin to regroup and inhabit my mattress. My adrenaline is pumping so much, I lose my fatigue.

Nauseated, I sit on a tiny metal stool bolted to the wall. *How will I sleep? How's my cellmate sleeping through the infestation and my arrival?* Copying his technique, I cocoon myself in a sheet and lie down, crushing more cockroaches. The only way they can access me now is through the breathing hole I've left in the sheet by the lower half of my face. Inhaling their strange musty odour, I close my eyes. I can't sleep. I feel them crawling on the sheet around my feet. *Am I imagining things?* Frightened of them infiltrating my breathing hole, I keep opening my eyes. Cramps cause me to rotate onto my other side. Facing the wall, I'm repulsed by so many of them just inches away. I return to my original side.

The sheet traps the heat of the Sonoran Desert to my body, soaking me in sweat. Sweat tickles my body, tricking my mind into thinking the cockroaches are infiltrating and crawling on me. The trapped heat aggravates my bleeding skin infections and bedsores. I want to scratch myself, but I know better. The outer layers of my skin have turned soggy from sweating constantly in this concrete oven. Squirming on the bunk fails to stop the relentless itchiness of my skin. Eventually, I scratch myself. Clumps of moist skin detach under my nails. Every now and then I become so uncomfortable, I must open my cocoon to waft the heat out, which allows the cockroaches in. It takes hours to drift to sleep. I only manage a few hours. I awake stuck to the soaked sheet, disgusted by the cockroach carcasses compressed against the mattress.

The cockroaches plague my new home until dawn appears at the dots in the metal grid over a begrimed strip of four-inch-thick bullet-proof glass at the top of the back wall – the cell's only source of outdoor light. They disappear into the cracks in the walls, like vampire mist retreating from sunlight. But not all of them. There were so many on the night shift that even their vastly reduced number is too many to dispose of. And they act like they know it. They roam around my feet with attitude, as if to make it clear that I'm trespassing on their turf.

My next set of challenges will arise not from the insect world, but from my neighbours. I'm the new arrival, subject to scrutiny about my charges just like when I'd run into the Aryan Brotherhood prison gang on my first day at the medium-security Towers jail a year ago. I wish my cellmate would wake up, brief me on the mood of the locals and introduce me to the head of the white gang. No such luck. Chow is announced over a speaker system in a crackly robotic voice, but he doesn't stir.

I emerge into the day room for breakfast. Prisoners in black-and-white bee-striped uniforms gather under the metal-grid stairs and tip dead cockroaches into a trash bin from plastic peanut-butter containers they'd set as traps during the night. All eyes are on me in the chow line. Watching who sits where, I hold my head up, put on a solid stare and pretend to be as at home in this environment as the cockroaches. It's all an act. I'm lonely and afraid. I loathe having to explain myself to the head of the white race, who I assume is the toughest murderer. I've been in jail long enough to know that taking my breakfast to my cell will imply that I have something to hide.

The gang punishes criminals with certain charges. The most serious are sex offenders, who are KOS: Kill On Sight. Other charges are punishable by SOS – Smash On Sight – such as drive-by shootings because women and kids sometimes get killed. It's called convict justice. Gang members are constantly looking for people to beat up because that's how they earn their reputations and tattoos. The most serious acts of violence earn the highest-ranking tattoos. To be a full gang member requires murder. I've observed the body language and techniques inmates trying to integrate employ. An inmate with a spring in his step and an air of confidence is likely to be accepted. A person who avoids eye contact and fails to introduce himself to the gang is likely to be preyed on. Some of the failed attempts I saw ended up with heads getting cracked against toilets, a sound I've grown familiar with. I've seen prisoners being extracted on stretchers who looked dead – one had yellow fluid leaking from his head. The constant violence gives me nightmares, but the reality is that I put myself in here, so I force myself to accept it as a part of my punishment.

It's time to apply my knowledge. With a self-assured stride, I take my breakfast bag to the table of white inmates covered in neo-Nazi tattoos, allowing them to question me.

"Mind if I sit with you guys?" I ask, glad exhaustion has deepened my voice.

"These seats are taken. But you can stand at the corner of the table."

The man who answered is probably the head of the gang. I size him up. Cropped brown hair. A dangerous glint in Nordic-blue eyes. Tiny pupils that suggest he's on heroin. Weightlifter-type veins bulging from a sturdy neck. Political ink on arms crisscrossed with scars. About the same age as me, thirty-three.

"Thanks. I'm Shaun from England." I volunteer my origin to show I'm different from them but not in a way that might get me smashed.

"I'm Bullet, the head of the whites." He offers me his fist to bump. "Where you roll in from, wood?"

Addressing me as wood is a good sign. It's what white gang members on a friendly basis call each other.

"Towers jail. They increased my bond and re-classified me to maximum security."

"What's your bond at?"

"I've got two $750,000 bonds," I say in a monotone. This is no place to brag about bonds.

"How many people you kill, brother?" His eyes drill into mine, checking whether my body language supports my story. My body language so far is spot on.

"None. I threw rave parties. They got us talking about drugs on wiretaps." Discussing drugs on the phone does not warrant a $1.5 million bond. I know and beat him to his next question. "Here's my charges." I show him my charge sheet, which includes conspiracy and leading a crime syndicate – both from running an Ecstasy ring.

Bullet snatches the paper and scrutinises it. Attempting to pre-empt his verdict, the other whites study his face. On edge, I wait for him to respond. Whatever he says next will determine whether I'll be accepted or victimised.

"Are you some kind of jailhouse attorney?" Bullet asks. "I want someone to read through my case paperwork." During our few minutes of conversation, Bullet has seen through my act and concluded that I'm educated – a possible resource to him.

I appreciate that he'll accept me if I take the time to read his case. "I'm no jailhouse attorney, but I'll look through it and help you however I can."

"Good. I'll stop by your cell later on, wood."

After breakfast, I seal as many of the cracks in the walls as I can with toothpaste. The cell smells minty, but the cockroaches still find their way in. Their day shift appears to be collecting information on the brown paper bags under my bunk, containing a few items of food that I purchased from the commissary; bags that I tied off with rubber bands in the hope of keeping the cockroaches out. Relentlessly, the cockroaches explore the bags for entry points, pausing over and probing the most worn and vulnerable regions. *Will the nightly swarm eat right through the paper?* I read all morning, wondering whether my cellmate has died in his cocoon, his occasional breathing sounds reassuring me.

Bullet stops by late afternoon and drops his case paperwork off. He's been charged with Class 3 felonies and less, not serious crimes, but is facing a double-digit sentence because of his prior convictions and Security Threat Group status in the prison system. The proposed sentencing range seems disproportionate. I'll advise him to reject the plea bargain – on the assumption he already knows to do so, but is just seeking the comfort of a second opinion, like many un-sentenced inmates. When he returns for his paperwork, our conversation disturbs my cellmate – the cocoon shuffles – so we go upstairs to his cell. I tell Bullet what I think. He is excitable, a different man from earlier, his pupils almost non-existent.

"This case ain't shit. But my prosecutor knows I done other shit, all kinds of heavy shit, but can't prove it. I'd do anything to get that sorry bitch off my fucking ass. She's asking for something bad to happen to her. Man, if I ever get bonded out, I'm gonna chop that bitch into pieces. Kill her slowly though. Like to work her over with a blowtorch."

Such talk can get us both charged with conspiring to murder a prosecutor, so I try to steer him elsewhere. "It's crazy how they can catch you doing one thing, yet try to sentence you for all of the things they think you've ever done."

"Done plenty. Shot some dude in the stomach once. Rolled him up in a blanket and threw him in a dumpster."

Discussing past murders is as unsettling as future ones. "So, what's all your tattoos mean, Bullet? Like that eagle on your chest?"

"Why you wanna know?" Bullet's eyes probe mine.

My eyes hold their ground. "Just curious."

"It's a war bird. The AB patch."

"AB patch?"

"What the Aryan Brotherhood gives you when you've put enough work in."

"How long does it take to earn a patch?"

"Depends how quickly you put your work in. You have to earn your lightning bolts first."

"Why you got red and black lightning bolts?"

"You get SS bolts for beating someone down or for being an enforcer for the family. Red lightning bolts for killing someone.

I was sent down as a youngster. They gave me steel and told me who to handle and I handled it. You don't ask questions. You just get blood on your steel. Dudes who get these tats without putting work in are told to cover them up or leave the yard."

"What if they refuse?"

"They're held down and we carve the ink off them."

Imagining them carving a chunk of flesh to remove a tattoo, I cringe. He's really enjoying telling me this now. His volatile nature is clear and frightening. *He's accepted me too much. He's trying to impress me before making demands.*

At night, I'm unable to sleep. Cocooned in heat, surrounded by cockroaches, I hear the swamp-cooler vent – a metal grid at the top of a wall – hissing out tepid air. Giving up on sleep, I put my earphones on and tune into National Public Radio. Listening to a Vivaldi violin concerto, I close my eyes and press my tailbone down to straighten my back as if I'm doing a yogic relaxation. The playful allegro thrills me, lifting my spirits, but the wistful adagio provokes sad emotions and tears. I open my eyes and gaze into the gloom. Due to lack of sleep, I start hallucinating and hearing voices over the music whispering threats. I'm at breaking point. Although I have accepted that I committed crimes and deserve to be punished, no one should have to live like this. I'm furious at myself for making the series of reckless decisions that put me in here and for losing absolutely everything. As violins crescendo in my ears, I remember what my life used to be like.

PRISON TIME BY SHAUN ATTWOOD

CHAPTER 1

"I've got a padlock in a sock. I can smash your brains in while you're asleep. I can kill you whenever I want." My new cellmate sizes me up with no trace of human feeling in his eyes. Muscular and pot-bellied, he's caked in prison ink, including six snakes on his skull, slithering side by side. The top of his right ear is missing in a semi-circle.

The waves of fear are overwhelming. After being in transportation all day, I can feel my bladder hurting. "I'm not looking to cause any trouble. I'm the quietest cellmate you'll ever have. All I do is read and write."

Scowling, he shakes his head. "Why've they put a fish in with me?" He swaggers close enough for me to smell his cigarette breath. "Us convicts don't get along with fresh fish."

"Should I ask to move then?" I say, hoping he'll agree if he hates new prisoners so much.

"No! They'll think I threatened you!"

In the eight by twelve feet slab of space, I swerve around him and place my property box on the top bunk.

He pushes me aside and grabs the box. "You just put that on my artwork! I ought to fucking smash you, fish!"

"Sorry, I didn't see it."

"You need to be more aware of your fucking surroundings! What you in for anyway, fish?"

I explain my charges, Ecstasy dealing and how I spent twenty-six months fighting my case.

"How come the cops were so hard-core after you?" he asks, squinting.

"It was a big case, a multi-million-dollar investigation. They raided over a hundred people and didn't find any drugs. They were pretty pissed off. I'd stopped dealing by the time they caught up with me, but I'd done plenty over the years, so I accept my punishment."

"Throwing raves," he says, staring at the ceiling as if remembering something. "Were you partying with underage girls?" he asks, his voice slow, coaxing.

Being called a sex offender is the worst insult in prison. Into my third year of incarceration, I'm conditioned to react. "What you trying to say?" I yell angrily, brow clenched.

"Were you fucking underage girls?" Flexing his body, he shakes both fists as if about to punch me.

"Hey, I'm no child molester, and I'd prefer you didn't say shit like that!"

"My buddy next door is doing twenty-five to life for murdering a child molester. How do I know Ecstasy dealing ain't your cover story?" He inhales loudly, nostrils flaring.

"You want to see my fucking paperwork?"

A stocky prisoner walks in. Short hair. Dark eyes. Powerful neck. On one arm: a tattoo of a man in handcuffs above the word OMERTA – the Mafia code of silence towards law enforcement. "What the fuck's going on in here, Bud?" asks Junior Bull – the son of "Sammy the Bull" Gravano, the Mafia mass murderer who was my biggest competitor in the Ecstasy market.

Relieved to see a familiar face, I say, "How're you doing?"

Shaking my hand, he says in a New York Italian accent, "I'm doing alright. I read that shit in the newspaper about you starting a blog in Sheriff Joe Arpaio's jail."

"The blog's been bringing media heat on the conditions."

"You know him?" Bud asks.

"Yeah, from Towers jail. He's a good dude. He's in for dealing Ecstasy like me."

"It's a good job you said that 'cause I was about to smash his ass," Bud says.

"It's a good job Wild Man ain't here 'cause you'd a got your ass thrown off the balcony," Junior Bull says.

I laugh. The presence of my best friend, Wild Man, was partly the reason I never took a beating at the county jail, but with Wild Man in a different prison, I feel vulnerable. When Bud casts a death stare on me, my smile fades.

"What the fuck you guys on about?" Bud asks.

"Let's go talk downstairs." Junior Bull leads Bud out.

I rush to a stainless-steel sink/toilet bolted to a cement-block wall by the front of the cell, unbutton my orange jumpsuit and crane my neck to watch the upper-tier walkway in case Bud returns. I bask in relief as my bladder deflates. After flushing, I take stock of my new home, grateful for the slight improvement in the conditions versus what I'd grown accustomed to in Sheriff Joe Arpaio's jail. No cockroaches. No blood stains. A working swamp cooler. Something I've never seen in a cell before: shelves. The steel table bolted to the wall is slightly larger, too. *But how will I concentrate on writing with Bud around?* There's a mixture of smells in the room. Cleaning chemicals. Aftershave. Tobacco. A vinegar-like odour. The slit of a window at the back overlooks gravel in a no-man's-land before the next building with gleaming curls of razor wire around its roof.

From the doorway upstairs, I'm facing two storeys of cells overlooking a day room with shower cubicles at the end of both tiers. At two white plastic circular tables, prisoners are playing dominoes, cards, chess and Scrabble, some concentrating, others yelling obscenities, contributing to a brain-scraping din that I hope to block out by purchasing a Walkman. In a raised box-shaped Plexiglas control tower, two guards are monitoring the prisoners.

Bud returns. My pulse jumps. Not wanting to feel like I'm stuck in a kennel with a rabid dog, I grab a notepad and pen and head for the day room.

Focussed on my body language, not wanting to signal any weakness, I'm striding along the upper tier, head and chest elevated, when two hands appear from a doorway and grab me. I drop the pad. The pen clinks against grid-metal and tumbles to the day room as I'm pulled into a cell reeking of backside sweat and masturbation, a cheese-tinted funk.

"I'm Booga. Let's fuck," says a squat man in urine-stained boxers, with WHITE TRASH tattooed on his torso below a mobile home, and an arm sleeved with the Virgin Mary.

Shocked, I brace to flee or fight to preserve my anal virginity. I can't believe my eyes when he drops his boxers and waggles his penis.

Dancing to music playing through a speaker he has rigged up, Booga smiles in a sexy way. "Come on," he says in a husky voice. "Drop your pants. Let's fuck." He pulls pornography faces. I question his sanity. He moves closer. "If I let you fart in my mouth, can I fart in yours?"

"You can fuck off," I say, springing towards the doorway.

He grabs me. We scuffle. Every time I make progress towards the doorway, he clings to my clothes, dragging me back in. When I feel his penis rub against my leg, my adrenalin kicks in so forcefully I experience a burst of strength and wriggle free. I bolt out as fast as my shower sandals will allow and snatch my pad. Looking over my shoulder, I see him stood calmly in the doorway, smiling. He points at me. "You have to walk past my door every day. We're gonna get together. I'll lick your ass and you can fart in my mouth." Booga blows a kiss and disappears.

I rush downstairs. With my back to a wall, I pause to steady my thoughts and breathing. In survival mode, I think, *What's going to come at me next?* In the hope of reducing my tension, I borrow a pen to do what helps me stay sane: writing. With the details fresh in my mind, I document my journey to the prison for my blog readers, keeping an eye out in case anyone else wants to test the new prisoner. The more I write, the more I fill with a sense of purpose. Jon's Jail Journal is a connection to the outside world that I cherish.

Someone yells, "One time!" The din lowers. A door rumbles open. A guard does a security walk, his every move scrutinised by dozens of scornful eyes staring from cells. When he exits, the din resumes, and the prisoners return to injecting drugs to escape from reality, including the length of their sentences. This continues all day with "Two times!" signifying two approaching guards, and "Three times!" three and so on. Every now and then an announcement by a guard over the speakers briefly lowers the din.

Before lockdown, I join the line for a shower, holding bars of soap in a towel that I aim to swing at the head of the next person to try me. With boisterous inmates a few feet away, yelling at the men in the showers to "Stop jerking off," and "Hurry the fuck up," I get in a cubicle that reeks of bleach and mildew. With every nerve strained, I undress and rinse fast.

At night, despite the desert heat, I cocoon myself in a blanket from head to toe and turn towards the wall, making my face more difficult to strike. I leave a hole for air, but the warm cement block inches from my mouth returns each exhalation to my face as if it's breathing on me, creating a feeling of suffocation. For hours, my heart drums so hard against the thin mattress I feel as if I'm moving even though I'm still. I try to sleep, but my eyes keep springing open and my head turning towards the cell as I try to penetrate the darkness, searching for Bud swinging a padlock in a sock at my head.

Printed in Great Britain
by Amazon